GAMBLE TO WIN

A Complete Guide
for the Serious Player

R. D. Ellison

A Lyle Stuart Book
Published by Carol Publishing Group

A Lyle Stuart Book
Published by Carol Publishing Group
Lyle Stuart is a registered trademark of Carol Communications, Inc.

Editorial, sales and distribution, and rights and permissions inquiries should be addressed to Carol Publishing Group, 120 Enterprise Avenue, Secaucus, N.J. 07094.

In Canada: Canadian Manda Group, One Atlantic Avenue, Suite 105, Toronto, Ontario M6K 3E7

Carol Publishing Group books may be purchased in bulk at special discounts for sales promotion, fund-raising, or educational purposes. Special editions can be created to specifications. For details, contact Special Sales Department, Carol Publishing Group, 120 Enterprise Avenue, Secaucus, N.J. 07094.

Manufactured in the United States of America
10 9 8 7 6 5 4 3 2 1

Library of Congress Cataloging-in-Publication Data

Ellison, R. D.
    Gamble to win : a complete guide for the serious
    player / R. D. Ellison
            p.   cm.
    "A Lyle Stuart book."
    ISBN 0–8184–0601–1 (hardcover)
    1. Gambling.   2. Games.   I. Title
GV1301.E45   1998
795—dc21   98–34296
                                                  CIP

Dedicated to Sharon Joan Pfeiffer

TABLE OF CONTENTS

TABLE OF CONTENTS

TABLE OF CONTENTS

TABLE OF CONTENTS

PART II: PROFESSIONAL TECHNIQUES

TABLE OF CONTENTS

TABLE OF CONTENTS

TABLE OF CONTENTS

xiii

TABLE OF CONTENTS

TABLE OF CONTENTS

SCORECARD PLATES

INTRODUCTION

*If you want the rainbow, you've got to put up with a lot of
rain.*
        —from TV show *Dawson's Creek*

It is a strange, reckless, precarious way to make a living. You
wake up, and think about the day's strategy as you go about your
morning routine. Then you head for the casino, where it's a holiday
for everyone but you.

It's different for you, because you can't participate in the fun.
You're looking for meat. Sustenance for one more day.

As you walk into the casino, you feel just a little bit terrified.
Knowing what you have to do today has that effect. I'm sure that's
what every soldier feels on the eve of the battle.

Experience has taught you to visit the casinos just once a day,
because if you win, your smartest bet is to take the money and run.
If you lose, you need time to clear your head, else you'll find that
you're reacting to the sting of that loss.

Inexplicably, the fact that you've won on nine of the last ten
days doesn't really boost your confidence. You still feel awkward
and helpless. It seems inconceivable that you could win yet again.
But that's the way you feel every day. One would think you'd be
used to it by now.

Up to the table you walk. You scan the layout, searching for
a target. Like always, you're confronted with the daunting task of
building the day's empire from scratch ✠

PART I

THE BASICS

1

INSIDE THE ARENA

Welcome to the world of Professional Gambling, the art of turning over money to generate income. Here, you will learn how one can maintain a consistent income by exploiting casino conditions that *favor the player,* and we will take you there using the most direct route possible.

Most of what you're about to read is information that can't be found anywhere else. What it takes to get started, what it takes to succeed and what it's like to live this life. You will learn about risk probabilities, systems and procedures, the implications of trends, and the art of building a bankroll.

It doesn't take a genius to understand this book, but you'll be in for the fight of your life, because everything the casinos do is calculated to separate you from your money as quickly as possible. It's their *job* to treat you like royalty while they systematically plunder your wallet.

Your workday is going to be spent inside a pool of sharks. Somehow, you're going to have to get what you need from them —before they get to you.

This is not easy money. To achieve success in this arena, it will take a great quantity of hard work, dedication and discipline. But if you stick to the program, you may discover that it offers the best income you could ever hope to get, without an inheritance, a lottery win, or a master's degree ✠

MONEY, STRATEGY AND DISCIPLINE

Money, Strategy, and Discipline. That's how you win in the casinos. You will need all three, but the latter most of all, because *discipline* is the foundation and the soul of professional gambling. Without it, you're just wasting time.

The very first test of your *Discipline* is to acquire a thorough understanding of every word on every page in this book. That is the absolute, humpity-dump, drop-dead minimum.

After *Discipline* comes *Strategy*. A fortune in gold won't help you earn more if you ain't got a plan and the will to see it through. This book takes care of that.

Finally comes *Money*. Necessary though it is, it's the least significant of the three. Why? Anyone in the world can get money, but few know a *Strategy* that will work, and fewer still have the *Discipline* to *make it work*.

Gambling professionally is hard work and pain. It's repetitious and petty, and monotonous as hell. There is no fun involved here. If you're determined to make a living this way, be prepared to spend much of your time in the cold part of town. Be prepared to discover the exact address of that beast they call loneliness. And especially, be prepared to live with the notion that mistakes will be made. Big, costly mistakes, that will put you in touch with the rage you never knew was inside of you.

If you can accept that; if you can truly live with that, maybe there *is* a part for you in this picture ✠

HITCHHIKING AND THE LAW OF AVERAGES

I think I was in the Eighth Grade when I became aware that a certain group of my classmates favored hitchhiking as a means of transportation home from school. These were the *malcontents,* who smoked, got into fistfights and wore black leather jackets. I never understood why they didn't take the schoolbus like everyone else, but it wasn't any of my business.

Until, one day when an errand happened to take me right past one who had his thumb stuck out, and I decided to strike up a conversation. It became my first exposure to the concept of the *Law of Averages.*

His name was Dennis, and maybe it was because he smiled a lot that I found the nerve to approach him. It hadn't occurred to me that doing so helped him get a ride more quickly.

"Hey Dennis, how's it going?"

"Not bad. . .what's up?" He glanced at me, but was focused on the passing traffic.

"Why're you hitchhiking?" I asked, seeking a quick answer. *"Why not take the schoolbus?"*

"I dunno. . .had some stuff to do. . ." Disdainfully, he flicked an ash from his cigarette. A car filled with girls passed by and he gestured in an attempt to get their attention.

"But. . .what if a car never stops?"

"That never happens." He continued to smile, but kept his gaze fixed straight ahead.

I was exasperated. *"How do you **know** that won't happen? How could you possibly know that?"*

He shrugged. *"I **always** get a ride after 20 minutes or so. . ."* (He was rapidly losing interest in the conversation.)

I looked at him with disbelief. How could he be so sure a ride would come? Then I thought about the timeframe. Imagine that! No matter where he was or what time it was, the car that would end up giving him a ride was twenty minutes away, making its way toward him like clockwork. It was a game a chance he *always* won; the only question was *WHEN*.

At the time, that kind of thinking was beyond my ability to fathom. *Never* would it have occurred to me to put unconditional trust in such an expectation. But Dennis appeared confident enough to convince me that he would succeed.

A few years later I tried it myself and learned that he was right. Sometimes the ride would come sooner, sometimes later. But it averaged out to twenty minutes, like he said.

What I learned since then is that in affairs of chance, it's only a matter of time before the *Law Of Averages* intercedes and begins to impose its will. Because, you see, behind the *Law Of Averages* lies a *statistical imperative:*

Given time, events will seek their proper place within their assigned probabilities.

Because of this, it would not be possible for an even, unbiased result, derived from the flip of a coin, for example, to win 500 consecutive decisions. Sorry. Not possible.

Now, everyone knows that the cards and the dice do not think for themselves. Consequently, every table decision is independent of the one before and the one after. But if this is true, where does the *Law of Averages* step in? Somewhere along the line, events are compelled to move toward their inherent probabilities. And this means that these events, when viewed in groups, are bending to a preordained will.

Exploitation of this phenomenon is the task of the gambler. Conveying its intricacies is the task of this book ✠

THE PATIENCE IMPERATIVE

A man was having a dialogue with God: *"Dear God, in your infinite wisdom, what is a million years to you?"*

Replied the voice from above, *"A million years is but one minute to me."*

The man persisted: *"Lord of the universe, in your infinite knowledge, what is a million dollars to you?"*

"A million dollars is but one penny to me."

"Well then, benevolent one," he responded, *"in your infinite generosity, could you grant me one of your pennies?"*

"I would be delighted to do so. . ." came the voice, *"if you can wait a minute."*

—C. Thomas Hilton

It is part of human nature to want things *Now*. This is but one part of your humanity you will have to learn to suppress before you can succeed.

The casino will be working against you in this regard, but you must not stray. Of all the clubs in your golf bag, *patience* is the one you will need the most.

Before you can learn to **Win**, you must learn how to **Not Lose**. The latter is far more important, for the casino will use every device at its disposal—and they have many—to ensure that you lose as big as the skies of Montana.

If you learn only one thing today, learn this: **Discipline** is all *that separates you from the losers and the fools.*

Save yourself a lot of pain and *learn this Now* ✠

THE RECOMMENDED GAMES

You should only pick fights you're sure you're going to win.

—Alan Rush, from TV
drama *Central Park West*

The (three) games recommended for professional play are **Roulette, MiniBaccarat** and **Craps.** They are considered superior to other games because, for one thing, their bets have *bet opposites.* The underlying principle of professional play is to *play to the trend;* bet the side that's *hot.* To do that, there have to be two sides to bet. *Blackjack* doesn't qualify because it's a one-dimensional game: if the dealer's hot, it matters not if you hit or stand, *you're gonna lose.* That's a disadvantage you don't need.

Of the three games, *craps* is the author's preference, because its primary bets carry lower house percentages than *roulette,* and it is more widely available than *minibaccarat.* But some readers may have a problem with its image, for they equate a *craps shoot* with a high-risk situation.

Indeed, craps is a volatile game that will carry you away in a wave of euphoria *if you let it.* This book will teach you how to stay detached from its intoxicating effects.

By its very design, craps is a game of *trends,* the one thing casinos can't control. You'll learn to capitalize on this. No one else at the table will make the same bets or play the same way as you. That is where much of *your* edge will derive.

But the other two games have their place as well. And as any seasoned player can tell you, the more viable options you have, the greater your chance for success ✠

A BLACKJACK ADVISORY

According to an abundance of books on the subject, blackjack is a game where a player can use skill to interpret the statistical data that unfolds as the cards in the deck are revealed, letting him know when to bet heavy. As it is an intriguing concept, I think you should know why I don't recommend this game.

There was a time when *card counting* actually worked, if the player could disguise the fact. But if caught, he'd be ejected from the casino. Today, many players use a less conspicuous counting method called *Overview,* which involves checking the ratio of the high cards to low cards. When 60% or more of the cards dealt out are low, they have a theoretical edge. But the casinos have adapted to the card counting problem by having the dealers shuffle whenever a player suddenly bets big. And this invalidates all his computations, no matter which counting method is used.

Another problem with blackjack is that a player is helpless against a hot dealer. Of course, he can move to another table, but he's likely to find the same thing: a dealer who draws five cards and ends up with 21 against his 20.

One way to get a clue about the game is to count the blackjack tables in any casino. There are an awful lot of them, aren't there? Why do you suppose the casinos have so many? Is it because they like giving their money away?

I never understood the appeal of blackjack, but there's one thing I'm sure of: there are a lot of suckers out there who think they can beat this game. But they don't win.

Bottom line: the house has the edge because the player has to act first. The dealer *reacts* to that result ✠

THE HOUSE EDGE DEFINED

Before moving on, we're going to have to take a look at that statistical vampire known as the *House Edge*. This is one concept you should understand with leaded crystal clarity, because it is what guarantees the casinos a winning position.

House Edge is the mathematical advantage casinos hold over players, by paying off winning bets for less than what would be paid to *fairly* compensate the risk that's involved. You see, there is a precise statistical probability for every bet you can make in a casino. If you were paid the exact inverse of a bet's probability every time, in theory neither you nor the casino would ever win in the long run. Both of you would just be turning over money.

The *house edge* is the unseen foe that never sleeps. It works against you with every bet you make, grinding away your fortunes with persistant malicious intent.

To illustrate, we'll look at the game of roulette. This game has 38 numbers on the layout: 1 through 36, plus 0 and 00. If you place a bet on one of these numbers, you'll be paid 35 to 1 for every winning bet. But wait a minute. There's only one chance in 38 that you'll win, according to its statistical probability. So, you're paid 35 to 1 for taking a 37 to 1 risk.

The difference is the *house edge*.

At American roulette, the house edge is 5.26%, which means that the casino will earn an average of $5.26 out of every $100 that is wagered, by virtue of that statistical advantage.

All games are structured to guarantee the house a favorable position in this way. But despair not. In Chapter 5, you will learn of its antidote, the *Player's Edge* ✠

THE DAGWOOD EDGE

I can't believe we had to go all the way to five out of nine.

—Dagwood Bumstead

FIGURE 1
The Dagwood Edge

Now that we've discussed the *House Edge,* let's take a look at the *Dagwood Edge.*

In Figure 1 above, Dagwood has opted to let a coin toss decide whether he will take a nap or give Daisy a bath. He wants to give each side a fair chance, but prefers one outcome over the other. How does he get what he wants? He keeps tossing the coin until the desired side wins a majority.

That, my friends, is the Dagwood Edge: *keep the game moving until the preferred side wins.* This is a simplified version of the *player's edge,* and its effectiveness would be hindered in real life by the *house edge,* but it helps make a point:

You have the capacity to think, react, stay in the game or leave. A gaming table cannot maneuver or react. It is reacted *upon.* THAT gives YOU a decisive advantage ✠

2

THE CASINO'S POINT OF VIEW

Those houses weren't built by giving money away.

—Dale Rabiner

In any competitive situation, it is important to understand the strengths and weaknesses of your adversary. What is the worst he can do to you? What is the worst you can do to him? Like any capable general in a wartime situation, you should be prepared for the full spectrum of strategic possibilities.

This applies especially in gaming, for your opponent has accumulated a track record that is worthy of the deepest admiration. One can learn from that kind of success.

It would most definitely be advantageous for you to learn to **think like a casino,** if only for the length of time it takes for you to grasp the logic applied therein.

Have you ever thought about the lengths to which casinos go to create an attractive and appealing destination? It would seem that no expense is spared to manufacture an environment that is the ultimate in hospitality, party atmosphere and glitter, wrapped around the charming *illusion* that you can *get rich quick* while living it up in a lifestyle of decadence and gluttony.

Donald Trump's Taj Mahal casino cost over a billion dollars to build. How does he pay for all that *atmosphere?*

This atmosphere, however, must not hinder the flow of dollars. Atlantic City casinos have no windows in the gaming area on the walls that would otherwise afford an ocean view. They want you to be undistracted when the money is flowing. That's why you won't see a clock from where you sit at a table game, and it's why some casinos pump fresh oxygen into the gaming area. The free drinks help loosen the players' grips on their wallets, and finally, the tokens used in the table games play down the importance of all that money you're putting at risk.

All this is calculated to trigger your compulsive nature. Over the years it has been refined to a science. And yet, after all that, the casinos would be content to win just a fifty-dollar profit from each player. Unlike nearly all their guests, they appreciate the power of the small return.

Now, you must realize that the casino has a huge advantage over the individual player, for the small return *they* get is multiplied times the thousands of guests that pass through their doors each day. But how many of these guests would be content with that same fifty-dollar win?

It is **greed** that destroys the players, and keeps all the casinos profitable.

Steve Wynn, owner of some of the most successful casinos in the world, including the Mirage, Golden Nugget and Treasure Island, was once quoted as saying that *the best way to make money in a casino is to own one.* Well. No point in arguing with that, but this book is for those who lack the $400 million to build their own. The next best thing is to become a *table game specialist,* and put your money at risk in much the same way as a casino.

The weapons casinos use to close the sale and guarantee their income are known as **Compulsion, Continuum** and **House Edge.** Before you go out there to challenge the giant, you should know about the weapons in its arsenal, and especially, their psychological effects on you, the player ✠

COMPULSION:
THE ENEMY WITHIN

Remember, the House doesn't beat a player. It merely gives him the opportunity to beat himself.

—Nick *The Greek* Dandalos

Compulsion is defined in the American Heritage dictionary as *an irresistible impulse to act, regardless the rationality of the motivation.*

The above definition has been abridged to reflect only the part that is relevant for this context. In casino gambling, it describes those less-than-noble personality traits the casinos will attempt to coax out of you: hedonism and greed.

Compulsion is a treacherous adversary, because to fight it is to fight your natural inclinations. Even seasoned professionals can succumb to this beast, for though they have learned to suppress it, it's always beckoning from the shadows.

When losing, it is natural to find yourself edging toward a state of panic. How are you going to absolve the losses you just incurred? You're hurt and confused, because someone just took your money away. How are you going to get it back?

Maybe now (after eight consecutive losses) is the time to *load up* and get back everything you lost with one *large, well-timed bet.* Yep; sounds like a plan.

Doesn't that sound like a plan?

This is what goes through one's mind. It's part of being human. The casinos know it. They wait for it. It's the reason for their success. Witnessing their guests self-destruct before their very eyes is part of their daily routine.

For those readers who wish to hear the outcome of that *large, well-timed bet,* there are three possibilities:

1) The player reached into his pocket but realized he was tapped out. The bet was planned but never made.

2) He lost that bet also, bringing his string of losses to *nine*. Don't think it can't happen to you.

3) He won, and was very pleased until his next crisis, when he tried it again and lost *big*.

If you're thinking result number three could have worked out, well, think again. Winning a bet conceived through one's surrender to *Compulsion* only serves to validate the habit, leading to severe consequences down the road.

Compulsion works against you when you're winning, too. When things are going well at the tables, one tends to feel invincible. This is your life's big moment. As the dice fly across the table, you imagine the headlines: *"Local man makes 35 passes at the craps table, shattering all records!"* This is the chance you've been waiting for all your life. You pick up the dice, and run through the list of ways to tell your idiot boss he can take that job and shove it. You'll never have to put up with his black-hearted, self-righteous, ritualistic power trips again!

Oops. You just heard the words *"Seven out, line away, eight was"*, and *poof*. . .the dream is gone.

Oh well. It was a

beautiful dream while it lasted.

Now if you can just figure a way to avoid losing *and* winning while at the tables, *Compulsion* won't be such a problem ✠

CONTINUUM:
THE UNBROKEN CHAIN

The applicable definition of **Continuum** is *any continuous extent or succession that has no arbitrary division.*

Casino games move quickly. Decision after decision occurs, and the action never stops. You may have just won a thousand with a bet at the roulette table, but you have no time to savor that victory or plan your next move. . .the wheel never stops turning. Do you give up your seat at the table, or temporize with a quick bet? This is *Continuum:* an absence of time to react to the never-ending succession of betting opportunities.

What about the players making smaller bets? They also fall victim because they stay too long. Within minutes, they lose the ability to keep pace with the wheel. And they seldom have the good sense to quit after that big score, *if* it ever comes.

My roulette sessions usually last 30–40 minutes. In that time I often witness a dozen players come and go. Most of them last just a few minutes, but they all seem to have one thing in common: they don't stop playing until they're out of chips.

Compulsion and *House Edge* also did their dirty work, but *Continuum* was the key player. The repetition and monotony of ongoing play pulled them in and turned them all into reckless, irresponsible, mechanical robots that moved without thinking. *That* is the hypnotic effect of that unconscionable foe known (only in this book) as *Continuum* ✠

HOUSE EDGE: THE STATISTICAL ADVANTAGE

Fear makes the wolf bigger than he is.

—God's Little Instruction Book

Meet the casino's most notorious weapon: the House Edge. This is what guarantees its profits. In theory, as long as the casino keeps the games moving it can do nothing but win, for the numbers will automatically fall in its favor. And that's all it takes to make a successful business enterprise.

In Nevada, some casinos advertise a 98 percent return on their slot machines. What does that mean? Well, for every dollar taken in, an average of 98 cents is returned to the player. How do they make money? Volume. If a casino's take from its slots is five million dollars a day, it will take in $100,000. Not a bad day's pay for a game that doesn't even require a dealer.

Figure 2 shows the *Statistical Casino Advantage* for games found in most casinos. These are arranged in order, with the best deals for the player at the top of the list.

For all its notoriety, *House Edge* is the least destructive of the three mentioned in this section. Be assured, a craps player who lost $200 in twenty minutes didn't do so because of the house edge. There are much worse demons to fear.

If you stick to the games (and the bets within those games) recommended in this book, you shouldn't have to worry (too much) about the residual damage arising from the *House Edge* ✠

STATISTICAL CASINO ADVANTAGE

GAME / BET	HOUSE EDGE
CRAPS: Pass or Don't Pass with double odds	0.60%
Pass or Don't Pass with single odds	0.80%
Patrick System, Pass/Don't Pass	0.92%
MINI-BACCARAT: (betting on) Bank	1.17%
(betting on) Player	1.36%
EUROPEAN ROULETTE with *En Prison:* Even money bets	1.35%
CRAPS: Pass Line or Don't Pass (only)	1.41%
CRAPS: Place bet on the 6 or 8	1.52%
ATLANTIC CITY ROULETTE: Even money bets	2.63%
CRAPS: Place bet on 5 or 9	4.00%
Buy bet on 4 or 10	5.00%
Lay bets (Any number)	5.00%
AMERICAN ROULETTE: All bets except Fiveline	5.26%
CRAPS: Place bet on 4 or 10	6.67%
AMERICAN ROULETTE: Fiveline bet	7.89%
CRAPS: Hardway 6 or 8	9.09%
Hardway 4 or 10	11.11%
Any Craps	11.11%
Any Seven (Big Red)	16.67%
MONEY WHEEL: All bets	11.00% & up
HORSE RACING: All bets	15.00% & up
KENO: All bets	22.00% & up

FIGURE 2

WHAT ODDS MEAN AND HOW THEY'RE FIGURED

In this business, you won't last ten minutes if you're not clear on this business of *Odds:* what they mean, why they change, and their monetary significance.

No place—I imagine—are *Odds* more closely watched than at thoroughbred racetracks, where you will find *Pari-Mutuel Odds,* which are determined by the bettors as a group. The mystique and allure of the ever-changing odds, in fact, figures prominently in the success of thoroughbred racing as a business. So this is where we will first look for definition.

Fig. 3 shows the range of odds commonly seen at racetracks. These prices show the return for a basic $2 bet. According to the chart, a winning 1–1 bet pays $4. Two dollars of that figure is your original wager; the other two represent your profit, which in effect works out to a 100% return on your investment.

So how are *Odds* figured? It's easy once you understand it. From Fig. 3, you can see that a 5–2 bet pays $7.00. For any odds, divide the second number into the first (resulting in the odds for each dollar wagered), then multiply it times two (since the minimum racetrack bet is two dollars), then add the return of your basic two dollar bet. Accordingly, the math for a 5–2 wager is:

$$5 \div 2 = 2\frac{1}{2} \times 2 = 5 + 2 = 7 \text{ dollars.}$$

This isn't as complicated as it appears, and once you know it, you can apply it to *all* Odds and to multiples thereof.

APPROXIMATE ODDS

Return on a successful $2.00 wager		
1-9 PAYS $2.20	8-5 PAYS $5.20	7-1 PAYS $16.00
1-5 PAYS $2.40	9-5 PAYS $5.60	8-1 PAYS $18.00
2-5 PAYS $2.80	2-1 PAYS $6.00	9-1 PAYS $20.00
1-2 PAYS $3.00	5-2 PAYS $7.00	10-1 PAYS $22.00
3-5 PAYS $3.20	3-1 PAYS $8.00	15-1 PAYS $32.00
4-5 PAYS $3.60	7-2 PAYS $9.00	20-1 PAYS $42.00
1-1 PAYS $4.00	4-1 PAYS $10.00	30-1 PAYS $62.00
6-5 PAYS $4.40	9-2 PAYS $11.00	40-1 PAYS $82.00
7-5 PAYS $4.80	5-1 PAYS $12.00	50-1 PAYS $102.00
3-2 PAYS $5.00	6-1 PAYS $14.00	99-1 PAYS $200.00

FIGURE 3

The reason Figure 3 is entitled *Approximate Odds* is that all racetrack *odds* fall within a range. If the final odds for a winning horse reads 5–2, for example, it will pay no less than $7.00, and as much as $7.80 (for every $2 bet), in increments of 20 cents. That's five different prices you could get from a successful bet (to Win) on a horse with 5–2 odds.

Racetracks do this for two reasons: *Simplicity* and *Breakage*. The *Simplicity* is to avoid the confusion that would occur if the track posted hundreds of different odds figures, and *breakage* refers to the slice the track pays itself when rounding *downward* to the next 10- or 20-cent increment as the payouts are tallied.

Racetrack odds are more precise than casino odds, which is why they were chosen to illustrate the concept. In a casino, a $2.00 bet on anything with 2–1 odds (for example) returns exactly $6.00. Never a penny more or a penny less.

As a final word, it is important to distinguish between casino odds of say, 8 *to* 1 and 8 *for* 1. The former returns 8 units profit for each unit wagered, *plus* the return of your original bet. The latter gives you 8 units for 1, period. Translated, 8 *for* 1 equals 7 *to* 1. Why are there two methods? For the same reason a $3.00 burger is priced $2.99: it sounds like a better deal ✠

SUMMARY: COMPULSION, CONTINUUM, AND HOUSE EDGE

Compulsion, Continuum and *House Edge* comprise the essence of the casino's arsenal, and should be feared in that order. In the absence of these three, casinos would need federal aid to thrive in our society.

The best way to handle *Compulsion* is to keep tabs on what you're doing, as if you're watching yourself. When you begin to deviate from the plan, it's time to bail out. Do so quickly before you get caught in the snare.

Continuum is manageable as long as you make it a point to pace yourself, and, not stay too long. Don't let the table put you in a trance. Stay on top of things.

Obviously, you should stick to games (and the bets within those games) that carry lower house percentages, for although the *house edge* is characterized as the least harmful of the *terrible three,* there lies the accompanying presumption that you have the good sense to avoid (as a general rule, but not as an absolute) those bets that carry percentages running into two figures.

The best way to avoid all three of these trappings is to make it a habit to keep your visits to the casinos as brief as possible, and, watch yourself like a hawk. You're part of a commando mission, raiding an enemy target. You need to strike quickly and deep, then get the heck out of there.

The ones who lose are the ones who stay too long ✠

3

NECESSITIES
AND REALITIES

Back in Chapter 1 you learned of the basics needed to become a credible player of casino games: *Money, strategy* and *discipline.* When you strip away the fluff, these are the essentials you'll need, but *getting started* is a bit more involved.

This is what's addressed in this chapter: the *necessities and realities* of a career in player-side gaming ✠

THE SYNCHRONIZATION
IMPERATIVE

Did I mention. . .that I never said this was going to be easy? There are some preparations that are necessary, for you to go from your present career to that of the future.

The first obstacle you will face is *Synchronization of the Four.* This is a reference to the four conditions that must be in sync for you to have any chance at success:

Don't even *think* about getting started unless Jupiter and Saturn are conjunct, the 13th of the month has passed, you're on good terms with both parents, and the skies are clear.

If only it was that easy. Actually, the four I mean, in the most basic terms, are *Time, Money, Access,* and *Strategy.*

1) **Time.** *You need time (away from a primary occupation, or any other potential schedule conflict).*
2) **Money.** *You need a bankroll, plus a second set of funds to carry you until you are financially secure.*
3) **Access.** *You need to live close to one or more casinos, or to allow for traveling expenses.*
4) **Strategy.** *That's what this book is for, but you need to add discipline for it to work.*

It is not easy to position oneself so that these four elements are synchronized. Trying to compromise any of these categories, however, is a sure-fire recipe for disaster:

If you're short on *time,* you will compromise your patience. If you're short on *money,* you'll be playing scared, throwing you off your game. And if you're short on *discipline.* . .turn out the lights, it's over, so long, good night.

Psychology plays a critical role in this script. It's a *must* that everything is going for you, *and you know it.* Without that edge, you're just another schmuck trying to get lucky.

And, uh, before you go making too many plans, like whether you prefer a red Ferrari or white, or if you should get a Lear jet, there's one tricky little question you should ponder:

Can you do it? Assuming that you'll succeed because it's something you want really, really bad. . .would be a grave mistake. Over ninety percent of those who buy this book will likely fail because they just haven't got what it takes to discipline themselves through the ordeal that I call a livelihood.

It's nice to dream, but before you step *into* the dream, see if you can find out if it's **real** ✠

THE PARTNERSHIP IMPERATIVE

Short as it is, this one page is absolutely indispensible. The concept presented right here is what separates this book from all those that couldn't get the job done.

The **Partnership Imperative** is pretty much what it sounds like: The *absolute need* for a partner or assistant. I hope this comes as not too much of a shock, but it is not realistic to expect that you can go out there and fly when you've never seen the cockpit. There is a training period that must be passed through. This cannot be emphasized too strongly, for I don't think it humanly possible for you, or anyone, to succeed without help.

To make this work, you need an associate who is *detached from the flow of the game.* You see, the one who places the bets must not be the one holding the purse strings.

This associate will come from one of two places: a friend or mate who follows your instructions *implicitly,* or someone you hire. Choosing who does what is not critical, as long as the one handling the money isn't doing the betting.

As soon as you arrive at the tables, the *treasurer* will start planning your exit. No joke. His immediate objective will be to seek the earliest possible moment for troop withdrawal while staying within procedure guidelines.

This page is just a preview—because this isn't the sort of thing to spring on one's readers in the final chapter, but please be advised: *This is what it takes* ✠

DO YOU HAVE
WHAT IT TAKES?

Speaking of *what it takes,* do you have it? Do you *think* you have it? Can you get it? Before you get in too deep, there are some questions you should consider about whether you possess the rare blend of qualities needed for the mission.

If you *strictly* follow the teachings in this book, you could end up making an exceptional income. But what you must do will go against the grain of everything you've ever done.

Do you have what it takes to become a robot, stripped of all senses and emotions? *Can you deal with* the monotony of a career that is devoid of fulfillment? *Have you prepared* a vocational alibi, the lie you will have to live to get along in a world that despises gamblers? *Can you handle* the management of an income that moves backwards as well as forward? *Can you deal with* having to be *right,* time after time, as a necessity to survive?

Can you sustain the loss of friends who are convinced you're on the path to self-destruction? *Do you have the guts* to carry large sums of cash through questionable neighborhoods?

Ever wonder why you've never met a professional gambler? The odds are, you don't know any. Why is that?

Success in this field carries a price that one can pay for only so long. Repressing one's natural tendencies. . .well, just isn't *natural.* Even the most accomplished veterans of the game eventually fall prey to vocational burnout.

The smart ones use their skills to raise money for business ventures *completely* unrelated to gambling! ✠

PROFILE OF A PRO

If professional gamblers *do* exist, what are they like? At what games do they excel? *How do they do what they do?*

The truth is, the ones who last the longest are those who have the most conservative income goals!

Professor Plum is a craps specialist who lives out on the west side of Las Vegas. He comes into town in the morning, plays for an hour or two and then goes home to work on his house. He had started with a bankroll of $1500 and played at the $5 level until he had won enough to play with the green chips. At that level, he needs to win only a handful of bets before he's $200 ahead and done for the day.

I asked him why he quit so early; why he didn't try for more. He said he didn't want to press his luck. But I persisted. *"Why not play two sessions every day? Wouldn't you make twice as much?"* His answer: *"I don't know."*

He may not have realized it, but his preoccupation with other projects probably figured largely in his success. He didn't have time to be greedy. But I already knew the answer.

Only when you've looked at the world through the eyes of a seasoned veteran of the game does the answer come through crystal clear and undiffused:

When you've lived that life, you have enough respect for your rival to stop challenging him *once you've gotten what you need.* The moment you quit for the day is the most cherished moment in the life of a gambler, because finally, you don't have to put any more of your ever-precious money at risk.

Success at gambling is a lesson in humility. Even someone who has made $2000 a day for the last ten years can never rest, can never coast, can never boast. He's flirting with disaster every time he sets foot inside a casino, and well does he know it. The day he becomes cocky is the day he goes down.

Ms. Scarlett represents the other side of the coin. I kept seeing her at the craps table at the Frontier (in Las Vegas) every night, and I finally decided I had to find out what her story was. She had long, blonde hair, but her general manner was crude and loud, like a biker babe.

She had been living there at the Frontier in a comped suite, but her room comp was about to be rescinded, for the casino had won back most of the $28,000 she'd won the past month playing craps. I asked her if we could talk, and she told me stories all night long. From these, and from seeing the way she spread out the greens whenever she thought she'd found a hot table, I was convinced that her stories were accurate. Her career, however, was very unstable. She would go from being very rich to very poor, very fast. Then back to rich. Hers was a rough-and-tumble existence, a study in chaos and life on the edge.

But none of this is what you wanted, or expected, to hear. You wanted James Bond, who picks up the dice, rolls a ten and says *"I'll take full odds on the ten, $300 on the hardway, $250 on the 11 and the limit on all the numbers, thank you very much,"* and walks away twenty minutes later with fifty grand profit and a busty babe in a low-cut dress. Right?

This isn't *Diamonds Are Forever*. This is real life. Besides, he was playing with *someone else's* money.

A real pro *never* plays that way, risking a huge amount on one outcome, and relying heavily on luck. Most look at it this way: Every bet is a seed planted. Some bear fruit, some don't. But you never know which one will do what.

The accumulation of good seeds, minus the bad, is what makes up your income. Your skill and experience assure you that in the long run, the majority will succeed ✠

THE IMPORTANCE
OF A LOW PROFILE

*The display of status symbols often indicates low self-esteem.
A self-confident person can afford to project a modest image.*

—H. Jackson Browne

Well then, how far off the mark *is* James Bond? Does real life even come close?

There is a picture:

He is a sharp dresser, immaculately groomed, and he knows every casino game inside out. He can quote the house edge for any game, is tops in his field, and feared by the casinos. He drives a turquoise-grey Ferrari, owns homes on both coasts, and is usually in the company of a glamorous blonde.

Feared by the casinos? *Right.* Disregarding that little gem, the casanova I've just described is beyond conspicuous all the way to flamboyant, and that's way off the map. Only the rich or foolish can get away with drawing that much attention to themselves, and in case you didn't know, they generally lose.

Remember, a casino is first and foremost a business. Seldom is their cash flow threatened, but when it is, they'll take measures to protect themselves. And that may include barring a player who has a habit of winning. A professional understands the importance of keeping a low profile, so as not to jeopardize the privilege of making money in a casino.

It comes down to a matter of discretion. Don't give them your name, don't use credit. Spread your action around to different casinos and different work shifts. Don't let the same floorperson see you winning too much, too often.

Casinos generally appreciate their image as places where money is recklessly exchanged, but they are watching every dime. You can always nab a big score *once,* but you better believe, they'll be paying close attention after that.

Some years ago while staying at Lake Tahoe, I financed the trip with my minibaccarat earnings. While at a table in Harrah's, a middle-aged Asian gentleman took a seat at my table and asked for a marker for $2000. While that was being processed, he asked the floorperson if the table limit could be raised from $1000 to $2000. The floorperson politely said he didn't have the authority to do so, but after a quick phone call the limit was raised. I watched this man play with a few greens stacked up at first, then his wagers quickly began to grow in size. In just a few minutes, he was making $1200 bets (by my rough count) with the black chips. I saw him lose one of those large bets, but it didn't bother him one bit. He appeared bored and distracted, as if he was just killing time. At one point he got up and left the table for a few minutes, leaving several thousand dollars worth of chips stacked on the felt.

Twenty-five minutes after arriving, he left the table with $7800 worth of value chips, and that was *after* paying off the marker. Once he was gone, I was at the table to witness the look of apology on the dealer's face as she recounted the damage to her superior. He was not a happy man. She just shrugged.

The next day that table was shut down. There was, in fact, no minibaccarat action in the whole casino. I asked when a table would open, and was told *Noon.* But it never happened. And three days later (when I left Lake Tahoe) there was no change in the situation. To this day, I have nary a clue how that man did what he did. If he was a pro, perhaps I could learn from him.

Then again, perhaps he could learn from me. He did well, but he won't get another chance in *that* casino ✠

HOW MUCH IS ENOUGH?

Money isn't everything, but it sure beats the heck out of whatever's in second place.

—attributed to Paul W. Bryant

As you have just learned, winning $8000 in a casino is all it might take to have your privileges revoked, if it's not a fluke induced by alcoholic overindulgence. But this raises the question: How much *can* you get away with?

Even when pursuing an aggressive income goal, I would advise that you try for no more than $1500 per day, and spreading the action around so that no table game loses more than $500 or so, except on occasion. And that assumes you can win that much in the first place, and *that* goal hasn't even appeared on your horizon. And don't forget: if you play for high stakes, there will be days when you'll *lose* that amount, or *more!*

When betting at high levels, your chief concern will be limiting your losses, but there will be times when it's okay to exceed the recommended figures. If a shooter is having the roll of his life at your table, casino personnel generally accept the fact that some of the more aggressive players might pull down five figures in an hour . . .but you won't run into that too often.

Many pros are content to shoot for a daily profit of $200 to $300, giving them a thousand a week. This goal is easily attainable for them, and it leaves time to pursue other interests. But perhaps most important of all, it keeps their betting levels within their *Comfort Zone. . . .*

THE COMFORT ZONE

If your bets aren't large enough to hurt you, it won't do you any good to win.

—Bill Lear

Imagine that you were playing a casino table game at the $5 level, and you had won $60 in thirty minutes. You had made a prior decision to keep your bets at the nickel level until obtaining some assurance that your experimental strategy was sound. As you were accumulating this information, you projected mentally to the figure you would have won had you played with the black ($100) chips instead of the reds ($5 chips). Sounds like a simple mathematical conversion, doesn't it?

Indeed it is, long as you're playing with figures in your head. But when you're using the black chips for real, your hands are gonna shake, your palms are gonna sweat, and you're gonna feel like you've just been stricken with the plague.

Now you've done it. You're alone, frightened, and in the dark. And it's all because you strayed too far from the warmth and safety of your own personal *Comfort Zone.*

At the nickel level, you were doing okay once you got past the first four bets, which were losses. Being down twenty bucks is no big deal, but if those bets had been made with blacks instead of reds, you'd be out $400, and you would *feel* that loss. Would you have done the same thing at that point, as you did with the red chips? Sorry to say, but there's a greater chance that you wouldn't. And that means that the $1200 figure you derived from your conversion would be false.

This is what happens when you play outside that venerable perimeter known as the *Comfort Zone*. Reaching your ideal betting level is a mentality that must be worked toward in stages. You're not going to make it in a single leap. Actually, you might *get there,* but you won't last.

While living in Las Vegas some years ago, I decided to go to the Frontier every night after work during a two-week period, in an attempt to pick up an extra $50 to $100 per night, playing craps. It worked great: at the end of twelve consecutive winning days, my bankroll had grown from an initial stake of $100, to over $1100. That was all the proof I needed. I was on my way. It was time to go for larger gains.

That's when the losses came. I tried to bet my way out of the crisis with even larger bets, using timing as an excuse to legitimize my compulsion. But the first night of playing at higher levels, I blew the entire bankroll I had worked so hard for two weeks to acquire, *plus* the original stake. Then, after licking my wounds, I pulled my ass off the pavement and tried again, managing to build up *another* $1000 over the next two weeks. . .only to lose *every last dollar again* on the night I chose to go for larger gains!

You know, you tell yourself that this just can't happen again. It just can't. To believe otherwise is to surrender to superstition. But what do you do when it *does* happen? How in God's name can you explain that to anyone?

How can you explain it to yourself?

Take note, readers. This is the kind of jerkwater runaround you're in for when you choose a career as a gambler.

My mistake was trying to move up too soon. If I'd waited until I had built up $3000 instead of just $1000, I *might* have had a prayer. I know it seems like an absurd extension of what should be necessary, but that's the way it is. Moving up through the ranks of betting levels is an insanely difficult proposition.

It seemed to me that my goals were reasonable, but I choked. Moral is, without a (seemingly) preposterous amount of discipline, you're gonna get whipped ✠

SUMMARY: NECESSITIES AND REALITIES

Everyone has talent; what is rare is the courage to follow the talent to the dark place where it leads.

—Erica Jong

If you are to succeed as a professional gambler, there's only one way it's going to happen: you're going to have to want it really, really, really bad. So bad, you would walk barefoot over hot coals, watch Toyota commercials all day long, or climb to the top of the Sears tower with suction cups.

You starting to see a picture here?

This is not the glamorous life. See, there's this one question: *Do you have the right stuff to succeed?*

Chances are, you don't. Odds are, you have

NO IDEA what you're in for.

But, how can this be worse than flipping burgers for a nickel ninety-five for some parasitic loon?

Trick is, for you to succeed, you have to win. Then you have to continue to win. You have to go to a higher plane than the rest of mankind. Any jughead can try it and fail. Millions already have. Did I say millions? I meant billions.

But *you* won't choke like the rest of those clowns. *You* have the right motivation, and your will is strong.

Takes more than that. But, maybe you're right. Maybe *you* are the one who can do it. We'll see ✠

4

FUNDAMENTALS
OF GAMING

*If you have built castles in the air, your work need not be lost.
That is where they should be. Now put the foundations under them.*

—Henry David Thoreau

Knowing what to expect of one's opponent is what separates the winner from the loser. Especially, when gambling in a casino, the better you understand common *table trends*, the better you can coordinate your game plan.

The key to successful gambling lies in the ability to anticipate trend development. What this means is that you should size up the table as you play, and chart a course in your mind that represents its logical destination. Then you act on that projection—for as long as you think you can continue to win.

If you don't get this; if this concept escapes you, I don't guess there's a future for you in this field. Trends are what make a career in gaming possible. Love trends as you love life itself, for they are your lifeblood. It's either that, or wait for the great white father to come cruising down the street, throwing moneybags out of the car. Or, you could wash dishes, sell shoes, or deliver pizza for a living. Lots of choices out there ✠

TRENDS IN GAMING

There are things we don't understand, yet they exist none-theless.

—Lt. Worf, from
Star Trek, Next Generation

It is said to be statistically proven that the house will win in the long run. Against *the crowd*, this is true. But the serious player knows that **trends are more powerful than statistical projections.** If this was not true, it is not likely that career gambling would exist in any form on this planet.

Trends are the most positive *and* negative aspects of the game. Any game. They represent the highs and the lows. To a seasoned player, they are like gods.

Back in the days when I believed in fighting the trend, I once made the 12-hour trip to Atlantic City, parked the car, and headed straight for the roulette tables of Trump Plaza. At one of the tables, I watched as black came up six times in a row. Most definitely, that table was ripe for a bet on red. Hell, it was overdue. By my way of seeing things (at the time), this was a *gift*.

My $10 wager lost when black appeared again, so on the next spin I bet $20 on red. I was brimming with overconfidence as I watched the little white ball circle the wheel. But it happened to land on another black number. Strangely, I was *gaining* confidence as I put down $50 on the next spin, but black won yet again. Time to bring out the cannon. I laid a bill ($100) on the table and said to the dealer, *"One black, on red."* In about a minute, I watched as my bet sunk like a stone, loss number four.

Well. This *had* to be a historical first. And I was there to see it happen. Surely this is front page stuff. But where's the reporter? Where's the camera crew?

There was only one other player at the table, a young lad who had been putting a $5 chip on black with every spin. *What a loser,* I thought, not quite getting the point that he had been winning the whole time.

Hesitating a little, the pitiful *loser* put another chip on black. Is he *nuts?* Does he expect black to win *again,* after 10 straight? *I'll* show him how it's done.

With the confidence of a man who'd seen the future and knew the result, I put $200 on red.

Sure was a long ride home.

My trip allotment was $400, and $380 of that was gone in six minutes, speculating on red to win just one time. Later, I learned that streaks of eleven are not that uncommon.

That was the *hardway lesson* in trends. Hopefully, you won't need to experience that for yourself.

There's a saying that is the law of the land for horseplayers: Once you spot a pattern, it's no longer the pattern. This is true for most players, because they're unable to see the big picture. They're looking for trends that are *localized and immediate.* They miss the larger portrait that's painted right in front of them.

In this line, you will frequently encounter (what appear to be) *historical firsts;* things you would not have thought possible had you not seen with your own eyes. In time, you will become inured to the incredible, and you'll expect the unexpected.

When things like that occur at the tables, don't run and hide. Chase it down. Take it for all its worth, for this is one way you *win* in the casinos. Just don't use that as *an excuse to abandon your discipline,* for that is how you *lose* in casinos.

Though these things defy one's imagination, they've always occurred and always will, as long as man and casino games endure. It's called the *defiance of rational explanation.* And believe or not, there's a logical reason for every bit of it. . . .

THE RANDOM WALK

Chance is always powerful; let your hook always be cast. In the pool where you least expect it, there will be a fish.

—Ovid

The concept of the *Random Walk* was introduced about three hundred years ago, and has been studied by some of the greatest men of modern science, including Albert Einstein. For brevity, this book will cover only the basic concept.

We will use the flip of a coin to illustrate the point. If you are standing in one place, and you've decided to move one step to the right after every *heads* decision, and one step to the left after *tails*, where will you be after, say, twenty decisions?

Most of the time, you'll end up close to where you started, but if you keep repeating the same trial, there will be times when one side may win fifteen out of twenty, for example, which would put you way to the left or way right.

If you persist, you'll get results that are even farther out, but as you do so, the totals for all decisions from each side will move closer to 50%. This is known as the *Law of Very Large Numbers*. There are books currently in print (that address the scientific aspects of random numerical events) which show the bell curve that is formed by cumulative trials.

Now, stop and think for a moment about the ongoing action in your average casino. At a craps table, the dice may roll 200 times an hour. Multiply that times 24 hours and then that result times an average of three active tables. That works out to 14,400 betting opportunities a day, just for the game of craps.

On that basis, with betting from all other table games added in, Trump Plaza in Atlantic City may well produce over 100,000 table game results every day.

From those 100,000 decisions, there will be a percentage that is skewed to the outer limits—when viewed in groups—and another percentage that isn't quite so far out but is nevertheless unique. Most of the time you'll get your even balance per the experiment. But keep in mind: while some tables are doing *this,* others are doing *that,* resulting in the occurrence of numerous *outer limit trends* at almost any point in time, in any active casino.

The seasoned player knows that all he has to do is play the games, and the trends will come to him. They're part of the natural order of things, especially in casinos, where trends live and grow in abundance. And some players (like myself) make it a point to *look for* specific trends, allowing one to (occasionally) bet with pinpoint precision. At the craps table, there are numerous outward signs that tell you whether the dice are likely to pass. At a roulette table, the scoresigns (used by the major casinos) tell you right up front what's going on at that table, and what's *been* going on for the last twenty decisions or so.

When you start to understand the dominion of *trends,* your outlook will change, and your game will improve ✠

TRENDS IN EVERYDAY LIFE

It may help you to understand trends in gaming if you are reminded that they are part of everyday living. People seldom think about it, but trends can in fact influence or even alter the direction of one's personal development.

Surely you've had days when everything went wrong, and then days when things went superbly. This is a truly remarkable trend, because it is not confined to a single category; it affects all that you do and everything you touch for an entire day!

Have you ever tried to purchase an item you don't often use, and can't find a store that has it in stock, anywhere in the city? Have you ever run an errand, and all fifteen traffic lights you had to pass through were green? Have you ever gone weeks without a date, then have two the same night? Or noticed that both of the local college basketball teams won last night's game by exactly fourteen points? Or that suddenly, you're seeing red convertibles, everywhere you go?

Maybe you haven't seen or experienced any of this, but I think you could relate to the concept.

You need to be aware of the existence of trends, because it helps you avoid being thrown off balance by a statistical fluke that may occur when your money is on the line: *Did you see that? The double zero came up four spins in a row!* So what? You can't let that throw you off your game.

If you pursue a gaming career, expect to be absolutely floored on a regular basis by trends that defy your imagination, and all manner of explanation! ✠

THE FIRE THAT NEVER DIES

Mozart: *How would you translate that?*
  Salieri: *Consigned to flames of wall.*
Mozart: *Do you believe in it?*
  Salieri: *In what?*
Mozart: *A fire which never dies, burning you forever.*
  Salieri: *(pause) Oh, yes.*

—from the movie *Amadeus*

There was once an experiment I performed in Atlantic City: I went from casino to casino, looking for a roulette scoresign with a *Reoccurring Single* trend in progress (coming up in Chapter 9). At the appropriate moment, I played one $25 bet and then moved on to another table or casino. Betting on that basis, I won twelve of fourteen wagers. The next day I tried the exact same thing, but encountered results that were radically different. (I quit for the day after losing seven out of seven bets.)

Those examples demonstrate the power of trends, for though my betting activity was not confined to a single casino, the trend was consistent, offering winners on the one day, then reversing its course on the following day. It reminded me of a *fire that never dies,* described in the quote above.

Moving from table to table can help one reduce the damage inflicted by the house edge, but keep your eyes on the big picture. If you keep getting whacked, **change the procedure to concur with the results the tables are disposed to give.** But in doing so, be sure to react *to the group,* not just the latest result.

You cannot win against the *fire which never dies* ✠

THE CLUSTER PRINCIPLE

FIGURE 4
Fourteen events, evenly spaced

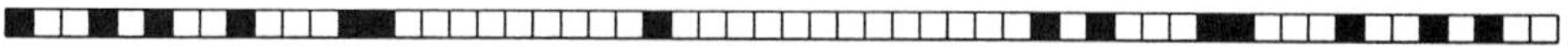

FIGURE 5
Fourteen events, randomly spaced

Through the years, people ask: *How can anyone hope to beat the house when the games are slanted in their favor?*

The need to provide a concise answer forced me to examine what I've been doing, which led to the definition of a targeting method for wagering that I call the *Cluster Principle.*

Figure 4 shows fourteen events, *evenly spaced* along a lateral continuum of 56 trials. If gaming events were assembly lines, the black squares would represent a one in four chance, meriting a 3–1 return to *equitably* compensate the risk.

Below it, Figure 5 shows fourteen events *randomly spaced* along the same continuum. This figure more closely approximates authentic table game results.

Take a good look at Figure 5. In the middle of the continuum there are two large gaps. Then look at the *impact* of those gaps on the *other* results. Because of the extended absence of that event, (which will frequently occur), the remaining results are compressed into tight groups, or *clusters.*

Now, in real life, it's not likely that Figure 5's dry spell would self-correct (so as to concur with the probability) by the 56th result, but this helps illustrate the *Cluster Principle:*

For every absence of a probable event, there is an equivalent compression of subsequent events.

This is kind of like saying that *what goes up must come down.* If, for example, an event that has a one-in-four expectation does not occur for one hundred decisions. . .*somewhere,* a deficit is accruing. Now, we all know the dice and the roulette wheel have no memory, but the fact remains: statistically, a deficit is mounting, and at some point that debt will have to be paid. *The Law of Averages cannot be defied into infinity.*

How do players win when the games are slanted toward the casino? They target the clusters. They wait until the table sends a message revealing what it's likely to do next, then make their play. That is, after all, why they came.

What does this tell you? Well, if an event isn't happening, don't chase it. Bet on it after it begins to show up and lay back when it fades. You won't catch a *cluster* every time, but if you make it a habit to wait for the right signals, you won't spend so much time chasing rainbows in the dark ✠

POSITIVE AND
NEGATIVE TRENDS

In gaming, all table patterns can be classified as belonging to one of the following groups:

1) ***Positive Trends:*** *Events that occur in clusters.*
2) ***Negative Trends:*** *Prolonged absences of an event.*
3) ***Neutral Table Patterns:*** *Ordinary event sequences.*

These were just discussed, though they had not been given names. Each one of these could be exploited in gaming situations, though most pros and semi-pros prefer *positive trends.* Then again, some do favor *negative trends.* No one I know bothers with the *neutrals,* at least not by design.

Positive trends refer to the *presence* of an event, in groups or clusters. *Negative trends* describe the *absence* of such an event, and *neutrals* are normal, uneventful table patterns.

Positive trends are more fruitful than *negatives,* because the aberration *favors* the occurrence instead of opposing it. Problem is, *negative trends* are easier to spot. When a number isn't hitting, it can be very obvious. Conversely, a *positive trend* may have run its course by the time its presence is realized.

This book advocates the pursuit of positive trends, because chasing negative trends is, in effect, *fighting the trend.*

If you specialize in certain table patterns or events, *positive trends* will be easy to catch in the early stages, for you'll be waiting for their arrival. Your snare will be set ✠

SUMMARY OF
TRENDS IN GAMING

Some years ago, I remember saying to someone, *"When you understand numbers, you understand life."* That may have just been some trash I was talking; I don't remember. But I think the same could be said for *trends,* though doing so will probably help you understand *gaming* more than life.

Trends, believe it or not, can help you see into the future. Such a vision is far from definite, but frequently solid enough to justify a wager. More on that in Chapter 9.

For me to suggest that *positive* and *negative trends* are both bettable situations may seem like a contradiction. But you see, both represent a deviation from the norm. This is when you should pay attention to subsequent developments, for they often herald the arrival of a new table pattern.

Some authors of gaming books don't say a word about trends. Others leave it to the reader to decide their importance. And I say that you cannot hope to succeed until you understand them, for they are at the heart of professional gambling.

Life's a gamble. Whenever you run a yellow light, put your moves on a babe or drink city tap water, you're just rolling the dice. There's a measure of risk in everything you do.

As long as you're doing all that gambling, you might as well make it pay. In today's world, your chances for success increase in direct proportion to how well you know the odds, and understand the power and implications of *trends* ✠

5

THE GARDEN OF RISK

To win, you have to risk loss.

—Jean-Claude Killy

It was the movie *Cocoon* that taught me a very memorable lesson about the relationship between *yin* and *yang*. In that movie, a group of extraterrestials had been using a swimming pool to store embryonic aliens. Some senior citizens were using that pool on the sly, and had noticed that the water gave them incredible vitality. But while they were gaining energy, the aliens inside the cocoons (under the water) were being robbed of their lives.

Initially, the seniors thought they had discovered a fountain of youth. But the real world isn't like that, is it? When somebody gains, somebody else will lose. Every time you push a button *down*, somewhere, another button is going to pop *up*.

So it is when you live in the *Garden of Risk*. Even if you are lucky enough to win, you cannot continue to do so with impunity, because your wins are causing somebody else to *lose*. And trust me on this: *nobody* likes to lose.

They say *discretion* is the better part of valor. It is also one of the unspoken precepts of the *Player's Edge* ✠

45

THE PLAYER'S EDGE

Neglect not the gift that is in thee.

—New Testament
I Timothy 4:14

As if a counterweight to the knowledge that your opponent is indomitable, it's a good feeling to walk into a casino and know that *you* have the edge. Now, a professional gambler—by definition—*has* to win more than lose. . .but exactly what *are* the contents of his little bag of tricks?

The *Player's Edge* consists of four points:

1) ***When losing, you can walk.***
2) ***You can vary the size of your bet.***
3) ***You can choose where to play.***
4) ***You can respond to the table results.***

Most people don't know what a huge advantage these offer. In effect, the casino is confined to linear movement while you can go anywhere you please. To elaborate:

1) ***When losing, you can walk.*** Casinos don't have this option. Can you imagine being stripped to the bone by a mob of greedy players while you stand there, powerless to stop them? Casinos face this dilemma every time a craps table heats up, or some high rollers get lucky at baccarat. There's not very much the casino can do—except go to the vault.

2) *You can vary the size of your bet.* Ideally, a player should bet low (or leave) when losing, and press up his bets when he's doing well. It's called *lose low, win high.* It's how you minimize losses and maximize your gains.

3) *You can choose where to play.* Frequently, there are signs that clue you in to the table's temperature or disposition. Some tables whisper, some shout. Of course, you never know what the future will bring at any given table, but you're better off if you make it a habit to be selective.

Also, you can take your business to where the best deals are. Not all casinos make the same payoffs for bets. Some pay 14–1 for the 3 or 11 at craps; others offer 15–1. Some pay triple for a field roll 12 while most others merely pay double. Some casinos have roulette scoresigns, some don't.

4) *You can react and respond to the table results.* Every table you will ever encounter is inanimate. It may seem otherwise, but the truth is, it does not and cannot think. *You* can adjust to the changing situation as the changes occur. *You* can bob and weave, thrust and parry, circle and pounce. The table cannot react to anything. It just grinds out random numbers, endlessly and forever. It is doomed to a life of being reacted *upon.*

Imagine that it had a life of its own. Imagine that it could fight back. For just a moment, imagine.

The *Player's Edge* is the sum of the points listed above, plus this very pertinent advice: *Be discreet about your wins and losses.* You can't afford to let the world know how much money you're turning over, because 1) there are people out there who would kill you for fifty bucks, and 2) the casinos can deny you access, if you prove to be a constant drain on their resources. If you seek a long and prosperous life, be sure to keep these in mind.

The point of the *player's edge* is to neutralize the destructive effects of the *house edge.* But your biggest *edge* will be sourced to your *discipline.* The same discipline, in fact, the casinos impose upon their obedient staff! ✠

THE COLDEST GAME

There is no law that says you cannot lose 100 consecutive bets.

—the Author

It may serve you to recite the words above, or burn them into your eternal memory. Of course, no player ever lost that many, because he'd be brrrroke long before he even got close. But fate and chance work in mysterious ways.

To illustrate the point, we will re-enact a trip of mine to Las Vegas in the early 1980's. My first buy-in was at a roulette table at CircusCircus. I was playing *Chinese Roulette,* a hodge-podge of even money wagers that had worked well for me in Atlantic City. At CircusCircus, however, fate was not so kind. I ended up losing *the first sixteen spins.* Yep. Sixteen.

You cannot imagine how that felt. Losing $100 was nothing. What got to me was battling an omnipotent force that could read my thoughts and cause the opposite result of my bet. . .*into eternity.* You see, I was playing a different outside bet with every spin, yet *mister opposite* kept pace with every step.

Granted, sixteen losses is far from a hundred, but you know, I never saw the **end** of that streak. If you put yourself in that place, you might understand that after loss twelve, it was like something from the Twilight Zone. But there's no reason the table can't do the opposite of what you do, indefinitely.

At the time, it didn't occur to me that this was the polar opposite of what worked so well in Atlantic City when I was playing the same strategy. It's not so strange *when you win!*

It is this type of situation that separates *discipline in gaming* from that which is needed in other areas of professional expertise. You have to take these aberrations in stride, just as the casinos do. It's either that, or take a bullet in the gut.

It's always amusing to see the house lose. A few years ago at the Sands in Atlantic City, I held the dice for about 40 minutes. The other players at the table were in a state of rapture; many of them made thousands from my roll. I was wondering when the boxman would complain that I was throwing the dice wrong, or get nasty in an attempt to shut me down. How was he going to explain the $40,000 hit that occurred on his watch?

He never said a word. He just sat there smiling, as if he was enjoying every minute—of *our* collective enjoyment. He knows that you've got to take the bad with the good, but more importantly, he realizes that in the long run, the casino will do nothing but win. This reminded me how important it is to *think like a casino* when things may not be going as you'd hoped.

You will *never* have to worry about being held hostage in a situation like that, while your opponents grow rich before your eyes. You will walk at the first sign of trouble. But it can't be done without discipline.

Well then, exactly what is *discipline?* In the simplest terms, it is a combination of patience, restraint and experience. It is the recognition that it's far easier to lose than win, and the extraordinary ability, when necessary, to suppress your natural inclinations. It is a tacit, unwavering commitment to stay the course and avoid the numerous temptations that surround you every minute of the day. And it's the coldest game you'll ever play.

One of the things that held me back for a good many years was misunderstanding the concept. I'd ask myself. . .*Now, what is the disciplined move to make in this situation?*

Don't give it a thought. This book spells out precisely what you should be doing. All you have to do is stay on track and follow the procedure. The wins will come ✠

A PREVIEW
OF WHAT TO EXPECT

Protect the downside, and the upside will take care of itself.

—Donald J. Trump,
from *The Art of the Deal*

Up till now, I have emphasized the downside to this career more than the benefits, because the glamorous image of gamblers propagated by Hollywood is an exaggeration. And the picture of gamblers in the minds of those who avoid the sport is one of avid losers. When the procedures outlined in this book are strictly observed, the truth will be found between these extremes, but I hesitate to paint too rosy a picture. One's pulse tends to quicken when cash flow is discussed, and there is no place for emotion in this arena. This logic should make more sense as you evolve from reader to participant.

In the following section, you'll learn about the recommended casino games, which are *craps, minibaccarat* and *roulette*. I hope you understand that this endorsement is not an unconditional seal of approval on these three games; it applies only to the methods that are specifically represented herein.

Before we get to the rules of play, however, you should have an idea of what to expect and how it may affect you, including some of the positive attributes that I am otherwise reluctant to express on these pages.

If you have been paying attention, you should know by now that there is no such thing as a sure bet, or even a smart bet. The closest you will ever come is what this book calls an educated bet. But even in such case, you never, ever *bet the farm* no matter how good the odds may be. Even if you have 99 ways to win and only one way to lose, *and* the return is 10–1, it's a bad bet if you're compelled to overextend yourself.

You don't need to rely on lucky wins. There's no good reason for you to take that kind of chance when you have the skill to make an exceptional living *without* heavy risk.

One of the paradoxes of gaming is how you will feel when you enter a casino as a seasoned player. Part of you feels a sense of pride that you can withdraw money from the casinos as if they were banks holding cash reserves in your name. The other part will feel weak and inadequate because once again you've got to put your money at risk, and frankly, the very thought makes you feel a little sick to your stomach. Yesterday, you were **right** many more times than not, just as you were all last week, last month and last year. But today, the counter has been reset to 000, and you have to start all over, building the day's empire from scratch. And who the hell are you to presume you can take on such an opponent, built from the losses of players spanning generations, who tried but failed to do exactly what you're about to do?

You're a proven professional, that's who. Your track record shows that you've attained a level of proficiency that few have ever known, and with that comes confidence, and power. You've paid your dues. You know how to exercise restraint in the heat of battle. Your work is interesting, even a bit enjoyable, but you know how to anchor that enjoyment with an awareness of what can go wrong and how quickly it can happen.

As you stride down the aisles, you shake your head as you watch the players lose themselves in malicious euphoria, for it reminds you of your destiny, should you become careless and forget about the treacherous undercurrents that silently erode the fortunes of those who play.

Some dealers would pay dearly to possess your skill. When the floorperson sees where you've chosen to sit, he might replace the dealer just because you happened to sit there. And the cocktail waitress brings you your favorite drink, *pineapple juice, no ice,* without asking.

Your life is good. You awake at nine-thirty and look out the window at the Atlantic Ocean. You listen to the seagulls as you stroll the boardwalk with your partner on your way to breakfast at the Showboat buffet, and there's no real hurry to go anywhere or do anything. Your workday might be over by noon or it might not begin until midnight. Your call. You have complete control over your life and how you spend your time. You do what you want, where you want and when.

Next week you'll go to the Bahamas where you'll earn just a bit less than your average back home, and you'll have lots of time to explore the cays on a sailboat or cruise the island on a motorbike. And next month you'll be traveling to Europe where you'll visit the French casinos at Trouville and Chamonix before heading to the Casino Ruhl De Nice on the riviera, and then to the Mirabeau hotel in Monte Carlo.

How do you get to that place? Like anything worth having, you can't jump right in there and expect to be fantastic. You can't succeed at anything in life without investing a great deal of hard work and discipline.

There are tricks that can assist you along the way, however. One I use is to remind myself of a quote from Donald Trump's first book, which appears at the beginning of this subchapter: ***Protect the downside, and the upside will take care of itself.*** No matter how good you get, never think for a minute that your opponent is no match for you. You'd best stay humble if the concept of survival carries any weight at all.

Balance is the name of the game. Believe in yourself, *and* in your opponent. And if you subscribe to the idea of *wealth without work,* you'd best get out now. As Ralph Waldo Emerson once said, *Only shallow men believe in luck* ✠

6

AMERICAN ROULETTE: RULES OF PLAY

Roulette is the most popular of the three recommended table games, and it is relatively easy to learn. It's a game of chance, but with selective wagering it can be converted to a game of skill for brief periods. You must, however, have an adequate understanding of trends, including knowledge of the different types, and roughly what frequency and duration to expect from each. Much of this can come only from experience, but there are exercises in this book which can speed the process.

Of the three games, you should spend the least amount of time at roulette. It carries a higher house edge than craps, and this edge is more destructive than the 5.26% might suggest. It's not a matter of settling for less when you win; quite often the house edge will change a (would-be) win to a loss, and it does so with no shame, right in front of your face.

All the same, roulette has two strong positives to offer: It's more widely available than the other two games, and it has wagering options that exist in no other games, including some you can create to suit your preferences.

Figure 6 shows the roulette wheel. The dealer spins it in one direction, then sets a small glass or plastic ball in motion going in the opposite direction. At intervals inside the wheel are 'baffles' that cause the ball to bounce randomly before coming to rest in a slot representing the winning number.

While the wheel is determining the winner, the dealer stacks the losing chips that were cleared from the table during the last spin, or he straightens chips for the current spin (to help avoid disputes over which numbers were covered). As the rotating ball slows down and seeks its destination, the dealer waves his hand over the layout to indicate *No more bets*. All wagers placed after this signal will be refused.

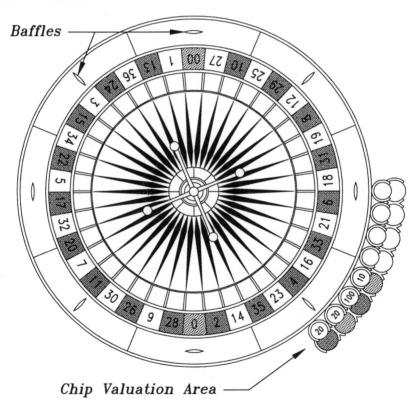

FIGURE 6
The Roulette Wheel

American roulette has eighteen red numbers, eighteen black and two green (the 0 and 00). European roulette has the same number of red and black numbers, but only one green number, 0. This cuts the vig for that version in half.

Figure 7 shows the roulette layout, upon which the bets, in the form of chips, are placed.

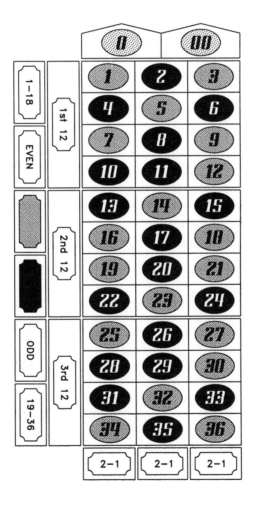

FIGURE 7
The Roulette Layout

After the wheel has produced a winning number, the dealer will place a dolly on the corresponding number on the layout, and begin clearing the table of losing chips in preparation for paying any wagers that might have won. From the moment the dealer signals *No more bets* to when he removes the dolly from the winning number, you cannot place any bets, or remove your winnings. You must wait until the payoff process is complete, which is official when the dealer removes the dolly. Remember this, if you prefer not to be scolded by the dealer.

The area with the 38 single numbers (36 red & black, plus the 0 and 00) is where the *inside bets* are made; the areas in the two adjacent sections are for *outside bets*. The table minimum applies to each of these areas *separately,* which means that at a $10 table (a table where the minimum bet is $10), you can't spread the $10 in minimum bets between these two; you must pick one or the other or play $10 in each. The table minimum and maximum bets are usually noted on a small placard next to the wheel.

Figure 8 shows the different returns possible from inside and outside bets at American roulette. The house edge for all wagers is 5.26%, with one notable exception: the inside bet at the top of the layout, called *fiveline,* carries a 7.89% vigorish, giving it the distinction of being the worst bet on the board.

The object of the game is to cover the one number out of 38 choices that becomes the winner, dictated by where the ball lands on the wheel. In your attempt to do so, you may cover as few or as many numbers as you wish. That's what's great about casinos: they don't care. They'll let you play all 38 if you want. Now, if you're a recreational gambler and have a hunch that number 17 will come up soon, you could play that number only, spin after spin, provided that you met the table minimum. This is called *longshot betting,* and that bet will pay 35–1 if you win.

If you prefer favorite odds, you could spread chips all over the board, covering twenty or more numbers. Or, you may prefer the *outside bets* that pay even money, such as red or even. Then again, you might like the 2–1 outside bets.

If you like *odds-on* wagers, you could play two of the 2–1 bets together and get really good coverage—and a very strong chance to win—but the payoff for this combination, which covers 24 numbers, is only 1–2 ($1 profit for every $2 wagered).

In between are numerous *inside* bets that pay 7–2, 5–1, 8–1 and 11–1, to name a few. The 7–2 bet just mentioned, by the way, is not listed in Figure 8, but can be constructed by playing two *corner bets,* which pay 8–1 separately. Roulette offers many ways to create bet returns of your liking.

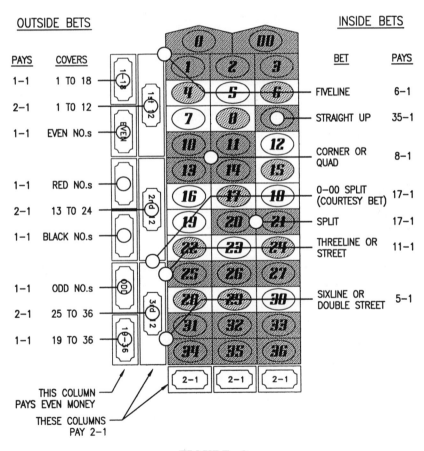

FIGURE 8
Inside and Outside Bet Returns

Please note that the inside bets shown in Figure 8 are merely examples; they are not fixed positions. Except for the *fiveline bet*, which *is* a fixed position, you can play them anywhere on the board. For example, the *split bet* shown needn't apply only to side-by-side numbers; it could be played on over-under numbers, like 26 and 29. Also, you can play multiple chips on any of the bets, or multiples of the bets themselves, such as three *sixlines* or five *corner bets*. The numerous playing options available at roulette are what help make this game popular.

Before taking a look at *outside bets,* this business of the *fiveline bet*—the one with the higher vigorish—should be clarified. I don't think the casinos set out to gouge the public when they made this bet available. More likely, they responded to public demand, because many players seem to like this bet. But since the amount of numbers covered by this wager (5) will not divide evenly into 36 like the other wagers, the corresponding payoff would end up at 6.2–1. That offbeat percentage (7.89%) comes from rounding downward to the next even bet return (6–1).

Moving on to *outside bets,* there are six that pay even money and another six that pay 2–1. The 2–1 bets don't seem to get much action, and I can tell you from personal experience that there seems to be a force loose in this world that keeps a player from being able to win this bet with reasonable frequency. Most players seem to be tuned into this, preferring the 1–1 bets instead.

Every even money (1–1) bet has an opposite. Red is opposite to black, even opposite to odd, and 1–18 (low) opposes 19–36 (high). With any of these wagers, there are 18 ways to win and 20 ways to lose. The extra two ways to lose, the 0 and 00 (which are not considered red, black, even or odd) comprise the house edge through simple numerical advantage.

Many players like even money bets because they think they can exploit a trend of some kind. In a situation where you have roughly an even chance to win, they wonder: how long can the wheel do the opposite of what they do? Well, it's thinking like *that* that's kept this country back *fifty years!*

Of all the even money bets, most players seem to prefer the red/black. Some will jump back and forth between the six, and some play several of them together. The only problem with that, however, is the zeroes. When they show up, all even money bets will lose simultaneously.

As Figure 8 shows, the even money bets are all situated in the outermost column on the long side of the layout. The 2–1 bets are located between them and the inside bets, and also on the short side of the board at the end farthest from the wheel. The latter are called *Column bets* and cover the twelve numbers in each of the three columns marked 2–1. These are the least popular outside bets. Most who play the 2–1s prefer the dozens, marked *1st 12, 2nd 12* and *3rd 12*, because it's easier to track a wide block of consecutive numbers than a long column.

That pretty well covers the bet types and positions except for one lone banana that isn't marked. For player convenience, casinos allow players to play the 0-00 Split on the *courtesy bar* (the line separating the 2nd 12 and 3rd 12). It may seem odd for an inside bet to be positioned amongst the outside bets, but it makes sense. Many players like to hedge their bets with coverage of the 0-00, but only a couple of them can physically reach the spot where that bet lies at the top of the layout.

Please bear in mind that the options shown in this chapter are not part of the book's recommended strategy. This is strictly an accounting of the rules, the percentages, and a handful of the betting variations that are possible.

Before selecting a table and making a buy-in, you really should take some time to observe the betting patterns of the players of this game. If you've never done this, I'm sure you will find this to be rewarding, or at the very least, entertaining ✠

VALUE CHIPS/TABLE CHIPS

Value chips, also known as *generic chips,* are casino tokens having a set monetary value, which can be used interchangeably at all table games within the confines of the issuing casino. They are made of high-impact plastic, are roughly the size of the old-style silver dollars, and are available in numerous denominations, the most common being $1, $5, $25 and $100. Not all casinos carry the full range, but most have those four, and have standard colors for them. The $1 chips are usually white, and referred to as *singles* or *whites.* The $5 chips are called *nickels* or *reds* and are generally red. $25 chips are green, and are called *quarters* or *greens.* $100 chips are always black, and are called *blacks.*

Of these four, the one that is least likely to be colored as noted is the $1 chip. They are white in most casinos, but I have also seen them beige, brown, yellow, light blue, dark blue and medium grey. If you happen to encounter these off-colors, you had best refer to them as *singles* or *dollars* instead of *whites.*

For the high rollers, many casinos have chips in $500, $1000 and $5000 denominations. And for the whales (very large bettors), some even carry $25,000 and $100,000 chips.

Now, there is another class of chips, known as *table chips,* or *house chips,* or *colored chips.* These are issued to roulette players (only), to help the dealer identify who bet what in the common betting area. These chips may not leave the table, and have to be exchanged for value chips at the end of play.

Incidentally, value chips are allowed at roulette, if there aren't too many players placing bets in the same section of the layout, or, if you are placing outside bets only ✠

THE BUY-IN

Before you can play table games in a casino, you must first make a *buy-in*, the conversion of cash to casino gaming tokens. But you need to seek out a suitable table: one with space to play, and having a table minimum that is compatible with your resources. You may recall that the table minimum is noted on a small sign located near the (roulette) wheel.

On that same sign, the *chip* minimum is often noted, which pertains to the minimum valuation ascribed to each of your chips. At a $5 minimum table, the *chip* minimum might be 50¢, which means you'd have to lay out at least ten of your chips each spin, to meet the *(per bet)* minimum. Most casinos I've been to recently have a $1 chip minimum at their $5 and $10 tables, although you can still find casinos in Las Vegas that have $1 and $2 minimums, with 25¢ chip minimums.

Not everybody chooses to play at the minimum chip level, however. Some might buy in for $300 and request a valuation of $5 for each chip. In that case, they would receive 60 chips, which is how many times $5 divides into $300.

Every table also has a maximum, which is designed to keep players from beating the house with extended betting progressions. In major casinos, the maximum is usually between $1000 and $3000 for outside bets, and $100 for any inside bet. Why the disparity between these two figures? Well, if a player lucked out and won a $100 bet straight up on one number, he'd be entitled to a $3500 payoff, which is in line with the $3000 the casino would have to pay a player for a (maximum bet) even money winner.

What it really comes down to is, the casinos don't want the chance that somebody might come along and hit a few straight up winners to the tune of $105,000 each, as the case *could* be with a $3000 *inside bet*. Frankly, I don't blame them. I don't think I'd like that kind of liability either.

When you've found a suitable table and have decided upon the dollar amount you wish to exchange for chips, lay the money on the felt and wait for the dealer to take notice. Worry not: he'll notice. When he does, tell him *"Five stacks of chips, please."* or whatever you want. A stack is 20, so five ($1 chip) stacks will cost $100, which is a popular buy-in figure for recreational players. You can request a certain color (provided that another player isn't already using it) but if you don't ask, the dealer will probably make that choice for you. These are *colored chips* we're talking about, not *value chips* (the latter being what dealers give you when buying in at other games like minibaccarat or craps).

Each player is assigned his own color of chips. Your chips might be light blue (the color I often get stuck with); the man next to you might have orange chips, and the lady next to him might have brown chips. She might have her chips valued at 50¢ each and the orange ones might be valued $5. He paid $200 to get two stacks; the woman paid $50 for her five stacks and you bought five stacks valued at $1 each, for $100. The value of each player's color is noted near the wheel in the *chip valuation area* shown in Figure 6. The dealer will set a sample chip for all active colors in separate slots, then place a numbered disk in the slots above those. These *valuation disks* have numbers imprinted on them representing the value of one stack, so the dealer will know how much to give each player upon cashout.

There is no minimum amount of play required; there have been times when I've bought in and then cashed out before playing a single spin, because of something I noticed at the next table. But the best time to cash out is shortly after the dealer has lifted the dolly (or marker) from the latest winning number, for he then has time to address the matter ✠

THE BANKROLL

Before making your buy-in, you're going to have to figure out where to get the money to do so. That money will originate from your *bankroll,* a special fund you create to be used exclusively for gaming endeavors.

The size of your bankroll depends on how much money you're willing (or able) to set up for this purpose. If your average buy-in is $100, for example, it is generally recommended that you back it up with a cash reserve that is twenty times that amount, which would work out to $2000.

Does this sound excessive to you? Me too. It's fine if you have the bucks, but this approach may not be for everyone. You might recall that back in Chapter 3, I made $1000 on two occasions, each time from a bankroll of $100. Realize, I wasn't a professional at the time, and, I had the luxury of playing or not playing as I pleased (since I lived in Las Vegas), but it does show another angle. If you try that, however, you're going to have to get lucky right out of the gate, and *stay* lucky.

My recommendation is to not exceed 1/10 of your bankroll for any buy-in, but be prepared for the worst-case scenario: the possible loss of your entire stake. It's not the end of the world, you know. You've always got next year.

There's just one thing you should keep in mind: your bankroll is your lifeblood. When it's gone, you're dead in the water. You're just a rotting corpse floating on the ebb tide. Because, nobody's going to lend you a dime once they know you gamble. You see, they do that to protect you from yourself ✠

THE SESSION

Now that you've procured a bankroll, your *session* can begin. This is the gaming activity in which you participate, in between the time you buy in and cash out. Ideally, your bankroll should be large enough to finance a number of *sessions,* each of which represents a financial tug-of-war between you and the casino. Your objective is to win the majority of these battles.

Why is your bankroll subdivided into sessions? The idea is to limit your losses in the event that you get caught up in a losing jag. Anything can happen in the short run. You need to make an effort to contain the potential damage so you don't blow your wad in one horrible and deeply regrettable moment.

How much money should you invest in a session? Depends on your betting level, how much time you want to invest and any other particulars that may affect your decision. Most *recreational* players buy in for $100 and play until it's alllllllll gone. Let's hope you can avoid *that* little trap.

How long does a session last? As long as you decide, or you and your associate together decide, or until you can no longer play because of some natural disaster such as an earthquake or tornado. Of course, armageddon, or, an invasion by evil martians, could also impact the duration of your session. Most of the time, it's your call. You might want to play for an hour or more, or you may seek only to lay down a single bet.

Ahead in this book there are exercises which establish betting parameters for typical gaming situations. Practicing with these should answer your questions pertaining to the duration and scope of your gaming endeavors ✠

THE SERIES

And now we come to the *series*. There's no end to all the stuff you have to learn, is there?

A series, pure and simple, is a wagering cycle or progression. It consists of either a single bet or a group of bets, whose number is predetermined by the player.

Some gaming authors say that a series ends only after a win occurs. I disagree. To me, a series ends when:

1) The last bet of a cycle is reached,
2) A convenient stopping point is reached, or
3) A win occurs.

My rules are more liberal, because I do things a bit differently than most. Sometimes, in order to thwart the misanthropic designs of the house edge, one must engage in a progression that is not necessarily confined to a single *table*, a single *casino*, or even, a single *day*.

Sometimes, this is what it takes to achieve the desired result. In this business, one must remain flexible ✠

THE WAGERING MANDATE

If you have been to a casino, you may have noticed that there is no place to sit except at the tables, the slot machines, or the bar. And if you take a seat at any of these, you can't stay for very long unless you pull some money out of your wallet.

This is the wagering mandate: *Seats are for players.* If you're not gonna play, you're gonna havta move along.

The main reason for this rule is that the casinos don't want the *players* to feel shut out because the tables are full when in fact some of the seats are filled by spectators. Many casinos enforce this rule only when necessary, meaning, when it makes good business sense because of crowded conditions in the gaming area. Others see it as a black-and-white issue.

This does not mean you can't play sporadic bets. If you don't mind standing, you can place a bet every tenth spin at the roulette tables, if you so desire. And the same holds true for all the other table games, as long as there is no other hindrance, such as a lack of room to put your bet at a minibaccarat table, or the roulette table has all of its colored chips assigned to other players, or there is no room to squeeze in at the craps table.

In recent years, I have noticed a policy shift in many casinos away from strict enforcement of this mandate, probably because of the increased competition. Very seldom does my partner Sharon get hassled for taking up a seat next to mine when I play. I guess the dealers suppose that we're married or something, and don't want to appear inhospitable.

But you should be aware of the *wagering mandate.* It's one of the facts of life in the world of gaming ✠

HEDGE BETS

Generally speaking, I am what you might call a hedge bettor. Meaning, I tend to play *hedge bets* more than the average player. I believe in their healing qualities.

Hedge bets are similar to auto insurance. In the event of a debilitative disaster, you're protected. You're entitled to immediate compensation.

Hedge bets are most useful when you have a large bet on the line, and don't want to risk losing it to a longshot fluke that could be easily covered with a small bet.

Example: You're playing a $300 bet on red at the roulette table, and the zeroes have burned your butt too many times. So you put a quarter on the *courtesy bar*. Now, you've protected your primary bet against a zeroes-induced loss, *and* given yourself two more ways to win (the hedge returns $425, giving you a $125 profit after deducting the $300 (primary-bet) loss).

When playing progressions, I frequently wait until my primary wagers reach the upper levels before activating hedge bets. That way, the expensive wagers are protected. But there are times when hedging isn't possible. If you're playing at the table minimum, you can't hedge because such bet should be smaller than your main bet, and the table minimum prevents you from doing that.

Hedge bets are common at roulette and craps, but they don't exist at minibaccarat. There is only one longshot in that game, and its occurrence has no impact on the other wagers.

Ahead in this book you will learn more about the application of hedge bets in craps and roulette ✠

THE ROULETTE SCORESIGN

Before the days of digital scoresigns at roulette tables, I considered the house edge for American roulette to be prohibitive. With the advent of technology that exposes the recent history of each roulette table, however, this game has moved into the realm of practicality for professional gambling.

This of course does not change or reduce the *house edge,* but it helps the *player's edge* immeasurably.

How so?

It exposes the *mood* of that table; its current trends and general disposition. This is valuable information that used to take twenty to thirty minutes to acquire.

I suppose this is one of the benefits of living in *the information age* ✠

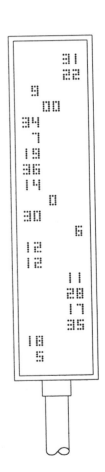

FIGURE 9
The Roulette Scoresign

CHARTING A TABLE

Formerly, the serious player had to invest time *charting* each table before *"making an investment"*. But when a charted table proved unsuitable, it would seem a wasted effort.

And yet it was often necessary.

Charting means tracking table results, which is usually done on a notepad or *scorecard* (available on request in major casinos), in search of a dominant trend. This is no longer a dire necessity in the casinos that have scoresigns, which divulge the last twenty winning numbers, or thereabouts.

The numbers on the sign are lighted, with the red numbers appearing *red* on one side, black appearing *yellow* on the other and the 0 & 00 appearing *green* in the middle of the two columns (see Figure 9 on the preceding page). This signage is located near the roulette wheel at eye level.

Newcomers to the game can't begin to imagine the difference these signs make. In two minutes you can size up a dozen tables and know which are ripe and which should be avoided. One table might show classic signs of the *reoccurring single*—of which you will learn later on—and be good for one or two large bets. Next to it might be one where the 00 showed up three out of the last ten spins, which you might interpret as *bad news*.

Now, if you play enough roulette, you will occasionally run into a scoresign that does not function properly. Never assume that these bad boys are infallible. All the same, they are a tremendous boon to the serious player, and should by all means be exploited. Taking advantage of a weakness freely offered by a competitor is an elementary tenet of good business ✠

THE MAGIC DOWNSIDE NUMBER

Early in my gaming career, I undertook the task of gathering information about roulette trends. Part of my research was directed toward finding the magic number for the downside of any given bet. In other words, what was the maximum number of spins an even money bet—for example—could go without appearing? Tee hee. I sought a number that could be relied upon in the absolute, so that if a table ever reached that figure, I'd be assured a winner on the next bet. Hahaha. That, of course, was before I understood trends. I guess I was thinking that eventually, the law of averages would begin *dictating to the table.*

When I played at a table in Las Vegas where red did not show for eighteen spins, I knew it was a lost cause. By the way, black didn't win all eighteen; two zeroes got in there.

During that period and beyond, I witnessed incredible things. A table at the Sands casino, for instance, where 0 or 00 didn't show for over 150 spins, next to one where they came up 7 out of 35. You can't fight trends like that.

Chances are, the day you pick to *bludgeon your way to a win* is the day a table trend *really will* make it to the evening news, and you happened to have backed the wrong side. Such is a professional gambler's worst nightmare.

Expect them every couple weeks or so.

My search for the *magic downside number* was a trip to nowhere, or, a place that looked just like it! ✠

MULTIPLE PLAYERS USING VALUE CHIPS

Suppose you used the scoresigns to locate a table that is perfect for an inside bet you'd like to make. You pull some nickels *(value chips)* out of your pocket and start to place them on the layout. Uh oh; there's a problem: Before you get the second chip down, the dealer informs you that you can't use those chips for the spin that's in progress.

Another player, it turns out, is using the same denomination of value chips to play inside bets. The dealer can't allow two players to use the same type of chips in the common playing area, lest there be a dispute over whose token won. He offers to exchange your *values* for table chips, but this means:

1) There has to be space on the table to set your new chips, since you can't put table chips in your pocket;
2) If you're taking a seat, you've just inherited the obligation to play every spin, and
3) You may have forfeited the chance to play that particular spin because of the time lost.

Some dealers can handle multiple players using value chips, but many won't allow it, period. It might help if you explain that you'll be playing the same sixlines every spin, but some dealers see it as a non-negotiable issue.

Just thought you should know that evaluating a table might involve more than just glancing at the scoresign ✠

SUMMARY OF ROULETTE

For those who play inside bets, as most recreational players do, the *zeroes* are not a concern. All they do is dilute the payoff. For *outside* bettors, though, it's a different story. For them, the 0 or 00 is poison with no antidote, for all their bets automatically lose. And if they hedge, that bet has to meet the table minimum all over again, for it's considered an *inside* bet.

In the US, the best place to play outside bets is Atlantic City, for the casinos there return half your wager when the 0 or 00 wins, *if it is an even money bet*. The 2–1 wagers aren't similarly blessed. If you're unable to get there, however, hold out for a casino that has scoresigns at the tables, if you can.

There is another roulette version called European Roulette, which has only one green number, the 0. This reduces the house edge in half, to 2.70%. In Europe, such tables often have *en prison*, a rule that defers the decision against even money bets—that lost to the 0—until the next non-zero number appears. In those cases, the house edge is halved again, to a very respectable 1.35%. Obviously, this is the roulette version you should look for first, for all strategies except those that focus *on* the zeroes. The problem is that these tables are scarce in the U.S. And when you do find them, they are likely to have a high table minimum (in the neighborhood of $100). And I don't expect a change in this trend, except that at this writing, the Monte Carlo casino in Las Vegas has four single-zero $10 minimum tables, but no *en prison*.

If—against all odds—the single-zero tables start cropping up in abundance, those are the ones to play ✠

7

MINIBACCARAT: BACKGROUND

After craps, baccarat has the lowest vigs of any game offered in a casino. *Minibaccarat* is formatted differently, but its vigorish and basic rules are identical. This variation has been chosen over baccarat as a recommended game because it moves faster, has lower table minimums, and is easier to enter and exit. All these reasons are relevant factors toward my choice.

At some earlier point in my career, I decided to restrict my play to just two games: craps and minibaccarat. I did this after observing that whenever I lost at one of those two, I could always rely on the other to bail me out and make things right. Of course, this trend didn't last forever, but it led me to conclude that these two games are more suited for professional play than roulette. But the game of minibaccarat is often hard to find outside of Las Vegas or Atlantic City. So I don't wish for my tutelage to lean too heavily on miniB.

Understanding how to play minibaccarat is what you might call a no-brainer. There are two sides, and you bet on one or the other; that's pretty much it. There is a third betting option called *Tie*, but it is not considered a primary wager.

Baccarat and minibaccarat are played with standard decks of playing cards, dealt from a multi-deck shoe that typically holds six or eight decks. One thing that sets this game apart from all others is the presumed obligation for the casino to supply scorecards for the participants. This is one game where the players generally will not or cannot function without this accessory.

Except for the layout markings, most miniB tables resemble those at blackjack, with a semi-circular shape and barstool seats. Some casinos, however, utilize low tables where the dealer is seated and the players sit in conventional chairs.

Unlike blackjack, miniB participants are not dealt individual hands by the dealer, and they don't have an option to hit or stand. Instead, a *community hand* is dealt (by the dealer) to each of the two sides, which are called *Player* and *Bank*. Before this hand is dealt, players bet on one side or the other.

Many who are new to the game mistakenly think that *Bank* represents the house, and a bet on *Player* is a bet *against* the house. Not true. These are the names of the two primary wagering options and nothing more.

Both *Player* and *Bank* (also known as *Banker*) return even money, and the only remaining betting option, called *Tie*, pays 8–1. Most gaming books quote the vigorish at 1.17% for Bank, 1.36% for Player, and 14.1% for Tie. Now, I'm not sure how they come up with these figures—for they involve a computation method that I don't trust—but I'll go along with those for now.

There is, however, one thing you should know about the vig and the game in general. After Player and Bank have each been dealt two cards, there exists the possibility that a third card will be drawn for either or both sides. The rules for the *third card draw* have been configured to give Bank a theoretical edge, because it *reacts* to the result of the Player hand. Because of this, Bank is (statistically) expected to win slightly more than 50% of all hands. To compensate this inequity, a 5% commission is levied against all bets on Bank *that win* (which means that, technically, the payoff for Bank is slightly less than even money).

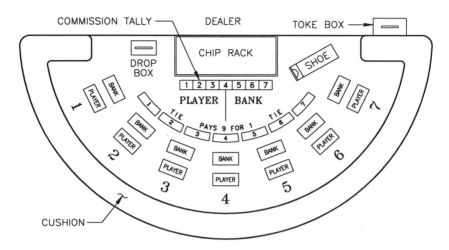

FIGURE 10
The MiniBaccarat Layout

The vigs of 1.17% and 1.36% quoted for Bank and Player apply *after* this commission has been accounted for.

The minibaccarat table shown above can seat seven players. The bets are placed in the rectangles marked *Player, Bank* and *Tie*. Incoming money for a buy-in is deposited in the *drop box* at the left, and tips for dealers are put in the *toke box*.

Gaming chips that the dealer uses to pay bets are stored in the *chip rack,* along with incoming chips (from players' bets that lost). The dealer dispenses cards from the *shoe* and puts them, face down in the areas marked *Player* and *Bank,* near the chip rack. After the initial draw of two cards for each side, the dealer turns them over and announces the result. If a third card is required, it will be placed face up next to the cards from the original draw.

Some casinos require the commission to be paid immediately after a bet on Bank wins, but most of them have the dealer keep a running count for each player. As the commission liability accrues, the dealer notes the amounts for each player in the area denoted *commission tally.* In that case, players are expected to settle those bills at the end of the shoe, or, when they depart ✠

RULES OF PLAY

The object of the game is to come as close as possible to the number 9. Each card is worth its face value, except for the 10 and all face cards, which count as 0. The Ace counts as 1. Jokers are removed from the deck, leaving 52 cards in each of the six or eight decks in the shoe.

Unlike blackjack, there is no such thing as a bust in miniB. If the point count exceeds 9, a digit is dropped, so that a would-be count of 14 becomes 4. Similarly, any combination of cards that total 10 would become zero.

The cards are shuffled at the beginning of each shoe and dealt face down, with the first card of each new hand going to Player, the second to Bank, third to Player and fourth to Bank. The dealer then turns over the cards and announces the result. At that time, rules for a possible *third-card draw* go into effect.

A point count of 8 or 9 on either side is called a *natural*, which shuts down the third-card option for either side from that point forward, though a natural 9 will beat a natural 8. If both sides are tied after options to draw (if applicable) have been exhausted, wagers on Player or Bank are a *push* (they neither win nor lose), but any bets on Tie will pay 8–1. When a Tie occurs, bets on Player or Bank can be left where they sit (to apply toward the next hand) or moved, or removed, or modified—as the player sees fit.

How do players usually handle a Tie? That varies with the individual, but I usually ignore it and leave my (Player or Bank) bet up for the next hand. I do, however, make an exception when I notice a trend where my bet will invariably lose after a Tie. Then and only then, I try to *play to the trend.*

RULES: PLAYER

WHEN PLAYER'S FIRST TWO CARDS TOTAL:	0-1-2-3-4-5	DRAWS A CARD
	6-7	STANDS
	8-9	NATURAL—NEITHER HAND DRAWS

RULES: BANKER

WHEN BANKER'S FIRST TWO CARDS TOTAL:	DRAWS WHEN PLAYER'S THIRD CARD IS:	DOES NOT DRAW WHEN PLAYER'S THIRD CARD IS:
3	1-2-3-4-5-6-7-9-0	8
4	2-3-4-5-6-7	1-8-9-0
5	4-5-6-7	1-2-3-8-9-0
6	6-7	1-2-3-4-5-8-9-0
7	STANDS	
8-9	NATURAL—NEITHER HAND DRAWS	

FIGURE 11
Rules For Third-Card Draw

Figure 11 shows how the *third-card rules* apply to Player and Bank hands. If you intend to play minibaccarat (or baccarat) with any degree of regularity, you may want to memorize these rules. I've caught more dealer mistakes at this game than any of the other two that are recommended; mistakes that convert a winning hand to a loss. When that does happen, you really lose twice: the loss that should not have occurred, plus the absence of the payoff for the win. It may have been a $25 bet, but the result is a $50 swing in your income for the day. That may be the absolute worst way to lose: from an unseen cause you never know about.

In fairness to the dealers, that paragraph should be qualified. Mistakes (by dealers) at any casino game are very rare. For every mistake, there are tens of thousands of hands (I'm guessing here) that are dealt mistake-free. There is no reason for paranoia, but it's always a good idea to stay alert ✠

THE TIE BET

Although minibaccarat offers the lowest vigs of any *stand alone* casino wagers, this applies only to the two primary wagers, *Player* and *Bank*. By contrast, *Tie* carries a vigorish of 14.1%, ten times higher. But as noted on page 74, I don't trust the vigs that are quoted for minibaccarat, because they differ from one book to the next, and particularly, I don't see how anyone can assign a statistical certainty to the occurrence of a Tie.

Those who do make a habit of playing Tie usually look for trends in much the same way as with Player and Bank, but these patterns are, of course, more sparse. Some players speculate that Tie will appear back-to-back or in clusters. Quite often I see real structure in the patterns, like a Tie occurring every other hand for eight hands, or every fourth hand out of twelve.

Is betting on Tie recommended? Not with much enthusiasm. Should you decide to do so, you should set up a separate fund for that purpose, else it will interfere with your efforts to manage the funds used for your primary (Bank and Player) wagers. Whatever you do, incorporate *structure* into your betting scheme, and avoid betting Tie on a random basis or a wild hunch, for that's when the vig steps in and goes to work.

If you are intrigued with the notion of betting on Tie, I would suggest that you establish an auxiliary bankroll for Tie wagering and bet small until you see results. Save your scorecards and analyze how you're doing when you're at home. If these bets prove to be a drain on your resources, either kick the habit, or use what you've learned to fine-tune the procedure. Just keep in mind that the high vigorish of this bet is not there to help you ✠

SIMULATIONS

Since minibaccarat has only three wagering options (unlike craps which has over two dozen), a few hypothetical hands might help you form a picture of how the game works:

1) Player has an Ace and a 3 for a total of 4. Bank has two 2s, which also totals 4. Since neither side has a *natural*, the chart in Figure 11 tells us that Player must draw a card when its point count is under 6. Player draws a 3, raising its total points to 7. Bank, having a total of 4, draws when the third card to Player is 2 thru 7. Bank draws a 6. 4 + 6 = 10, which converts to zero. Player wins, 7 over 0.

2) Player has 5 and 3: a natural 8. Bank has 2 and 5 for a total of 7. No third card should be drawn for Bank against a natural (whether it be 8 or 9), so Player wins, 8 over 7.

3) Player has 2 and 10 for a total of 2. Bank has 6 and a king for a point count of 6. Player then draws a 9, revising its total to 1. Bank stands and wins, 6 over 1.

4) Player has 9 and 5 = 14, equals 4. Bank has a jack and a 9 for a natural 9. Bank wins, 9 over 4.

5) Player has a jack and a queen = 0. Bank has a king and a queen which also equal 0. Player draws another jack, and Bank draws an ace. Bank wins, 1 over 0.

These examples should be sufficient to give you the general idea how the game is played, but it wouldn't hurt for you to play out a few practice hands with a deck of cards, to help acquaint you with the rules of the third-card draw ✠

THE BANK TRAP

I should have known there'd be a price to pay.

—Alice (in Wonderland)

As previously stated, Bank wins slightly more than 50 percent of the time. This is because the rules have been configured to give Bank an edge. And I can just picture the light bulbs glowing in the heads of newcomers to the game. I hate to spoil the fun, but those lights, actually, are not all that bright. The premise *sounds* plausible: *When in doubt, bet Bank.* Forget the 5% commission; what really counts is having that edge, right?

Bad plan. You'd have to play over a hundred hands to carve out a *theoretical* edge of just *one hand*, presuming that the statistics fall perfectly into place. And that seldom happens in the real world. Truth is: *trends are a lot more powerful than an edge that slim.* There's no reason a table couldn't favor *Player* for a whole week, through nothing more than a fluke.

But in the long run, Bank will win more, right? Everybody assumes it will, and the rules were designed to make that happen, but does it really? I wouldn't touch that bet. See, what's *intended* to favor Bank doesn't always do so; there's no guarantee these rules won't work against Bank. Now if you take every minibaccarat table in the world and do a yearly tally, I'd guess that Bank would come out ahead. But you won't live long enough to see its equivalent in real life, and the five percent will turn your ass into shredded wheat while you're waiting for the *golden monkey*. From a practical standpoint, *that edge does not exist.*

Reminds me of a time I was playing minibaccarat at Caesars in Atlantic City. A well-dressed man was standing next to my seat, pulling out hundreds from his pocket, betting on Bank. He was mostly losing, so his wagers graduated from a few hundred to over a thousand. His pockets were pretty deep, but I gotta admit that it was painful watching him lose like that. After he was down about $7000, I turned to him and said, *"Why're you fighting the trend? This is a Player table."* He said nothing as he laid $2500 on Bank. Ten seconds later it was gone.

"Maybe you're right," he mumbled as he paid his commission and walked away. He seemed to be in a bad mood.

Some of the shrewdest players of casino table games—in my experience—are Asians. They seem to favor minibaccarat, and it makes good sense: it has the lowest vigorish of any game except craps, which strains one's discipline. So it occurs to me that they have chosen wisely. But many of them allow themselves to be suckered by an illusion: they love Bank. They think it's the smart move. But it's a trap.

The game has been designed and promoted to make a player think that betting Bank will give him an edge. But that edge is too damn insignificant to be of any practical value. It works for the casinos, though: their clientele seem more than happy to pony up the five percent!

Sorry, all you *Asian-high-rollers-who-adore-the-Bank:* you're all victims of advertising. If you don't believe me, try this little experiment: walk up to ten different tables, and place a *dry bet* (an imaginary wager) at each one. Bet on the very first hand that you would have had time to play as a live bet. When you tally up the results, compare how ten bets on Bank would have fared against ten on Player, and don't forget to deduct the commission for all winning Bank wagers. You may be surprised at what you find.

Obviously, anything could happen in an experiment like this, including the fact that you might come to see why I always bet on *Player* for my minibaccarat *one-shots!* ✠

SUMMARY: MINIBACCARAT

Minibaccarat is a study in patterns. You wait for something that looks promising and follow it. That's why scorecards are such a necessity: you need to stay tuned to the localized trends as well as the larger picture (emerging more clearly with each passing hand). Is it a *Player* shoe or a *Banker* shoe? Is it laden with streaks or inveterately choppy? Once you have sized it up, try to make the most of it while the shoe lasts.

Your scorecard is an invaluable aid in helping you see what has happened, and what you might expect. Never throw away your scorecards, for they can familiarize you with gaming patterns and provide insights into weaknesses in your playing style.

But you should know, there are some things about this game that are deceptive. The images attached to the words *Player* and *Bank* would seem to have a subliminal effect. Do you want to bet on the fun-loving loser, or the powerful institution? Makes the 5% sound like small potatoes for the privilege of siding with a winner. Also, *Bank's* theoretical edge is another deception. That edge is just a flyspeck, but the players pay its 5% commission with a smile. Who do you think is fooling whom?

Because of its structure and its depth, I prefer craps for the majority of my wagering activity, but I'm sure that many readers will prefer minibaccarat, especially after reading Chapter 9, which tells how one can use table patterns to extrapolate future results. The game you choose for your primary wagering activity is up to you, but put your emphasis on the game that is most *practical*, rather than the most *enjoyable* ✠

8

CRAPS:
RULES OF PLAY

It's not hard to locate the craps tables in any casino; If you hear spontaneous cheering, there's a good chance that one of the craps tables has been blessed with a hot shooter, that winningest of animals that is like a god to the players.

If you want to see the face of *Compulsion,* you'll find it first at the craps table. Craps enthusiasts are by nature the loudest and most undisciplined players you'll ever encounter, because the game was specifically designed to ignite the short fuse of player emotion. Your success as a *table game specialist* may depend, in fact, on your ability to rip out that burning fuse before it has a chance to influence your judgement.

Bank craps is played with a pair of dice that are precision ground to ensure uniformity. The shooter throws the dice across a felt-lined table surrounded by a wall. To ensure a random result, the table crew insists that the shooter toss the dice so they bounce off the far wall before coming to a rest. At the top of the wall is an armrest with trays to hold the players' chips.

Many would-be participants seem to be intimidated by the complicated appearance of the layout, but it's not that difficult to learn this interesting, fast-moving game ✠

CRAPS PERSONNEL

Most craps tables are manned by a crew of four, consisting of a *boxman,* a *stickman* and two *dealers.* This does not include the *floorperson,* the *pit boss* and an auxiliary dealer who works in shift rotation with the other two dealers and the stickman. Please see Figure 12 on the following page.

The **Dealers** each work a side of the table, taking bets from the players and making payoffs. Also, they forward the customers' money to the *boxman* during a buy-in.

The **Stickman** stands in the middle of the table on the same side as the players, moving the dice with a long stick that is bent on one end. He calls out the dice results, hawks proposition bets and frequently advises dealers of payoffs.

The **Boxman** is the one seated, usually wearing a suit and tie. He is responsible for selling the gaming chips, depositing incoming cash, and settling disputes that may arise. He also checks the dice whenever they accidentally go off the layout.

The **Floorperson** is the next one up the chain. He's the one who usually takes your player's card so that your level and duration of play can be noted by the *pit bookkeeper.*

The **Pit Boss** oversees all the tables in the pit, which is the inner area formed by a group of table games. Any matters that can't be resolved by the other personnel are his domain.

During non-peak hours, or in smaller casinos, you may come across craps tables that are staffed only by a stickman and one dealer, for economy. In such case, the dealer may request that you situate yourself on the side he's working ✠

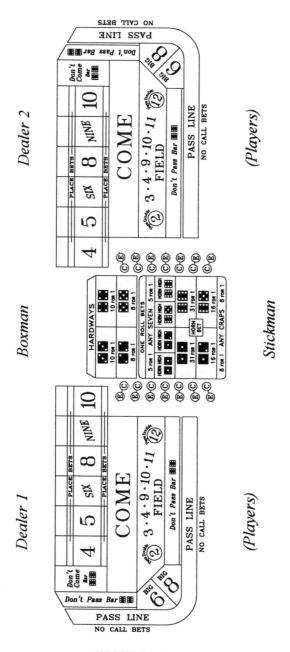

FIGURE 12
Craps Layout

CRAPS TERMINOLOGY

There are a number of gaming terms that apply only to the game of craps, which you should know before we get too deep into the territory. These definitions are brief, so if some of them don't quite make sense right now, they should when you come back to them after finishing this chapter.

The *Shooter,* as you have probably guessed, is the one who is rolling the dice.

A *Pass Line* bet is the most popular and basic bet made at the game of craps. It pays even money. A player must put down a pass (or don't pass) bet to qualify as a shooter. The objective of a pass line bettor is to first establish the point, then roll that number one more time before a 7 is rolled.

The *Point* is any one of six numbers: 4, 5, 6, 8, 9 or 10.

The *Come-out* is that period of time between when a shooter first gets the dice and the point number is rolled. (There are five non-point numbers that could be rolled (2, 3, 7, 11 & 12), which can extend the come-out period.

A *Natural* is one of two numbers: 7 or 11, which (if rolled during the come-out) wins instantly for all pass line bettors, and pays even money.

A *Craps* is a 2, 3 or 12, rolled during the come-out. This is the opposite of a natural, for it causes an immediate loss during the come-out for all pass line bettors.

A *Seven-out* is when a 7 is rolled after the point is established, but before the shooter has thrown a repeat of the point number. When this happens, the shooter forfeits the dice to the player to his left, who becomes the new shooter.

A ***Don't Pass*** bet is basically the reverse image of a pass line bet. Here, you are betting *on* the 7 to be rolled before the point is repeated. And since the 7 is the most frequently rolled number, the odds are that you'll win this bet more often than lose. But there is a serious downside that goes with the package. You lose when a 7 or 11 is rolled during the come-out, which can be responsible for *numerous* consecutive losses, at times. And it gets worse: The one thing that isn't an exact mirror image of the pass line bet is this little twist: A *craps* 2, 3 or 12 (which causes a loss to the pass line bettors at the come-out), *doesn't necessarily win* on the don't side. The numbers 2 and 3 do, but the 12 is a push (a tie with the house). So, during the come-out, the don't pass bettor has *six ways* to lose instantly (to a natural 7 or 11), *three ways* to win (from a 2 or 3), and *one way* (from the 12) to end up with a push.

The ***Free Odds*** bet (often called *Odds* for simplicity) is one big reason why the pass line bet is so popular. After the point is established, casinos allow you to add a supplemental bet, which pays according to the actual statistical odds for that number to be rolled. This bet pays 2–1 if 4 or 10 is the point; 3–2 for 5 or 9, and 6–5 for the 6 or 8. This is the only bet available in any casino that carries no house edge whatsoever. It is offered as an enticement to players, but it is not a stand-alone wager; it's only allowed as a tack-on bet to your basic pass or don't pass wager.

Note: On the *right* side (*pass line* betting), playing the *odds* bet is referred to as *taking odds*. On the *wrong* side *(don't pass)*, it is called *laying odds*. When you *lay odds*, the return on your bet is not so hot; you get less than even money. Laying odds against the 4 or 10 means betting $40 to win $20 (1–2); on the 5 or 9 you must put up $30 to win $20 (2–3), and for the 6 or 8 it is $24 to win $20 (a 5–6 return).

Lastly, a ***Line Bet*** is simply a *pass* or *don't pass* wager. This is mentioned only to let you know you can play either one, if you happen to have the dice forwarded to you, and the stickman insists that you put down a *line bet* ✠

THE CRAPS PROCEDURE

The game commences after a player arrives at a table and makes a buy-in, which involves dropping money on the layout near a dealer, or signing a credit marker. Remember that the cash must be dropped on the layout; the dealer can't take it from your hand. When buying in, tell the dealer *"Change only"*, to let him know that you're not trying to place a cash bet on the wager nearest to where your money was dropped. After forwarding the cash to the boxman, the dealer will place the appropriate amount of chips on the layout in front of you.

After you receive your chips, you're ready to place some bets. If you are the only player at the table, you have no choice but to be the shooter, else there will be no game. But to qualify as a shooter, you must first put down a pass line or don't pass wager. If there are other players present, however, you can gesture to the effect that you'd like to pass the dice.

Should you decide to be the shooter, you will select two of the five or six dice that the stickman initially offers, and fling them across the layout so that they bounce against the cushioned end wall that is farthest from where you stand. The stickman will call out the result, then wait for the dealers to pay any bets that may have won on that roll, then push the dice back in front of you with his stick, and you repeat the procedure.

Eventually, you will *seven-out* (roll a seven during midgame), at which time you forfeit the dice to the player to your left, unless there are no others at the table. If you're alone, you can shoot all night, long as you've got money ✠

DICE COMBINATIONS

On the following page, Figure 13 shows the 36 combinations that are possible from a pair of dice. Each number (2 through 12) can be rolled in just so many ways. These are the mathematics from which the odds and payoffs are derived at craps.

At the center of the paradigm lies the number 7, which stands taller than the rest. There are six ways this number can be rolled, which makes it the champ. The 6 and 8, which are sister numbers to each other, are the next ones down the chain, then come sister numbers 5 and 9 and so on. Sister numbers are pairs having the same probability. The numbers 6 & 8, 5 & 9, 4 & 10, 3 & 11 and 2 & 12 are all sisters. But there's another reason they're linked: Whatever number appears on the top (of a pair of dice) is the sister to the number you will find on the bottom.

To help you understand these probabilities, let us compare the 7 to the 10. According to Figure 13, the 7 can be rolled six ways, and the 10 three ways—out of 36 possible ways. So, statistically, the 7 is twice as likely to come up as the 10. Which may shed light on why the casinos compensate successful bets on the 10 at a rate close to 2–1: to match the probability, minus a small commission (which helps cover their expenses). The same figures apply to the sister number of the 10, the 4.

Fighting the almighty seven is what makes this game tough— *and* interesting. Occasionally the seven will disappear for a while, during which time an aggressive player can reap fantastic rewards. But it's an uphill battle for the players most of the time, which is one reason casinos prosper in our society.

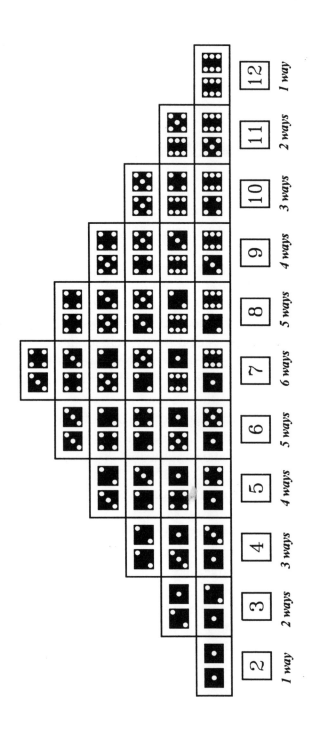

FIGURE 13
Dice Combination Paradigm
(36 Possible ways)

What about playing the other side, where the 7 is your friend? Isn't that the closest you can come to being the house? Perhaps so, but playing *don't pass* is no picnic. Don't forget, the house has a built-in edge no matter which side you pick.

The only way you can beat the casino at its own game is to exploit that which they are powerless to control. *You have to follow the trends* wherever they may lead—on both sides of the game—for as long as they persist in abundance.

Inevitably, some readers will have difficulty with one of the aspects of dice combinations. For the number 3, as an example, what's the difference between dice that read 1 & 2, and a reading of 2 & 1? Isn't that just one combination?

It is not. Imagine that one die is red and the other is brown. When 3 is rolled, sometimes the 1 will originate from the red die and other times from the brown. Those are two out of 36 possibilities, and all combinations must be accounted for to establish true odds. If the 3 was derived but one way, it would have the same odds as the 2. And that would throw all the odds and payoffs into a state of disarray, which may well cause a reactionary breach in the fabric of statistical certainties of the universe.

You don't want a reactionary breach, do you? No no. I don't think you want that.

This'll help: if a pair of dice was a horse race, the 7 would be the favorite and the 2 & 12 would be the longshots. All the other horses would carry odds in between ✠

WAGERING OPTIONS

PASS LINE: The *pass line* is unquestionably the most popular of all the betting options at craps.

The unshaded portion of Figure 14 shows how the *pass line* would appear on the right side of a craps table. Please note that the bet labeled *Free Odds Bet* is placed right behind the pass line bet. *Free odds* is an auxiliary bet that can be made as an accompaniment to a *pass line* bet, and it is technically the fairest bet you can make in a casino, for it carries no house edge.

To signify the *point* number (which is derived from a dice roll), a *puck* is placed on that number. In this figure, 4 is the point. After a decision is reached against that number, the puck is flipped over (to the OFF side), and placed where shown.

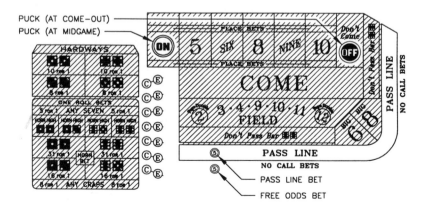

FIGURE 14
The Pass Line

At a typical active craps table, there are six or seven players on each of the two sides, and most, if not all, of the bettors have a bet down on the pass line.

"We're coming out," barks the stickman, pushing the dice to the shooter, who picks them up and throws, say, another four. *"We're out on four,"* the stickman says, as each dealer takes his puck out of the *don't come,* flips it over to the white side *(On),* and places it in the *"4"* box on the layout. At this point, the players at the table add their *free odds* bet, which they couldn't do until the *point* (in this case, 4) was established.

Now the *midgame* begins, where some of the bettors put up secondary wagers, called *place* bets, on other numbers. But the fate of all bets now rests in the hands of the shooter. His objective is to roll the four (again) before the seven, and if he succeeds, the players win along with him. If a seven comes up first, all pass line bettors lose and the player to his left inherits the dice, and *"comes out"* after the dealers retrieve the losing bets.

As each player *sevens out,* the dice move clockwise around the table to the next player. Any players who don't wish to shoot can indicate so with a hand gesture, in which case the stickman will offer them to the next player.

This is really all there is to the central wager made at the game of craps. The shooter rolls a number, which becomes the point, then tries to roll it again before a seven. He might get a bonus if he rolls a *natural* (7 or 11, which are instant winners during the come-out), or he may get stung by a come-out craps (a 2, 3 or 12, which are instant *losers* during the come-out). But all he's really trying to do is roll two of the same number, with any amount of other numbers in between, as long as one of them isn't a 7.

The most notable quirk in the rules of this game is that the 7 *wins* during the *come-out,* but *loses* after the point is established. This is one of the strongest enticements of the game: during the come-out period, pass line bettors have twice as many ways to *win* instantly (via a *natural* 7 or 11), than *lose* instantly, by virtue of a *craps* roll of 2, 3 or 12.

DON'T PASS: Near the table with the twelve players betting pass line is another table with four players. The shooter has a bet on pass line, but the others are betting don't pass. After three rolls he sevens out, and shortly, the stickman offers the dice to the next player, who refuses them. So the stickman pushes the dice to the player beyond him, who hesitates, then moves his bet from don't pass to pass, and picks up the dice.

This is a typical don't pass table, also known as a *cold table.* Fewer players; everyone betting against the shooter; no one wants to *be* the shooter. Don't pass is the opposite of pass, so when one side wins the other loses. And in that spirit, don't pass bettors are not excitable, enthusiastic, or abundant.

Most craps tables have no more than one or two don't pass bettors, if any. And sometimes you'll come across an ice-cold table that the bettors refuse to acknowledge: player after player sevens out, but each one thinks he can make the point. That's why the player, two paragraphs back, switched his bet from the *don't pass* to *pass* when the dice came to him. He hesitated because he knew the table was cold, but after a moment's thought, he decided that maybe *he* could change it.

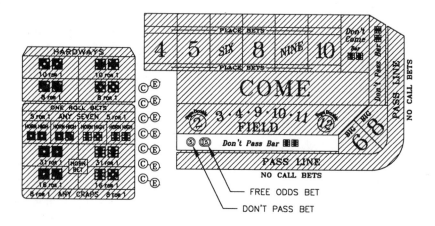

FIGURE 15
The Don't Pass

What about the one who refused the dice? Most craps players feel that *shooting from the don't* is betting against oneself. You see, the casino treats only the pass line winners as winners. If you shoot from the don't and make the point, the stickman pronounces it a winner, even though you lost! I think this is done to steer the crowd away from the bets with the best chances to win.

When playing the don't, the odds are on your side once the point is established, but getting past the come-out is the trick. The 7 and 11 will kill your bet instantly during the come-out, and there is a much greater chance of that, than for you to win from a *craps* (where only 2 or 3 will win; the 12 is a push). And, there's always the chance you'll get whacked with five straight *naturals,* which can be extremely frustrating.

Most of the time the don't bettor has to endure a tedious grind, for he must settle for low bet returns in exchange for owning a piece of the betting favorite. And when things don't go his way, matters can spiral out of hand with alarming speed, for it may take up to two wins to compensate a single loss. But then there are times when the dice will go all the way around the table, and no one can make a point. It's times like those that life is good for the don't better; all he's gotta do is ride the big wave until it dies, then leave after the first loss.

There are those who specialize in betting the don't; Nick the Greek was a back line player. But such types are usually quiet and withdrawn. They don't want to enrage the pass line bettors, whose *losses* help finance the don't bettor's *wins.*

If not for the extreme risk one faces during the come-out, the don't pass would or should be the number one choice of betting options for those who approach casino gambling as a business. But that come-out can be lethal to those who haven't got the seasoning to weather the storm.

Fortunately, there is a way to take advantage of the superior positioning the don't side offers—without heavy liability. That's coming up in Chapter 13 ✠

FREE ODDS FOR PASS LINE: This is the only bet that carries no house edge. You have to make a line bet to qualify for the privilege, but still, it's the best bet in the casino.

Understanding the concept of free odds may seem difficult for some, but it's really just three numbers to memorize. We will first look at how free odds apply to pass line bets.

Let's say a shooter has just made his point as you stroll up to a craps table. After the dealer finishes paying the winners, you drop $100 on the layout and say *"Change only."* The dealer takes your money and pulls a stack of (twenty) reds from the boxman's chip supply, or he might take them from his own stack. The stickman says *"We're coming out,"* as he pushes the dice back to the shooter, while plugging some proposition bets. After placing the chips in your rail, you pull one out and drop it in the area marked *pass line* on the layout, directly in front of you.

Your focus is now on the come-out roll. You have eight ways to win (from a 7 or 11) and four ways to lose (via 2, 3 or 12) on the next roll. The odds are in your favor, but there's a greater chance (67%) that your bet won't be immediately affected if the shooter rolls a point number, which he does, a 5.

As the stickman announces *"We're out on five,"* the players around the table put up their free odds, as shown in Figure 14 (back on page 92). Now, let's hold up a minute.

The *Free Odds* bet is allowed (as a tack-on to a pass line bet) *after* the point is established, and pays according to the statistical probability for that point to be rolled (versus the probability of a 7), as denoted below:

POINT	PROBABILITY	RETURN	$5 PAYS	$10 PAYS
4 or 10	1–2	2–1	$10	$20
5 or 9	2–3	3–2	$6 PAYS $9	$15
6 or 8	5–6	6–5	$6	$12

FIGURE 16
Free Odds for Pass

Figure 16 shows that the probability for the sister numbers of 4 and 10 is 1–2. If 4 was the point, there are but 3 of the 36 dice combinations that produce a 4, while the 7 can be rolled in 6 ways. The probability is 1–2 because for every (1) way you have to win, there are 2 ways to lose. The house pays 2–1, the inverse of 1–2, to compensate the risk you take fighting the 7. Moving across the Figure 16 chart, you can see that a $5 bet pays $10 (a 2–1 return), which is your profit, paid alongside the return of your original bet. Therefore, you end up with $15 for every $5 that is wagered on a successful free odds bet against a point of 4.

If a 5 or 9 is the point, the probability that it will be rolled before a 7 is 2–3, so the casino offers a return of 3–2. This is where it gets a little tricky: a 3–2 payoff on a $5 bet would come out to $7.50, and most casinos won't deal in anything except round dollar amounts, at least for bets like this. So they allow [insist on] a $6 *free odds bet* to accompany a $5 *pass line bet,* because a figure divisible by 2 is needed to enable payoffs in even dollar amounts. This $6 bet will return $9. (Divisibility is not a problem at the $10 level, for that amount *is* evenly divisible by 2.)

Finally, we come to the 6 and the 8, which have a probability of 5–6, just a hair below even money. For your risk, you get paid 6–5, just a hair above.

Returning to the game we were playing, you were about to put up your free odds against a point of 5. Since your pass line bet is $5, you should put $6 on the other side of the line, or $10 if you wish to take *Double Odds,* which is permissable in all major casinos. Now if the shooter rolls a 7 before a 5, both your pass line and odds bet go down, but if instead he rolls a 5, you will win $5 for your pass line bet plus $9 for *(single) odds.* That is your profit, which the dealer sets next to your original bets.

These are good deals. You get every bit of your money's worth on all of them, and although you are contesting the seven— which is more probable—there are times when the seven is off duty. This window of opportunity may be small or large, but it's what all *right bettors* (pass line bettors) look for.

FREE ODDS FOR DON'T PASS: For those times when you want the 7 on your side, *free odds* are available for the don't side as well. The return is always less than even money, but you'll be positioned to win the majority of the time.

The probability and return numbers are the exact inverse of the payoffs one receives when playing the *Do* side. If a house edge was attached to odds bets, the two would not concur.

Notice that the *$5 PAYS* and *$10 PAYS* headings have been replaced with *1x & 2x PAYS*. Since you're now on the reverse side, the constant ($10, as in *$10 PAYS*, for example), is the amount *won* instead of the amount *bet*. And casinos allow you to put up enough money to *win* single or double odds, as a basis for sizing your bet. So, to add double odds to a $5 don't pass bet on the 4, for example, means putting up $20 to win $10.

True, it's a crappy return, but this is what the house pays *you* when you win a *pass line* odds bet on the 4 or 10!

For the other numbers (5, 6, 8 & 9) the penalty is not so huge, but the compensating factor is that those bets won't win as often. All the same, it's nice knowing the 7 is on *your* side.

The only flaw in this bet is that your don't wager must first make it past the come-out for you to be able to win from a 7. And, since the *craps* number 12 doesn't win at the come-out (the lone exception to the perfect inversion), you have only three ways to win versus eight ways to lose.

Luckily, there is a way to minimize this downside, as you will learn ahead in this book.

POINT	PROBABILITY	RETURN	1x PAYS	2x PAYS
4 or 10	2–1	1–2	$10 PAYS $5	$20 PAYS $10
5 or 9	3–2	2–3	$9 PAYS $6	$15 PAYS $10
6 or 8	6–5	5–6	$6 PAYS $5	$12 PAYS $10

FIGURE 17
Free Odds for Don't Pass

COME: In Figure 18, the *Come* areas are not hard to find. The lower section is where the bet is placed, and the numbered boxes are where that bet will be sent by the dealer, once the destination is established on a subsequent roll.

A *Come bet* is identical a pass line bet; it's *when* the bet is made that sets it apart. At any point after the come-out, you can drop a chip in the come box, and the next number rolled is the point for that wager. The dealer then moves your bet from the come box to one of the six point number boxes. That number (whatever it is) becomes the point for that bet. You can then add a *free odds* bet, which he'll set atop your relocated come bet, slightly off center to maintain separation between the two bet types.

Players who like lots of action often play new come bets and take odds with every roll of the dice, but usually not for very long. One little 7 will bring them all down.

There may be times when it is advantageous to play come bets aggressively. When a hot shooter is scorching the table and you've already made enough profit to put some serious money out there, you might earn a handsome reward. But be advised, there may not be a more efficient way to unmask the evil face of Continuum than playing a never-ending stream of come bets.

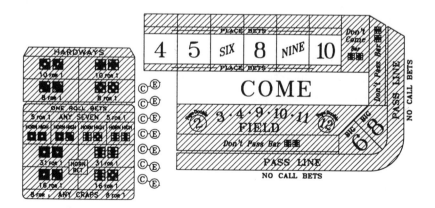

FIGURE 18
The Come Bet Areas

What attracts players to come bets is the multiple come-outs. Remember, a pass line bet has terrific prospects to win during the come-out because the 7 gives the player an instant win. Well, the same goes for come bets. Meaning, as your pass line bet loses to a *seven-out*, your come bet might win from the *come-out seven*, thereby defraying the cost of that loss. But don't forget: if you were playing come bets all along, every one that got past the come-out (and is still active) would fall **HARD** to the seven.

The biggest flaw in the come bet is that (unlike *place bets*) once the bet is up, it's up to stay. You cannot remove or reduce it. And there will be times when you'll wish you could.

This description of come bets is intentionally brief, because I don't wish to invest valuable space talking about a type of bet that is adored by compulsive gamblers, and, which has the potential to trigger those inclinations in others.

There are times when come bets *are* recommended, if one takes care not to get carried away. One such time is for a procedure called *Multi-Line*, described in Chapter 13. The only other time is to capitalize on a hot shoot, *providing* that you're financing those bets with money that was recently won.

DON'T COME: *Don't come* is the inverse to *come* in the same way that *don't pass* is to *pass*. The player drops his bet in the don't come box, and after the point *(for that bet)* is established, the dealer puts the bet *behind the line* (the uppermost part of the *point* boxes), at which time free odds can be added.

Most bettors who play don't come do so as an expansion of their don't pass bets. They like the idea that (unlike come bets) their bets *win* simultaneously, and *lose* one at a time.

Betting the don't come is a study in precision timing. If the shooter sevens-out (against the primary point) too quickly, it will nail the don't come bet as it is coming out (and vulnerable to the 7), but too long a roll will shoot down all the bets like ducks in a row. If you pace yourself you might do OK, but one needs a good deal of experience to play this bet successfully.

FIELD: The *Field* is another conspicuous area of the craps layout, and it must look rather tempting to the beginner. Here's a bet that covers seven of the eleven numbers, never pays less than even money, and sometimes pays 2–1.

Obviously, there's a catch, or everyone in the world would play the field. The answer of course is that the four numbers not covered are the most frequently-rolled combinations.

Consider the 7, a non-field number, which by itself can be rolled in as many ways as field numbers 2, 3, 11 & 12 *combined*. What you're doing is comparing seven *semi-longshots* with the top four *favorites*, and the latter have the edge.

Field bets are one-roll bets, which means that a win or lose decision will be rendered on the next roll. They carry a house edge of 5.55%, except in some casinos where a 3–1 payoff on the 12 is offered, reducing the vigorish to 2.70%.

Most books say the field is a sucker bet, noting that the craps table offers much better deals—which is true—though there are times when it pays to bet the field. Sometimes, field numbers show up in strings of seven or more. One time, in fact, I made $160 from a three-stage parlay of a $10 field bet.

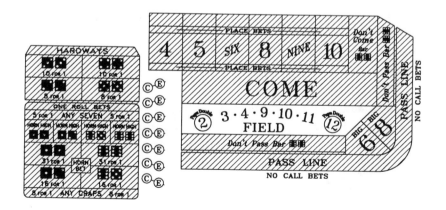

FIGURE 19
The Field

Figure 20 shows the dice combination relationship between field and non-field numbers:

FIELD NO.	COMBINATIONS	WAYS ROLLED	PAYOFF
2	1 + 1	1	2–1
3	1 + 2, 2 + 1	2	1–1
4	1 + 3, 3 + 1, 2 + 2	3	1–1
9	3 + 6, 6 + 3, 4 + 5, 5 + 4	4	1–1
10	4 + 6, 6 + 4, 5 + 5	3	1–1
11	5 + 6, 6 + 5	2	1–1
12	6 + 6	1	2–1

NON-FIELD	COMBINATIONS	WAYS ROLLED
5	1 + 4, 4 + 1, 2 + 3, 3 + 2	4
6	1 + 5, 5 + 1, 2 + 4, 4 + 2, 3 + 3	5
7	1 + 6, 6 + 1, 2 + 5, 5 + 2, 3 + 4, 4 + 3	6
8	2 + 6, 6 + 2, 3 + 5, 5 + 3, 4 + 4	5

FIGURE 20
Dice Combination Comparison

The number of ways field numbers can be rolled comes to 18 (the 16 shown plus 2 to compensate the 2–1 returns on the 2 & 12). But non-fields can be rolled 20 ways, giving the house a 20–18 advantage. But you probably know by now that any team with the 7 on their side is gonna be tough.

PLACE: *Place bets* can be made on any or all of the six point numbers (4, 5, 6, 8, 9 and 10). Each bet stays active until a 7 is rolled (which kills it), or until you decide to call it *off* (render it inactive), or have it physically removed from the layout. The appeal of place bets is threefold:

1) *Each bet can win a multitude of times.*
2) *Each pays better than even money,* and
3) *They can be added or removed throughout the game.*

The figure below shows *where* the dealer positions place bets on the layout. In this illustration, three bettors have *placed the 5,* and there is room for five more bets. The positioning of place bets corresponds to where the players stand around the table. Anyone making place bets should learn the arrangement (in the course of playing) so he can keep an eye on his bets.

FIGURE 21
The Place Bet Area

NUMBER	WIN PROBABILITY	RETURN	HOUSE EDGE
4 OR 10	1–2	9–5	6.67%
5 OR 9	2–3	7–5	4.00%
6 OR 8	5–6	7–6	1.52%

FIGURE 22
Place Bet Probabilities And Returns

The return for place bets is just a notch below what you would get for your odds bet on a pass line wager. A place bet on the 4 or 10 pays 9–5, which is just below the 2–1 odds bet return. The 7–5 return on the 5 or 9 is just below the 3–2 return for those numbers, and the 7–6 payoff for placing the 6 or 8 is the tiniest possible notch below the 6–5 free odds return. The 1.52% house edge on a *placed* 6 or 8 is a terrific deal, since these numbers are the most frequently rolled of all numbers except the 7. Most players favor placing the 6 and the 8 over the other numbers.

To a beginner, this may sound fantastic: a bet that pays better than even money, wins indefinitely and can be taken down at any time. . .*where's the downside?*

There are two: first of all, the 7 is seldom very far away from any point in the game. In my experience, placing four or more numbers acts like a magnet for the 7. Even trying to find a window in which you can place six numbers just long enough to catch one or two hits seems like nothing short of impossible most of the time. The second reason, is that Continuum does some of its dirtiest work to place bettors. Like come bets, place bets offer a chance to cash in six or seven times a minute if you have several numbers covered. It's great when the 7 has packed up and split for the coast, but that's the exception, not the rule.

If it's hard resisting the temptation when the rest of the table is cashing in on place bets, just remember that those are the same players that keep the casinos profitable!

Place bets on all numbers except the 6 and 8 should be of an amount that is divisable by five, because the 7–5 return on 5 or 9, and the 9–5 for the 4 or 10 have a 5 as the second digit. (The first number of bet returns represent what you *get paid;* the second is what you *risk* to get that amount.) So, when placing the 4, 5, 9 or 10, any bet amount not divisable by 5 will result in the player getting shortchanged in the course of rounding.

Place bets on the 6 or 8, however, must be divisable by 6, for the 7–6 return requires it. You *can* place the 6 or 8 for $5, but your return will be even money, as the dealer will surely point out to you. A 7–6 return means you get paid $7 profit for a $6 bet, which is a strange bet return; not seen anywhere but at a craps table.

On those rare occasions when you're lucky enough to catch a red-hot table, there's nothing like place bets, pressed up as you win, to help you make a lot of money fast. According to Robert Wagner, a former CEO of the Claridge in Atlantic City, his casino once took a $500,000 hit by a player capitalizing on a hot roll.

But don't be fooled. Place bettors are often the biggest losers of all. Moderation is the key ✠

BUY BETS: As an alternative to place bets, casinos allow you to *Buy* the number and get paid full odds, minus a 5% commission. For some numbers, this is a good deal.

Now, for the 6 and 8, this option makes no sense because the house edge for placing those numbers is 1.52%, well below the 5% commission. Same for the 5 and 9, with it's 4% vig. But the vig for placing the 4 or 10 is 6.67%. Here, the *buy* option looks pretty good, as long as your bet is $20 or more.

Why $20? Most casinos insist on a $20 minimum for buy bets, because they don't want to bother making change from a $1 chip that would be used to pay the commission. Others simply charge a $1 minimum, in which case the bettor would pay more than 5% through rounding. So, for bets under $20, buy bets are either not allowed, or not profitable to the player.

How do buy bets compare with place bets in dollar amounts? *Placing* the 10 for $25 would return $45, but *buying* the 10 would involve paying $26 ($25+$1 commission) to get a (2–1) $50 return. A net of $49 for $26 certainly beats $45 for $25.

Buy bets aren't marked on the layout, but are positioned by the dealer in the point boxes (like a come bet), with a *buy* button set on top to clarify the wager.

Switching over to different bet types at different intervals may sound confusing, but once you've been around the block a couple times, it'll be second nature to you.

LAY BETS: Several years ago in Atlantic City, I was passing through the craps section at Trump Castle, looking for an opportunity to make the last bet of the day. I stopped at the $25 minimum table, which had only one player, a heavyset dude who had just rolled two consecutive 7s. I watched him roll a third 7, and said to myself, *This table is perfect for a lay bet.* I had my money ready and was expecting him to then roll a point number, but he rolled another 7, his fourth. Then he proceeded to roll two more, and boy, I was nearly salivating in anticipation of the (seemingly) sure bet I was about to make.

On the seventh roll, comes a 10. Damn! Not the number I wanted. Too expensive to lay. But a decision had to be made, so I put $310 on the table and said *"Lay the 9."* On the next roll I won $200 when the shooter sevened out.

Looking back, it would appear that I was not as aggressive as I could have been. Instead of winning one wager, I could have won five, for every 7 he rolled would have represented another win. Then again, an *Any Seven Parlay* (ahead in this book) would have given me a truly handsome return.

But I was nonetheless pleased. The day's final wager was successful, and it was time to go eat. There was no way I could have anticipated such a trend from a random walk-up to a table; my bet was practical and sensible. But this story helps me illustrate a point: that was about as sure a bet as I have ever seen, yet there is *never* a sure bet. That's why I went with the 9 instead of the 10. Less risk to the bankroll.

Lay wagers are bets that can be made at any point during a game, and they pay the true *odds* minus a 5% commission. You can make a lay wager against any (or all) of the six point numbers. This bet wins if a 7 is rolled before the number you have chosen to lay odds against, but after it wins, the dealer will (probably) take it down immediately. If you want the bet back up, you have to tell him (or her) so.

Why did I feel the 10 was too expensive to lay, and choose the 9 instead? Just like the *odds* bets, the payoff ratio varies according to the number. I was seeking the middle ground between a safe, and lucrative bet. Please see Figure 23, below:

NUMBER	COST	WIN	PROFIT
4 OR 10	$40 + $1 ($41)	$20	$19
5 OR 9	$30 + $1 ($31)	$20	$19
6 OR 8	$24 + $1 ($25)	$20	$19

FIGURE 23
Lay Bet Cost And Profit

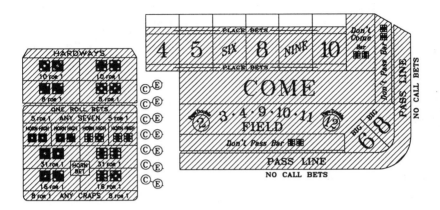

FIGURE 24
The Lay Bet Areas
*(Also referred to as **Behind The Line**)*

To make a lay bet, drop your money on the layout and tell the dealer (for example) *"$31 no nine"* or *"Lay the nine,"* and give him the proper amount (or a multiple thereof), as denoted in Figure 23. He will remove the $1 commission—which you have included—and put the remaining chips *behind the line* (the area shown in Fig. 24) for that number. Fig. 23 shows the cost of laying the six numbers for a bet large enough to win exactly four units in each case. For every $20 (four units) you attempt to win, the commission is $1. Most casinos don't allow lay wagers at levels below those shown in Figure 23 because of the problem making change from a $1 chip. But if allowed, you would be paying more than you should through rounding, which is not a good idea anyway.

To determine the amount of money needed for bets at other levels, you must know the odds of the desired number, then add the 5% house commission. Calculating the *No Nine* wager I made at Trump Castle was easy: The payoff is 2–3, so you need three units ($300) to win two ($200), then you add $5 for the (5%) commission for every $100 you stand to win.

The value of this bet lies in the fact that you can bet on the side of the seven (and *against* the number of your choice) without having to go through the come-out gauntlet, which is no piece of cake for back line bettors. The only penalty is the 5% commission, which strikes me as a reasonable price to pay, for the privilege of getting your man on base.

Laying the 5 or 9 returns 2–3 as stated; laying the 4 or 10 pays 1–2, and the 6 or 8 pays 5–6. As you can see, the 4 or 10 are costly to lay, but lay bets against the 6 or 8 pay close to even money. Quite a difference. I picked on the 9 because it felt safer than laying the 6 or 8, which are statistically the most likely numbers to be rolled *after a seven*. But I didn't want to pay the huge *one-for-two* penalty that accompanies the 10, regardless the better odds. And there's another reason I didn't want the 10. Back-to-back rolls of the same number frequently occur, and I didn't want to take that chance on my day's last bet.

That being the case, I felt safer with the 9.

BIG 6 / BIG 8: *Big 6* and *Big 8* bets do not appear on layouts in Atlantic City, but you'll find them in Nevada and on most riverboats, in the corners of the layout, between the field and the pass line. These bets are positioned by the player, pay even money, and stay active until they win or lose, however many rolls that may take. If you bet on Big 6, for example, you will win if a 6 is rolled before a 7, unless you pull up your bet, which is permitted. The same, of course, applies for the Big 8.

Why would anyone play these bets (with their 9.09% vigorish) and settle for even money, when they can place the same numbers (for 1.52%) and get a 7 to 6 return?

Well, either those people are too timid to disturb the dealer, too lazy, or else they're profligate morons who don't know better. But these are just theories of mine.

Most Las Vegas casinos carry Big 6 and 8, but not Bally's. They feel these bets insult the intelligence of their clientele. And that's how you should see it, if you're serious.

PROPOSITION BETS: These are located in the center of the layout (except for some bets which are not marked), and are made by the stickman. So, when making a proposition bet, toss your chips toward him, not the dealer.

As common practice, these bets should not figure prominently in your betting routine, for they've been mathematically constructed to favor the house in a lopsided manner. Nevertheless, there are times when they have their place, for exploiting conspicuous trends or hedging primary wagers.

Please refer to Figure 25 for all proposition bet descriptions in the upcoming pages:

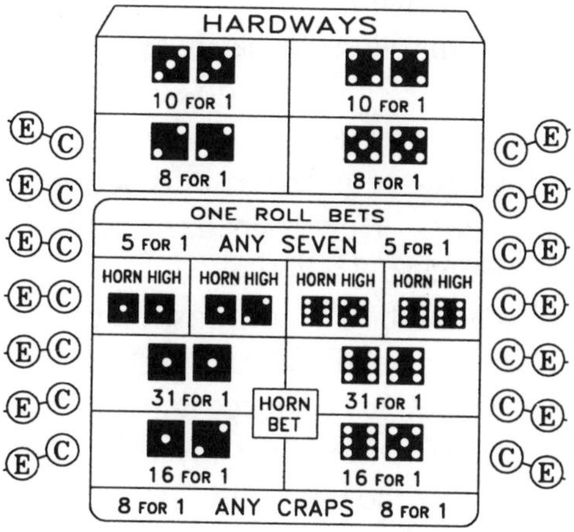

FIGURE 25
The Proposition Bet Area

HARDWAY: Back on page 49 I referred to a time I held the dice for 40 minutes at the Sands in Atlantic City. During that roll, a player at the other end of the table had the *Hard 6* and the *Hard 8* covered with $50 each. At some point I rolled a hard 8, and he was paid $450, and then later he made another $450 on a hard 6. In gaming, those are called big, lucky wins.

Hardways are bets made that *doubles* will show up on the dice (for any of the four *even* point numbers) before a 7, or an *easy* way. A *Hardway 6* (also called a *Hard 6)* is a dice showing of 3 and 3; an *Easy 6* is any other combination adding up to six, such as 4 and 2. For the hard 6 or 8, the payoff is 9 to 1 and the vig is 9.09%. For the hard 4 or 10, the return is 7–1 with an 11.1% edge. Unless the player specifies otherwise, these bets are always working during midgame (after the come-out), and usually *off* during the pass line come-out. Don't be fooled by casinos offering *10 for 1* or *8 for 1.* They equal *9 to 1* and *7 to 1,* respectively.

How do you know when a hardway number will be rolled? If any of you readers know, please write to me, care of the publisher. I'll pay handsomely for that information if it's reliable!

Most players seem to bet the hardways whenever a shooter is having an extended roll. I think they do so because they are money ahead, and feel lucky. Why not go for it?

Then again, some are prodded into action after hearing the stickman's *commercials.* He's trained, of course, to promote the bets most advantageous to the house.

Are hardways good bets? For most players, they are not, for they are merely seeking the thrill of catching an occasional longshot, but most of their money gets sucked into that whirling tidepool called the house edge. Others like myself make use of them as hedge bets when playing the back line. In such case, I *do* consider them useful, if played *selectively.*

For example, a large don't pass bet against the 8 will give you five ways to lose (if an 8 is rolled) and six ways to win (if a 7 is rolled first). The odds are marginally on your side. If however you put a small hedge on the hard 8, you now have *seven* ways to win versus *four* ways to lose. That sounds better to me, though I admit that I often skip the hedge to save money.

How big should you hedge? Just enough to get most of your money back, should your bet go down to a hardway.

Are hardway bets otherwise advisable? Not really, but if you find a way to make them pay, I won't try to stop you.

ANY CRAPS: *Any Craps* is a one-roll bet that covers the three numbers called *craps* during a come-out. It wins if a 2, 3, or 12 is rolled, and pays 7–1.

This bet is most often played as a hedge to protect a pass line bet against an immediate loss from a craps number (rolled during the come-out). You'll still lose your pass line bet, but you'll win the *any craps* bet for what could be a net gain.

Most players prefer playing the pass line *bareback,* that is, with no hedge. The ones that do use it usually put up $1 for every $5 or $10 wagered on the pass line. Others forego the hedge until their first *craps* loss, *then* they start hedging.

Is it a good bet? Most books say no, because of the 11.1% house edge. But it's one of my favorite bets.

When playing pass line, I want to get my man on base. Why risk everything on one roll? When hedging the pass line, there's one thing you know for sure: no way can you lose on the next roll. You'll either win from a natural, or from the hedge, or witness the establishment of the point. For that brief moment in time, you're covered sixteen ways to Sunday.

Few things in life will make you feel like a bigger loser than when you keep getting hammered at the come-out of a pass line bet. That's when the odds are totally in your favor, but bad trends are always out there, waiting to trample your face in the mud.

The best way to play *any craps,* is to hold off until you lose to a craps roll. If it looks like it's the start of a major *craps roll* trend, keep playing it for awhile, for protection. If not, it may be best to stop playing it. This helps reduce the house edge, because you're responding only to the immediate need.

When you've played this game awhile, you will come to realize that extended come-outs (four or more successive craps/naturals) are pretty routine. When that occurs, the other players are riding a monetary roller coaster—losing, winning, losing, winning—while you're making money every step of the way.

Everyone has their own theories about *any craps,* but as I see it, *that's the way to do it.*

HORN BETS: A *Horn* bet is a one-roll combination bet that covers the three *any craps* numbers (2, 3 & 12) plus the 11. This bet is accepted only in dollar amounts that are divisible by 4, for each of the four units wagered pays according to the return for that number. Most casinos pay 15–1 for the 3 and 11, and 30–1 for the 2 and 12. The vigorish for the 3 and 11 bets is 11.1%; for the 2 and 12 it is 13.89%.

A wager that covers four longshots might sound good, but the problem is that the return from the number that wins is diluted by the other bets that automatically lose. Two shots at a 30–1 return and two at 15–1 *sounds* good, but all you're really getting is 3–1 for the 3 or 11, or roughly 7–1 for the 2 or 12.

Most players who bet the Horn do so after a Horn number is rolled (expecting a repeat from that group), or as an expanded hedge during the pass line come-out. But the point of a hedge bet is protection. Why finance coverage of the 11, which is a pass line winner anyway?

There aren't a lot of good reasons to make this bet. No, wait. There aren't any *good* reasons. None!

HORN HIGH: This bet was designed to maximize the efficiency of the *Horn* as a shearing tool for the bleating, blinking, bacchanalian sponge-heads who don't know better than to play it. Oops! I hope I didn't offend somebody there.

Rather than deal with a four-unit bet, the player can call out *"Horn, high eleven,"* for example, and throw out a nickel. This gives an extra unit of coverage on whatever number may be desired. It caters to those who are either too lazy to bother with the change, or else they feel that calling out the bet makes them sound like they know what they're doing.

I admit, it *sounds* impressive.

Check the face of the boxman the next time you hear someone call out a bet like that. Chances are he's got a big smile on his face, because he knows he just reeled in another fish without having to put any meaningful bait on the hook.

WORLD BETS: This bet is something of an enigma, for it is seldom mentioned in gaming books, and it doesn't appear on the layouts. Only by playing the game and hearing it called out do you acquire an awareness of its existence.

I have a theory on why it isn't shown on the craps layouts: the casinos are too embarrassed to proclaim it a legitimate bet, because it's even worse than the *horn*. Yep, that's right.

The world bet *is* a horn bet, plus a fifth unit going to the *any seven*. The idea is to cover every number that isn't a point number, meaning, all the *craps* and *naturals*, wrapped up together in one sweet, silly little wager.

This bet is as dumb as they come. If a 7 is rolled, all the bet pays is enough to finance replacing the bet. You don't make a *dime* off the fact that you won. And of course the extra unit dilutes all the other payoffs even further. Forget about it!

THREE-WAY CRAPS: Imagine, if you will, the horn bet minus the yo (11). There you have it: *three-way craps*. Like the horn, each bet is paid as a separate wager, and the vigorish is as stated for those three numbers of the horn bet. Some players prefer this option over any craps as a pass line hedge, because the return is better if a 2 or 12 is rolled, and I suppose they like those little bonuses from time to time. But, the bet also costs more, and has to be made in amounts that are divisible by three.

If you are seeking to hedge the pass line, stick to the flat 7–1 return of *any craps*. It's much more versatile.

TWO-WAY CRAPS: If you play enough craps, you'll eventually hear someone call out *"Two-way craps,"* and you might wonder what it is. Actually, it's not a bet in the typical sense. What that bettor is doing is requesting an any craps for himself and another for the dealers, as a toke.

When I'm doing well at the table, I generally call out *two-way craps* enough times to ensure that they win with me once or twice. But that's up to the individual.

C&E BETS: If you refer back to Figure 25 on page 109, you will see a series of connected circles with the letters *C & E* imprinted therein. The *C & E* stand for *Craps* and *Eleven,* and the circles are fanning out to more or less aim themselves towards the bettors, so it's clear whose bet is whose.

The *C & E* bet is exactly what it appears to be: a bet that covers *any craps* (paying 7–1) and the *11* (paying 15–1), if one of the four numbers (2, 3, 11 or 12) comes up on the next roll. It is basically a condensed *horn,* and considered to be a two-unit bet, but the stickman will accept nickel bets, giving $2.50 coverage on each. Also, you can bet either one individually.

This wager is usually made by pass line bettors during the come-out, and it's surprising how many players are suckered into playing it, for it is half hedge (against a craps roll) and half bonus (adding to the come-out win if an 11 is rolled). It is presumed that the only reason this bet is played is because the stickman snags a few pigeons after promoting it.

Again, you've got the problem of the payoffs being diluted by the other bet component, for the two cannot win simultaneously. But if this bet is separated, suddenly it makes sense. There are times when you may want to bet any craps, and there may be times you'll want coverage of the 11. Both can serve as hedges, but for different bets. In a case such as this, the stickman will place your bet in the applicable circle.

As a combination bet, the C & E stinks. But as separate bets, the C & E have legitimate places in this world.

PROPOSITION LONGSHOTS: If you can imagine taking the horn bet, lighting its fuse and exploding it into four separate bets, you'd end up with *Proposition Longshots.* You have *Aces* (the 2), *Midnight* (the 12), *Ace-Deuce* (the 3), and the *Yo* (the 11). The 2 and 12 each pay 30–1 and the 3 and 11 return 15–1 in *most* casinos. But take note: some casinos pay only 29–1 and 14–1, respectively. And they describe these bets as 30 *for* 1 and 15 *for* 1, in an effort to disguise their sleaziness.

Oops. Did I offend some casinos? I'm sorry.

The vigorish for the 2 and 12 is 13.89% and for the 3 and 11 it is 11.1%. Some who play these bets are looking for a *repeater*, so they bet on the *ace-deuce* (3), using the appearance of the 3 as their wagering trigger. Now I realize I'm disgracing myself when I say this, but it seems to me that the 3 and 11 *do* frequently come up in pairs, or one after the other. And I suspect that one could make a living chasing these longshots. But you'll never understand these intuitions until you've played the game.

Like the horn bet, which is the accumulation of all these options, these are one-roll bets made through the stickman, and can be bet individually or in groups. I've played all of them on different occasions, for different reasons. You may decide that some of them are beneficial to you as well.

PS: If you hear someone call out *High/Low,* this is a bet on the 2 & 12. Similarly, *Ace-Deuce/Yo* equals 3 & 11. And *Boxcars* is sometimes used to request a bet on the 12.

HOP BETS: At this writing, *Hop* bets are not available in Atlantic City, and I doubt that you'll find them on the riverboats, but they *are* offered in Las Vegas. But then, what isn't offered in Las Vegas? They'll give you odds on how many times your weiner dog takes a dump, if you give them the right data.

A Hop bet is a one-roll wager on a specific dice combination that can occur in two ways, such as 5 and 4 (equaling a 9). A *Hop Hardway* is also a one-roller, but on a number that can be rolled only one way, such as 5 and 5.

Payoffs for these bets can vary from 14–1 to 15–1 for the Hops and 29–1 to 30–1 for the Hop Hardways. The vigs for these wagers range from 11.1% to 16.67%, no bargain.

One of the first times I heard this bet called out, it was the player to my right requesting *"4 and 4 on the hop"* as he tossed a nickel to the stickman. The next roll was a 4 and 4, and the man didn't even blink. Until I figure out how he did that, I think you'd be better off avoiding this bet.

ANY SEVEN:

This is the worst bet on the table, bar none.
>—John Patrick, p. 118,
>**John Patrick's Craps**

Avoid this bet at all costs.
>—Edwin Silberstang, p. 189,
>**Guide To Casino Gambling**

An inadvisable, sucker proposition.
>—Tom Ainslie, p. 102,
>**How To Gamble In A Casino**

Of all the bets at craps, this is the ultimate, the very worst.
>—Arthur S. Reber, p. 83,
>**The New Gambler's Bible**

If you read the above, it certainly appears that a compelling verdict has been reached on the *Any Seven*. Poor little Any Seven, the bet that nobody likes.

What's wrong with this bet? Isn't 7 the number that destroys all those pass line bets, place bets, and field bets? Wouldn't it make sense to align oneself with the *Great Destroyer?*

Not when the bet pays only 4–1 for taking a 5–1 chance! That's 16.67% you're fighting, the toughest edge at the craps table. This bet is soooo bad, you shouldn't even say its name out loud—during midgame—at the table where you make it.

Any Seven is a one-roll proposition bet that pays 4–1, but you are advised to ask for it under the name of *Big Red*, except during the come-out. Why? You'll live longer. You want to keep living, don't you? Well then, don't infuriate all the pass line bettors who dread hearing anything that sounds remotely like that unmentionable word *'seven'* between come-outs. Even if someone asks you the time at 7:17 pm, just point to your watch, or say you don't know. That's the way it be, Beverlee.

Now that you know what a thoroughly rotten and despicable bet the *Any Seven* is, this should be a good time to inform you that everything you know is wrong. Clearly, this will be a hard sell, but I'm going to try to vindicate the Any Seven.

To help you understand why my opinion of Any Seven differs so sharply from that of the experts, let us first take a hard look at why they don't like it:

Is it the 16.67% house edge? You got it. To them, 16-plus tells the whole story. To advocate the Any Seven is to reveal one's stupidity. Turn the page, close the book.

Now take a look at the other side. It is an indisputable fact that the most likely number to be rolled *consecutively* is the 7. But what about three, four, or even six in a row? Happens all the time. My records show that if you play craps for six hours, there's a good chance you'll run into *six* triple sevens, and one of those is likely to go to four-in-a-row. And if you continue to play, it's just a matter of time before you run into five, and six.

Ahead in this book, you'll learn about the *Any Seven Parlay,* which will help you make $100 from a $5 bet, simply because you anticipated a routine table condition.

Betting *selectively,* you can turn the *worst bet on the board* into a sweet deal. But you gotta stay from the dogma.

SUMMARY OF PROPOSITION BETS

Most knowledgeable people seem to agree that *proposition bets* are bad news, for they were designed—through mathematical advantages—to favor the house more than the mainstay bets. But it's not as simple as all that.

To a pro, every bet at the craps table—with a few exceptions—is like a surgical instrument. Each has its specific function, and collectively, they widen one's range of alternatives. Some of these options are expensive, so they must be used discriminately. But to proclaim them all to be monsters based on numerical figures is bad advice for aspiring professionals.

Proposition bets enable a player to capitalize upon trends that occur randomly yet routinely in any casino. They are the tools that help one maximize his efficiency. I have seen tables where every shooter rolls at least one 7 at the very beginning of his come-out. That's a catchable trend. Are you going to ignore a predictable wagering opportunity that could enable you to bet with pinpoint precision and reap successive 4–1 returns. . .*because you fear the 16.67% house edge?*

The exploitation of trends in gaming is what professional gambling is all about. To do the job right, you need access to every device at your disposal. Proposition bets, costly though they may be, can often work to your advantage.

Casinos are helpless against the wild swings of the dice that occur every day. This is where *your* advantage lies. Make the most of it, 'cause it's sink or swim in this business ✠

A COME BET ADVISORY

Another area where I disagree with the experts is with respect to the matter of *come bets*.

According to most experts, only the bets that have the lowest vigs are worthy of play. Come bets with double odds fit the bill with their 0.6 percent house edge. . .

But they are a trap. Casinos would truly love nothing more than to have their craps pits filled every day with inveterate come bettors. They gladly accept the chump change they get from the proposition bets, but when the come bets start to fall, it makes all that penny-ante stuff worthwhile. Now, at the right table, come bets can make a lot of money fast. Just don't expect the fun to endure. In time, you'll see the precipitous ledge upon which they stand for what it is: a shockingly weak, unstable and inadequate reef against the voracious jaws of the indomitable seven.

The big flaw in come bets is that no matter what you decide, you can't remove your basic bet. Like a wounded meadowlark in the speed lane of I–95, it's there to stay.

The other flaw is that although come bets carry the same low vig as pass line bets, there is no limit to how many you can make, and the house edge is *multiplied by its original figure* with each new bet. When you accelerate the number of bets within each line bet cycle, the house edge begins to eat you alive!

As I said back on page 100, there are only two times when I advocate come bets: for *Multi-Line* (coming up), and, to capitalize on a hot roll. At any other time, and for any other reason, you're taking on more risk than you need ✠

SUMMARY OF CRAPS BETS

Now that you know all the betting options for craps, don't you wish you understood the game?

No tutorial can substitute for one hour of the real thing, and this book is no exception. But if you follow the teachings herein, you can't go too far astray.

Your training period will entail practice games to simulate—and casino visits to observe—live games. And for those who really take their new career seriously, it wouldn't hurt to pick up some other books on the subject. Most of them weren't written for or by professionals, but they'll enhance your understanding of the games. A very good source for gaming titles is the *Gambler's Book Shop* in Las Vegas, at 1-800-522-1777.

This chapter is intended primarily to demonstrate how the game is played and the available options. Some of these options are better than others, but most of them have their place, at some point or another. To do the job right, you need access to all the tricks. And that includes proposition bets. As this author sees it, the bigger your portfolio of betting options, the more effectively you'll be able to *tame the trends*.

When you bet *selectively*, you won't feel the house edge, for your bets are triggered only when a specific trend has been spotted. This helps you *weed out* the decisions that *would have been* losses —which *would have represented the house edge*.

Most players are clueless to the wagering opportunities that are constantly presenting themselves at the tables. You will learn how to capitalize on the trends that breed these opportunities, for that is the specialty of this book ✠

PART II
PROFESSIONAL TECHNIQUES

9

USING PAST EVENTS
TO PREDICT
FUTURE RESULTS

It is the business of the future to be dangerous.

—Alfred North Whitehead

Earlier in this book, we noted that every gaming decision is independent of the previous one. That is to say, the roulette wheel, the cards, the dice: have no memory. But that doesn't prevent them from *acting* as if they did.

When an even money proposition wins seventeen in a row, it *seems* deliberate, but *how* the pattern originated is not important. It's *what you do with the opportunity.*

When a dominant trend is active, you can use *past events to predict future results*—with pinpoint precision, at times. Indeed, it is *possible* for one to foretell the next sixteen table game decisions, but realize, it is nothing more than good guesswork. The person doing the guessing must be prepared for that pattern to bust at any point along the way. As I've said, *there are no sure bets,* and that includes bet number ten, from a streak of seventeen ✠

THE FIVE PRIMARY EVEN MONEY PATTERNS

Figure 26 illustrates *The Five Primary Even Money Patterns,* which can be applied to even money wagering options for roulette, minibaccarat, and to a lesser extent, craps.

When one of the patterns below is identified at the table (in an early stage), it is frequently beneficial to match it stride for stride. Most patterns don't last very long, but the ones that do can make up for a lot of fruitless wagers.

P1

RED	BLK
•	
•	
•	
•	
•	
•	
•	
•	
•	
•	
•	
•	
•	

P2

RED	BLK
•	
•	
•	
•	
•	
•	
	•
	•
	•
	•
	•
	•
	•

P3

RED	BLK
•	
•	
•	
•	
•	
•	
	•
•	
•	
•	
•	
•	

P4

RED	BLK
•	
	•
•	
	•
•	
	•
•	
	•
•	
	•
•	
	•
•	

P5

RED	BLK
•	
•	
	•
	•
•	
•	
	•
	•
•	
•	
	•
	•
	•

FIGURE 26
The Five Primary Patterns

The *Five Primary Patterns* from Figure 26 have been assigned the designations P1 through P5. These comprise the range of the most elementary and easily recognized *even money trends*. They should be memorized, for they are constantly reoccurring in table games all over the world. Some day, you may wish to specialize in some or all of these:

P1   This is the most basic trend. Often called a *streak*, it is simply an extended group of duplicate table decisions. Very easy to spot. A P1 pattern must have at least four consecutive decisions, and has no fixed upward limit.

P2   This is an expanded version of the P1, where the streak that started on one side continues on the other. As long as both sides win four or more consecutive decisions (in one group), such a trend would qualify as a genuine P2 pattern.

P3   This is another variation of the P1, but in my experience it is more common than the P2. In this pattern, one of the two sides has complete domination—with the exception of an occasional blip on the opposite side.

P4   The P4 is one you'll see everywhere you go. You can't avoid it. Some, of course, last longer than others, but the zigzag pattern of the P4 is perhaps the most common of all those described on this page.

P5   This is an expanded version of the P4, where the zigzag pattern occurs in pairs instead of single hits. It may be a bit difficult for you to believe that patterns like this routinely prevail for ten or more decisions, but it's true.

If you are able to get to Atlantic City or Las Vegas—where roulette tables are grouped in bunches—you will eventually see *all* these patterns on their scoresigns ✠

PLAYING THE FIVE PRIMARY PATTERNS

The delineation of the *Five Primary Patterns* originated from a need to define the patterns that are regularly seen at minibaccarat. Most players of that game, I imagine, know about the Five Primary Patterns, though I haven't seen them documented elsewhere. But the players' awareness of their existence is chiefly why minibaccarat players use scorecards, *and,* why it would be unthinkable for casinos to *not* make these scorecards available.

Any patterns that are applicable to minibaccarat can also be applied to even money roulette bets, like red/black, even/odd, and high/low. There was a time when I tried to keep on top of all three of the even money categories at roulette, thinking it would give me three times the betting opportunities, but instead I found myself fighting a war on three fronts that ultimately proved to be too much. You're better off fighting one war at a time.

The most lucrative patterns for me are P3 and P4, because they are easier to spot and more abundant. A P1 is often exhausted or nearly so by the time I notice it; and P2*s* and P5*s* are more rare than the others. But the P3 is fairly catchable. You just wait for the blip, then play some two or three-stage parlays on the anticipated resumption of the streak. And the P4 is also good for parlay bets, or, just riding the wave till it dies.

Some players specialize in one, two, or perhaps all of these patterns, by seeking them out in the early stages of development, then taking up hot pursuit.

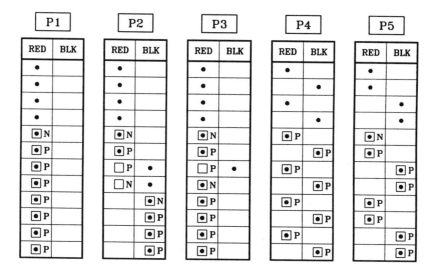

FIGURE 27
Playing The Five Patterns

Figure 27 shows how I recommend playing the five patterns. I usually wait until a pattern is in its fourth stage before presuming the trend is viable, and begin with a *Neutral* bet (denoted by an *N*). If that bet succeeds, I then venture a *Pattern* bet, denoted by a *P*. Neutral bets are tentative bets made to test the water, which are usually about half the size of Pattern bets.   There's a good reason for this: The trend you are pursuing will often break immediately. When you begin with a *half-bet,* you minimize your risk on the initial wager, and if it wins *but the next bet loses,* you've earned enough from *that* win to abate the subsequent loss.

Please note that:

1) The P4 doesn't require a Neutral bet.   This pattern is so common that I start out with a full-size bet.

2) Whenever you suffer a loss—but expect a continuation of a pattern, don't return to Pattern (full size) bets until you first win a Neutral (half size) bet.

3) Since the P3 is a more common pattern than P2, I follow up on midstreak losses as if I expect a P3 to ensue.

EVALUATION:

| P1 |

The P1 is a specialty for some players. Any streak of four or more could serve as a trigger to launch a series, which may take the form of Neutral/Pattern bets (as just described), *parlay* or *paroli* bets (coming up next chapter), or simply riding the trend with flat bets until it dies. (Note: I seldom bother with these until they reach the fifth or sixth stage.)

| P2 |

The P2 has the dubious distinction of being less prevalent than perhaps all the others, with the possible exception of the P5. Therefore, when a P1 streak dies, I presume that if the table is inclined to continue streaking, a P3 is more likely than a P2. All the same, you should know of its existence.

| P3 |

The P3 is my personal favorite for *parlays*. A *parlay* is a bet that is created by adding the proceeds of a previous winning bet to that original bet, forming a new, larger wager. In this case, I wait for the *blip* (the end of a P1 streak), then begin a two or three-stage parlay on the expectation that a P3 will arise from the ashes of the P1. On this basis, a three-stager would net $150 from a $10 bet. More on *parlays* in Chapter 10.

| P4 |

The P4 is my favorite for flat bets, though I frequently try a one-stage parlay (in an attempt) to maximize my gains. It is surprising to me how few players capitalize on this little gem, because P4*s* are always out there. This is the one pattern that I don't need to see four previous stages before venturing a wager. Usually, I pick up on the P4 as soon as the thought occurs to me (after seeing at least two stages of the zigzag.)

| P5 |

The P5 is pretty easy to follow. It is actually a variation of an *encompassing trend* known (only in this book) as the *Reoccurring Double,* of which you will also learn very soon. The P5 is suitable for flat bets and short parlays.

SECONDARY PATTERNS

The *Five Primary Patterns* aren't all that are out in the world. Next come *Secondary Patterns,* shown in Figure 28. These trends are more complex, but structured nevertheless.

Although I have given these names, they are not worthy of memorization. They are shown only to illustrate the repetition that prevails at the tables. Any one of these patterns could dominate the table activity for ten, fifteen or twenty decisions. Patterns like these are what minibaccarat players are looking for when they track the table results with scorecards ✠

P6		P7		P8		P9	
RED	BLK	RED	BLK	RED	BLK	RED	BLK
•		•		•		•	
•		•		•		•	
•		•			•	•	
	•		•	•			•
	•		•	•		•	
	•	•			•	•	
•		•		•		•	
•			•	•			•
•			•		•	•	
	•	•		•		•	
	•	•		•		•	
	•				•		•

FIGURE 28
Secondary Patterns

PATTERN/NEUTRAL/ ANTI-PATTERN

Although roulette even money bets are nearly identical to minibaccarat bets (disregarding the house edge), the betting methods of those who play the two are not at all alike. Those who play the roulette bets seem to favor fighting the trend, while the minibaccarat players appear to conduct themselves more like pros. But that's not all that's different. The numerical patterns within the games themselves don't seem quite the same, perhaps because there is no miniB equivalent to the roulette zeroes, whose presence may hinder the natural flow of events in two-sided situations. Still, the precepts that are used in minibaccarat can be successfully applied to even money roulette wagering.

Most experts at minibaccarat, I believe, employ a wagering technique that involves *following the pattern*. To help them see the big picture, they keep track of the table results on a scorecard. And quite a few of them, like myself, see all table patterns as belonging to one of three groups:

1) **Pattern:** *Table decisions that have a structured sequence, (e.g., a primary or secondary table pattern).*
2) **AntiPattern:** *The opposite of Pattern results (which would result in losses for Pattern players).*
3) **Neutral:** *A table trend that is in a state of transition, as old patterns die and new patterns emerge.*

Most tables are dominated either by *Pattern* or *AntiPattern* trends. *Neutrals* exist within both.

The *Neutrals* are simply interim table decisions that occur when patterns overlap, at which time a player should acquire more evidence (from the table) before making a wagering commitment. *Neutrals,* as defined herein, comprise perhaps 10 to 20 percent of all table game results. When a table is in such a state, there is *no hope* for you to make an intelligent wagering decision. Your best bet is no bet, if possible, and your *next best move* is to bide your time with a wager that meets the table minimum.

Theoretically, every table is slanted to favor *Pattern* trends or *AntiPattern* trends, though I believe that the former is the rule for the majority. What you want to do is identify *which one* it is, then cater your play to that trend.

How do you play **Pattern***?* Well, you just look at what the table's been doing, and try to match up the most recent results with one of the Patterns (P1 through P9) we've just covered. When you lose, this often signifies a shift to a new pattern, which will occur on an ongoing basis as you play. Until a new trend has been identified, the table is essentially churning out *Neutrals.* Playing *Pattern* involves jumping from one P number to the next, while seeking a transition that is as seamless as possible.

How do you play **AntiPattern***?* This is a bit harder. You have to first visualize what the *Pattern* move would have been, then do the opposite. This is tougher than it sounds.

How do you know which one (Pattern or AntiPattern) to play? There's one real effective way to get a clue: if you're not winning, it may be time to swim the other way.

Whenever I play sit-down roulette or minibaccarat, I start out with the presumption that *Pattern* bets will work. But when losses start to mount, I ask myself: *Is this a fleeting aberration, or are these the symptoms of an AntiPattern table?*

In such a case, the serious player has three viable alternatives: continue what he's doing, switch to AntiPattern, or walk. All the information he has gathered at that table, and some yet to be discovered, helps him make that choice ✠

ENCOMPASSING TRENDS

You have just learned about Primary and Secondary Patterns, which are small groups of gaming results. Now, step back a few paces and take in a larger view.

While the primary and secondary trends are vying for mastery, a larger portrait is taking shape, which may last for thirty, forty or even a hundred decisions. It's important that you don't ignore the *big picture* that emerges along the way ✠

THE REOCCURRING SINGLE

For a period in the early nineties, the Palace Station casino in Las Vegas was my favorite place for playing minibaccarat, because (for whatever reason) their tables always seemed to treat me right. But there was one memorable session I had there, during which time I dodged a bullet, and learned a lesson in doing so. This lesson can be applied to minibaccarat or (even money bets at) roulette, and it led me to the discovery of the *Reoccurring Single*.

At the time, I had noticed that Bank was hitting in singles and Player in multiples. That is, for the last fifteen or more hands the table favored Player, so that whenever Bank won it was only for a single hand before the trend reverted back to Player for another group of multiple hits.

At the time, this struck me as an *opportunity*. I opted to play *follow the Bank* (using a *Bank* win as the wagering trigger), based on the expectation that (the *law of averages* would see to it that) a multiple hit would soon occur.

This observation was made after Bank had three single hits; when Bank won another single decision I followed up with a larger than usual bet on Bank. No good. Player won the next two, then it came to Bank once again. I duplicated my previous bet, but it turned out to be another bust. By the time Bank reappeared, my follow-up bet was not as large, for the table was wearing me down. And Bank lost *again*, making it *six straight single hits*, amidst a veritable sea of Player wins.

I was attempting to deprogram myself away from the thought of my losses and the chase itself, when Bank happened to snare another single win, its seventh. At that point I jettisoned all my discipline and loaded up on Bank. It was time, doggonit! It *had* to win. If necessary I would *make it win* through the force of sheer determination.

Guess what? It worked. And Bank went on to win five of the next seven hands, which I exploited before leaving shortly thereafter with a moderate profit.

But I was twice a fool.

Once a fool, for losing my discipline, and once again a fool for my skewed perception of that opportunity.

For it later occurred to me that I could have latched onto the Player side for a hugely lopsided majority of wins, rather than fight the trend and settle for one.

This is what happens when you lose sight of the big picture: the one you really want is the one you miss.

Figure 29 is a facsimile of the scorecard used during that session, dated 11-30-91, at 7:05 pm. For clarity (in conveying this pattern to readers) I have not included my original notations, and all Ties have been removed. (This is done to make the pattern a little clearer to newcomers to the game.)

ЯDE BACCARAT SCORECARD			
P	B	BET	CP
•			
•			
•			
	•		
	•		
•			
•			
	•		
•			
•			
•			
	•		
•			
•			
•			
	•		
•			
•			
	•		
•			
•			
	•		
•			
•			
•			
•			
•			
	•		
	•		
	•		
•			
	•		
	•		
	•		
•			
	•		
•			

11-30-91
7:05 PM
PALACE
STATION

FIGURE 29
The Reoccurring Single

At the time I was using a customized scorecard that had a stylized monogram. *P* stands for *Player;* *B* for *Bank,* and *CP* is *Cumulative Profit.* These days, I seldom use my own scorecard at miniB; scorecards are always abundant at casinos where miniB is offered, and that makes one less thing to carry. And, using *their* scorecard is less conspicuous. However, since I am accustomed to the *Player* column being on the left side, I revise the titles when a casino scorecard shows *Bank* on the left. That way, there's less chance I'll mistake *which* side is doing *what.*

The *Encompassing Trend* approach to following the pattern is more complex than just matching a configuration stride for stride. You need to see the big picture. In this case, it means recognizing the dominant trend favoring Player at that table. During the heart of that run, Player won 19 of 25 decisions. It was inexcusable for me to miss something so obvious.

Whenever I pass a roulette scoresign and see an example of the *reoccurring single,* I take note if it isn't at a late stage of the trend. Such table is usually ripe for a substantial *one-shot.* Very seldom do I miss at those tables.

How does one best exploit this pattern? You do the opposite of what I did in the story. Instead of betting on the side (that's churning out single hits) to go for a double, bet on the *continuation* of that pattern. Meaning, if Bank is coming up with single hits, wait until Bank wins again and then place your follow-up bet on Player. Then keep doing that for as long as you think you'll win, or until you lose, or 50,000 miles, whichever comes first.

It wouldn't hurt for you to seek out the *RS* next time you pass some roulette tables. Doing so will help train your eye to see the world like a professional; to spot the patterns that are most easily convertible to large sums of cash, by those who know what to look for and how to play them.

Identifying the *reoccurring single*—as a means of gaining a speculative advantage—ultimately led me to the discovery of the *Reoccurring Double,* coming up ✠

THE REOCCURRING DOUBLE

The *Reoccurring Double* is pretty much what the name says: a reoccurrence of double (or multiple) hits on one or both sides of an even money proposition. It would be more technically correct to call it the *reoccurring multiple,* I suppose, but that phrase just isn't catchy enough.

Figure 30 shows a classic *reoccurring double,* which took place during a session at the Barbary Coast in Las Vegas in 1993. Initially, the table generated a choppy back and forth pattern (P4, from the *five primary patterns*), but then settled into a multiple-hit trend for a number of hands, followed by another (though brief) P4, then back to the streaks.

Are reoccurring doubles very common? They're everywhere. *How do you exploit them?* Just wait until the switch (from one side to the other), then *bet on the same side.* The trick is catching the table while the trend prevails. *Is it lucrative?* I suspect you could make a living from exploiting the *RDs* alone.

Figure 31 shows another fine example of an *RD.* By wagering on the side that switched (for one bet *right after the switch),* one would win eight out of nine bets. In Figure 30 (for comparison), one would win eight out of ten, *if* that player commenced playing the *RD after* the first streak began.

Both the *RS* and *RD* can give a player an edge, by enabling him to hit a wagering target with pinpoint accuracy. And although these two patterns are more generalized than the classic P5 pattern that showed up at the start of Figure 31, they are more suited to high level wagers, if played selectively. The serious player should always be watching for them ✠

ЯDE BACCARAT SCORECARD

11-16-93
7:30 PM
BARBARY
COAST

P	B	BET	CP
•			
	•		
•			
	•		
•			
TIE			
•			
•			
	•		
	•		
	•		
•			
•			
•			
	▲		
	TIE		
	•		
•			
•			
TIE			
	•		
	•		
	•		
•			
•			
	•		
•			
	•		
	•		
	•		
	•		
	•		
	•		
•			
•			
•			
•			
	•		
CASH OUT			

FIGURE 30
The Reoccurring Double

ЯDE BACCARAT SCORECARD

9-20-93
12:20 PM
PALACE
STATION

P	B	BET	CP
SHUFFLE			
	•		
	•		
•			
•			
	•		
	•		
•			
•			
	•		
	•		
•			
•			
	•		
TIE			
•			
•			
TIE			
	•		
	•		
	•		
	•		
	•		
	•		
	•		
	•		
•			
TIE			
•			
	•		
CASH OUT			

FIGURE 31
A Classic P5 Pattern

SUMMARY OF PRESCIENCE IN GAMING

In this chapter, you have learned about:

1) *The Five Primary Patterns*
2) *Secondary Patterns*
3) *Pattern, Neutral & AntiPattern Trends*
4) *Encompassing Trends*
5) *The Reoccurring Single*
6) *The Reoccurring Double*

Together, these comprise a powerful arsenal for any player of even money propositions. Add a bankroll, some experience and a *generous amount of discipline,* and you've got just about all you need to write your own paycheck. It won't happen overnight, but this information, right here, is a good part of what's been missing from all the strategies devised through the years by men who knew all along that *somehow,* casinos could be beaten.

How do you apply this information? For starters, re-read every page of this chapter. Make sure you understand every nuance of what's been said, and then do some experiments. Perform trials. Do whatever you must to seek *validation* for the specific techniques that pique your interest.

Be curious. Be skeptical. Be bold and courageous. *Find a way* to get the answers you need, so that when you go out there for real, you'll be as ready as ready can be ✠

10

MAXIMIZING YOUR ADVANTAGE

Them that has, gets.

—American expression

Now that you can predict the future, don't stop there. Take charge. Maximize your advantage!

As noted in the *Player's Edge,* a key advantage for a player is the ability to fluctuate the size of his bet. This is large. This is where you can capitalize on the fact that tables are reacted *upon.* You're the hammer; the table is the nail. Now, let's be honest: which would you rather be?

Unfortunately, there's a tiny catch. You need an awareness of *professional techniques.* That is, you must know *when* to do *what.* That's what *this* chapter is for ✠

PRESS AND PULL

One of the most basic techniques used by professionals is one called *Press and Pull*. In short, it means *press* up your bet size as you win, then *pull* back a profit at intervals.

Press and pull is suitable particularly for extended sit-down sessions of even money bets, like those found at minibaccarat or roulette. This book advises against making a habit of prolonged sessions, because it is easier—under those circumstances—for one to be seduced by the virulent effects of *Continuum*. Instead, readers are advised to keep sessions brief, more like a commando operation than playing a game. Should you discover a way to make sit-down sessions work, however, don't let me discourage you. . .as long as you take responsibility for that risk.

Getting back to the subject, *press and pull* is most effective when one is already winning. It helps you get the most from those gains, and prepare yourself for end of the ride.

Let's say you're playing at the $10 level, and you're enjoying an extended series of wins. Instead of $10-$10-$10-$10, you could increase your bet by a nickel with each win, then regress to the original bet after two hits. Your betting pattern would change to $10-$15-$20-$10. The *press* helps you maximize your gains while the *pull* locks up a profit as you go. In this example, you gain $55 instead of $40. In time, such gains will add up.

Press And Pull is a broad concept which has many offshoots. *Combination bets, parlays* and even some *progressions* are all part of the *press and pull* family. Once you know them, you'll be able to *maximize your advantage* ✠

THE PARLAY: The *Parlay* is one of the neatest tricks ever devised for players. It involves adding the entire profit from a bet that just won to the original bet, resulting in a new, larger bet. This is often called *let it ride,* though this concept is different from that of the casino game of the same name. Parlay bets can be made in one or several stages.

A *one-stage parlay* is the most common type of parlay, and is usually applied to even money bets. An example would be to bet $10 on an even money proposition and win, then add the $10 you won to the first bet, so that you're now placing a $20 bet. If that should win, you have received a 3–1 return from that pair of bets. If you then follow up with a $10 bet, you've defined the essence of *press and pull:* you *pressed* up your win, then *pulled* back its size to the original level, guaranteeing a profit for the series. The trick is, your first two bets have to win.

A *two-stage parlay* is much more difficult to attain, but it's much more lucrative if you succeed. It pays 7–1, and works like this: your initial $10 bet wins, so your next bet is $20. If that bet wins, your next bet is $40. If all three bets win, you end up with $80 from a $10 bet. But this is not easy to do, nor is it easy to *get yourself to do.* You see, every win is precious, so to risk forfeiture of two consecutive winning bets is a lot easier to plan on paper than to actually do. But there is a middle ground between the *one-* and *two-stage parlays,* which I prefer when betting aggressively. In this book, it is known as the *RE Parlay.*

THE RE PARLAY: I have christened this parlay with my initials, but I'm sure it's been done. I just haven't seen it in print or called by a specific name. It's a two-stage parlay, but you pull back enough from the second stage to recoup your original bet. Works like this: a $10 bet wins, so you then bet $20. If that wins, you press your bet to $30, which is $10 less than the collective amount. It that stage loses, you have no profit, but mercifully, you have also avoided a loss.

This allows you to bet aggressively with less risk—returning your original bet just before the third stage, where you fight the heaviest odds. It pays 6–1, just one notch below that of a two-stage parlay, where *everything* is risked at *every* stage.

MULTIPLE PARLAYS: Anything beyond a *two-stage parlay* is pretty rare except at sports betting, and those are sucker bets. Getting a win is not something you can pinpoint with a high degree of reliability; therefore, to seek *an unbroken chain of wins* (exceeding three)—in which a single loss at any point along the way will cause the structure to collapse—is regarded as a fool's game by those who understand the probabilities.

To let you know, however, the following are the returns for even money parlays that exceed three stages:

PARLAY	RETURN	$10 PAYS
4 Stage	15-1	$160
5 Stage	31-1	$320
6 Stage	63-1	$640
7 Stage	127-1	$1,280
10 Stage	1023-1	$10,240

FIGURE 32
Multiple Parlay Returns

These are noted for your reference only. I realize these figures *sound* good, but they are fundamentally unattainable.

My philosophy on parlays is that there will *never* come a time when it makes sense to exceed three stages. And none of the pros I know ever go beyond two.

Leave the multiple parlays to the recreational gamblers. They have no chance for long-range success anyway, so let them enjoy the fantasy. The pros stick to what's realistic.

INTERMEDIATE PARLAY: This one is a cross between a two- and a three-stage parlay. The *Intermediate Parlay* allows one to seek aggressive gains, but is more conservative than the *RE parlay*.

This parlay involves a three-stage series. If you win at the first stage, you use the profit to double your bet. If the second stage also wins, the third bet is at the same level as the second. Win or lose, the series is over at that point, and if you made it to that last stage, you're guaranteed either a small or large profit. At the $10 level, it looks like this: $10-$20-$20, and your profit is either $10 or $50. After that, you regress to the $10 level and remain there, or begin a new parlay series.

This parlay is my recommendation for those who are not content with the two-stage parlay. If all three stages are successful, the return is 5–1.

PAROLI: *Paroli* is another word for parlay, but in some circles it pertains to lightly-seasoned pasta shells that are filled with meat and covered with tomato sauce. No wait. . .that's *ravioli*, not *paroli*. Sorry. I keep confusing them.

In days long gone, a *paroli* was a more aggressive version of what is now called a *parlay*, but was limited to two stages. This involved adding the profit of a winning bet to your original wager, *plus* a duplicate of the first bet. If the first wager won, this bet series would read like this: $10–$30. The return is 4–1, which is not too shabby for a one-stage parlay. Obviously, one must have a fair amount of confidence that the final wager will succeed. What it accomplishes is a trade-off of the risk, relative to a two-stage parlay. You are risking more money at the second level, but the duration of the risk is reduced from three wagers to two. There are good and bad points to each approach. But then, such could be said about most anything ✠

COMBINATION BETS

Combination bets are just one-stage parlays, but I denote them as such when they are applied to the *five primary patterns* (from Figure 26, back on page 124). Patterns P1 through P5 are ideal for this type of wager when betting is commenced at the fifth stage as shown in Figure 27. This two-stage bet pays 3–1.

Why make a distinction? It is my opinion that parlay betting should be automatic at these stages (as shown below in Figure 33) unless your table shows a strong propensity for short-lived patterns. In that case, you may have to wing it, but I feel that this is a sound wagering practice in general. If you get the feeling that the pattern you are following may hold up a while longer, repeat the process indefinitely until the wins stop. Please note that *combination bet* Type 1 applies to three pattern types (P1, 2 & 3), while the other two apply to a single *P* pattern.

TYPE 1		TYPE 2		TYPE 3	
FROM P1, 2, 3		FROM P4		FROM P5	
PLAYER	BANK	PLAYER	BANK	PLAYER	BANK
•		•		•	
•			•	•	
•		•			•
•			•		•
• 1		• 1		• 1	
• 2			• 2	• 2	

FIGURE 33
Combination Bets

SUMMARY OF MAXIMIZING YOUR ADVANTAGE

When you combine knowledge of *patterns* (from Chapter 9) with an awareness of *press and pull, parlays* and *combination bets,* how can inert, unresponsive artifacts like gaming tables have a chance in the world?

Trust me, they do. They've foiled some of the most brilliant minds in history, because there are times when *non-reaction is the most effective way to react.* Sometimes, in trying to outsmart your opponent, you end up outsmarting yourself.

All the same, an experienced player who has knowledge of all these offensive techniques can frequently accomplish some amazing things in a very short period of time.

Even though *Press And Pull* is the vaguest of all the concepts noted in this chapter, it was chosen as the introductory subject for a reason: while working, it is this kind of mentality that you should keep in your thoughts at all times. When is the best time to *press* your bets, and when should you *pull* back to guarantee your profit? Just keep thinking: *press and pull, press and pull.*

Parlays are offshoots of *press and pull,* but are more rigidly defined, and there are several to choose from. *Combination bets* and *progressions* (which we'll get to soon) are also instrumental in helping the seasoned player maintain his edge.

These, however, are all *offensive* instruments, and as every soldier knows, you need a good *defensive* mechanism to coordinate with your offense. That's next ✠

11

YOUR DEFENSIVE ARSENAL

Back on page 8, it was noted that *before you can learn to win, you must learn how to **not lose**.* What that says, is that even the most dynamic offense in the world means very little, if it is not supported with an *outstanding* defense ✠

SESSION LOSS LIMITS

Of all the weapons in your *defensive* arsenal, none are more requisite to your success than strict adherence to your *Loss Limits,* as they pertain to each session, and each day.

Loss limits are your most cherished allies. They are there to protect you from yourself and from the evil you would do in their absence. They are what separate you from the losers, charlatans and fools. They confer the protection you absolutely need to do the job you have to do.

Now if you only knew what I'm talking about.

The concept of *session loss limits* is pretty simple. Before buying in at any table, you must visualize a figure in your head that represents the maximum damage you are willing to sustain in the event that things don't go well. When swimming in a pool of sharks —as you'll be doing every workday—you have to acknowledge the possibility that one of them just might manage to remove a pound of flesh. You see, those sharks have been *trained* to strip away all removable wealth from everyone who enters the gates, and they're pretty good at what they do.

Loss limits are your most important line of defense. Until you learn this, life will be one long struggle in the dark.

Those who succeed at casino gambling and those who write how-to books about it, all have their own theories about loss limits. It's not a black-and-white matter. Many authors advocate setting your loss limits at a figure that represents *half* your buy-in. That means, you're going to stop playing when half your chips are gone; the remaining half are never to be used. According to them, it is psychologically bad to leave the table with empty pockets, or to bet down to your last chip.

The underlying principle of that argument makes sense to me, but what's important is finding a way to mitigate the downside, and settling into something that works for you. Whatever your feelings happen to be, it is essential that you set up a mechanism to keep you from chasing your losses.

Different situations call for different tactics. When playing a sit-down session at roulette, I usually start thinking about leaving when half my chips are gone, like they say. But I don't play many sit-down sessions in the first place. At craps, I allow myself *the option* of exhausting my buy-in, and making a secondary buy-in that amounts to half the original figure. That's because my craps buy-ins are generally smaller, and, it's a volatile game from which you can swing back quickly. But after doing so, if things don't turn around quickly, I'm out of there. My recommendation is that you seek a method that works for you, and then (before every buy-in), *make a promise to yourself and stick to it.*

What's really important is this: never, ever let yourself *get into the habit* of pulling money out of your pocket when you're losing, like you're feeding a vending machine. *That* is what those esteemed authors are trying to get you to avoid, and their point is well taken. The exception I make for craps is *planned,* and enacted only when the table shows late-inning potential ✠

DAILY LOSS LIMITS

Just as important as the *session loss limits* (that have just been discussed) are *Daily Loss Limits.* Before starting out each day, you should set a predetermined figure that represents the absolute *max* you're willing to lose that day—in your quest for disposable income. If you don't do this, it's almost a sure bet that one day, you'll find yourself draining every single bank account you have, all because you had a bad day and ended up in a panic-stricken frenzy to bail yourself out of the mess you created. Believe me, you have the capacity to do this.

Some (like myself) are forced to set up all kinds of bankroll safeguards, so that only so much money can be accessed from any and all sources in a given period of time. Chances are, you're going to have to do the same. This subject is covered ahead in *Bankroll Safeguards* (Chapter 18).

Generally speaking, *loss limits* (of any kind) represent the contract you negotiate with yourself in advance. Like the LAPD, they are there *To Protect And Serve.*

Never underestimate their importance. Everybody has his own preferences in managing his career, but without loss limits, you're gonna need a slick answer to the question:

What do you want on your tombstone? ✠

WIN GOALS

There was a time while living in Las Vegas that I tried an experiment. Playing minibaccarat only, I'd buy in for $120 and play at the $10 level until I got four units ahead. Most of the time this meant going for five units ($50), to allow for paying my commission bill and a tip for the dealer.

Since I lived right behind *Harrah's*, I started there, then moved on to the *Imperial Palace, Flamingo Hilton, Barbary Coast* and finally *Bally's*. All these casinos were pretty much part of a contiguous chain, and I'd work my way up and down the boulevard. On this basis, I was able to record fifteen straight winning sessions. But this frequently led to some very brief sessions—like, under two minutes. That's how long I spent at a table at the *Imperial Palace,* where the dealer had just shuffled and *Player* came storming out of the gate with a full head of steam. I always bet on Player right after the shuffle, and Player won every hand that I was there to witness. Since I anticipated that occurrence and parlayed two of my bets, my cash-out was a larger-than-usual $70, in spite of the brief duration of that session.

That first day—during which time I won all of my sessions—I made $284 in the first six sessions, took a break, then had four more, resulting in a total gain of $430 for the day. It seemed easy at the time, and it is—as long as you continue to win. But the losses will come, and when they do, those sessions can also be very brief. The worst part is, you have to win three to compensate a single loss (if you go through your entire buy-in). Still, it's easier to win more sessions than you lose if you keep them short, and watch yourself carefully after each loss. You don't want any loss to poison your mood and lead to a *string of losses.*

What does this have to do with *Win Goals?* Well, the purpose of that story is to illustrate the power of the small return. In those sessions, I had set a *win goal* of four units, which was not difficult for me to attain. When your goals are conservative, you can often reach them quickly. Then, you move on to the next session and continue the process.

Win goals are your *second* most important lines of defense, and again, the concept is simple: when you get ahead at the tables, you need to take steps to ensure that you leave the table a winner. The worst mistake you can make is to press your luck, and give all your winnings back to the house—and then some.

Leaving the table a winner is achieved by locking up your gains as you go, then going for more in stages.

Before the buy-in, along with setting the amount you'll allow yourself to lose before retreating, you must also set a figure that you feel you can *realistically* win. The former is your *loss limit;* the latter, your *win goal.*

In doing so, you're able to visualize the full spectrum of what might occur. That's what it takes to win ✠

SETTLE FOR 90

One thing that helped me win fifteen consecutive sessions during my *settle-for-small-gains* experiment is something I call the *Settle For 90* rule.

Necessity was the mother of *this* invention, for at some point I got tired of repeatedly being 90% of the way to my *win goal,* then losing everything I had won while trying to get that last ten percent. That was before I was tuned into locking up a profit, but it was amazing how many times it happened.

The point is: it's not worth it to obsess over an arbitrary figure when you're so close. You must take what the table gives you and be thankful it wasn't a loss. You did good. You gambled and won. Don't press it.

In the fourth session of my *small-gains* experiment, I quit when I had battled back to a $32 profit. That session was a difficult challenge, and I felt lucky to avoid a loss. True, I was a bit shy of my *win goal,* but I said to myself. . . *"Close enough."* As I see it, *settle for 90* bailed me out.

Settle for 90 also serves as a secondary line of defense, in the event of a catastrophic failure of your *loss limits.* When you have logged some real time at the tables, I'm sure you'll come to make use of this rule as an alternate safety net.

The whole purpose behind manuals like this is to help you to avoid all the costly errors that were dearly paid for by those who went before you into the dragon's lair.

All I can do is make the effort! ✠

THE REALITY CHECK

It is unwise to be too sure of one's wisdom. It is healthy to be reminded that the strongest might weaken and the wisest might err.

—Mohandas Gandhi

Considering the importance I assign to *loss limits* and *win goals,* some readers may feel that these deserve more than the sparse number of pages devoted to each.

I don't wish to understate the value of these precepts as they pertain to gaming, but there is an overriding principle that covers both, called the *Reality Check.*

Oh, really?

The *reality check* is a promise to yourself to keep all gaming activity strictly monitored. You must question the wisdom of the choices you're making *every single minute:* Are you accomplishing what you set out to do? Have you adhered to the procedural rules? Are you in complete control? You must watch yourself like a hawk, because the minute you let go is the cast-in-stone minute your career begins to unravel. And once it begins, it will gather momentum like a steam locomotive on a downhill run.

You need to ask yourself these questions, almost constantly: Am I winning at this table? Is this table helping me or hurting me? If you are losing, you ask: Is it a loss I understand? Or is the table churning out some bizarre trend that's keeping me off balance, or worse, *filling me with rage?*

They can do that, you know.

Once a minute is a hard figure. A serious figure. But that's how often you need to step outside yourself and take a look at that idiot who's risking *your money*. What the hell is he doing? Is he on top of things? It's *imperative* that you challenge every bet he makes and every decision he contemplates.

If you're the one placing the bets, this job is your partner's responsibility, but learning to monitor your own behavior will help. It's never a bad idea to have a backup.

So what is the procedure for watching oneself?

The thought came to me while playing minibaccarat years ago at the Claridge in Atlantic City. At some point I noticed that I had an audience. A woman in her twenties was standing next to me, and when I glanced up she asked me some questions about the game. She said it looked like fun.

She wanted to play, but the table was full, so I offered to add her chips to my bets, slightly off center.

She had only two or three Reds in her hand when we started, but after twenty-thirty minutes she had maybe fifteen. About then, it struck me as a good time to cash out, and I invited her to check out some other casinos with me. That's when she said her bus would be leaving soon; she was just killing time.

Things might have turned out better for me, but the encounter helped me see the value of an objective, detached stance while at the tables. If you think about it in terms of helping a pretty girl make money, it's easier to gain the objectivity you need to make good things happen. I realized then that it was easier for me to help *her* than to help myself. With my guidance, she *quintupled* her "buy-in" in less time than it took for me to *double* mine.

Setting up your own *reality check* means reminding yourself before walking up to the tables that you're going to take a time out, every minute, to evaluate how you're doing. Think about what's at stake: an exciting career in which you can earn perhaps six figures, or back to the drudgery of the old job.

Think of how your life will change, if only you can find the strength to keep from screwing up ✠

SUMMARY ON DEFENSE

Anything that can go wrong will go wrong, and at the worst possible moment.

—Murphy's Law

Gaming is a tricky business. The tables do not think or react to anything we do, and yet legions of men and women are foiled, time after time, generation after generation, by these inert objects. Are we being outwitted by those who have no wits?

So it would seem. But what really happens is we let our guard down. We are unprepared for the unexpected, for it doesn't seem possible for passivity to be so shrewd.

Even after spending a lifetime on the player side of the tables, any veteran of the games knows that he'll never have seen it all. Around every corner in time lurks a new surprise, waiting to shock and amaze us all.

Your best defense is to remain humble. To acknowledge that the element of surprise is on the side of *the other guy*. Expect the worst result at the worst possible moment. If you continue to think in those terms, there may be hope.

Have a plan, and follow through on it. Don't let yourself be swayed by all the flukes that are swimming about, looking for fresh meat. Stay in control.

Most important: watch yourself. Be ready for the beginnings of your own self-destruction at any moment, and get away before the molehill becomes a mountain.

Be prepared for the challenge of a lifetime, each and every day you spend time in a casino ✠

12

SYSTEMS IN GAMING

Most gaming books contain at least a few *systems,* which are close-ended strategies that are designed to afford the player a superior chance to win over random wagering. Some are simple and some are rather elaborate; some work only half the time and some hardly ever fail. But the ones that seldom fail are usually dangerous: when you lose, you lose *big.*

The unpredictable nature of trends pretty much guarantees that no system is infallible. With enough discipline, however, one might be able to scratch out a living by using this system or that. But you'll be fighting tremendous odds, and your life will be as cold and hard as arctic ice.

This book doesn't advocate systems, though some advanced players may be able to make them work when combined with other procedures. Still, the focus of this book is on techniques that give you the best possible chances at the tables. You will be taught to make decisions like a pro, and you'll see the world much as they do. But you'll have to learn to take your losses in stride and accept the fact that some days you just can't win.

Nevertheless, this book would not be complete if it didn't let you know what systems are out there, along with an evaluation of their weaknesses and strengths ✠

EVEN MONEY SYSTEMS

Most system players prefer even money wagers, for they are found at all major table games, and offer a frequent win rate. They are the most basic wagers found in gaming, and are commonly the backbone of a professional's repertoire. Knowing about the systems designed for these bets should enhance your general understanding of the available options ✠

MARTINGALE: As systems go, this one exists in a class by itself, for it's the brainchild of at least a billion gamblers. I'm ashamed to admit that I invented it, *after* it had been invented by the billion I just spoke of. When I say *invented,* I mean it was an original idea, but as ideas go, this one is a dog. I pity the fool who donated his name to this system.

The Martingale was designed for even money wagers, and the concept is disarmingly simple: when you lose, you double the size of your wager. If you keep losing, keep doubling. When you win, the betting cycle is consummated and you regress to the bet amount you started with.

Neat idea, huh? As long as you don't lose more than, say, seven bets in a row, you'll never lose a series. Now, I can imagine how good this might sound to someone who has never played live bets in a casino, but there's a really big flaw here. Any seasoned player knows that losing streaks of nine or ten consecutive even money bets are not uncommon. For the sake of argument, let us project the amount you would need, to cover a series that produced a win on the eleventh bet:

Your first bet is $5; when it loses, you go to $10. Then, go to: 20–40–80–160–320–640–1280–2560, and finally 5120. Financing those bets costs over $10,000 *just to manage a $5 profit* at the end. But the problem is getting a waiver against the table maximum in the midst of all that. And that's not real likely.

Atlantic City casinos generally offer wide ranges between the table minimums and maximums; even the $5 (minimum) tables often have a $3000 maximum. But many other places aren't so liberal. In places like those a Martingale progression that commences with a $5 wager would reach the table maximum somewhere around the seventh step. What I'm saying is, the 11–stage series I projected is not really possible, *even if* you were foolish enough to attempt it. That's what we in the business call a *flaw*.

Granted, you could set up an arbitrary ceiling of six wagers (which would cost $315 for a complete cycle), and, you might be able to win hundreds of bets before losing a full series. But you're only postponing the inevitable. The day will come when you can't win five bets before getting sucked into a full-blown series loss, and then it happens twicemore before you quit for the day. That's when you start seeing the truth about cats and dogs.

Through the years, I've performed many, many thousands of numerical trials, and do you know what I've found? On average, no matter how many stages you use, you'll encounter a full series loss at roughly the same rate it takes to earn enough units to pay for it. And when you figure in the house edge, the two sets of figures correspond almost exactly. Isn't that a hoot?

MINI-MARTINGALE: The mini version is much less destructive than its cousin, because it is limited to three stages. At the $5 level, the series is 5–10–20. If you don't win at the third stage, write off the series and start over.

A full series costs $35, which is a massive improvement over the thousands a Martingale *could* cost, but there are two problems: You have only three chances to win, and, it will take seven wins to compensate one series loss.

At a choppy table, a MiniMartingale could keep you winning indefinitely. But when the table patterns change, you're gonna get a load of buckshot in your butt.

Some quasi-professionals specialize in the MiniM and have days when they do okay. But if you're seeking long-range success, this ain't the ticket.

All the same, you could do worse. I've been known to use it at times. Playing the MiniM is like speeding through a yellow light. If you don't do it too much, you may be able to dodge the man for some time. But when you get nabbed, lay off.

ANTI-MARTINGALE: Finally, we come to the last of the Martingales. Once these are out of the way, we can move on to something more meaningful.

The AntiMartingale is the mirror image of the Martingale. You double your bet only when you *win,* not when you lose. Then at some arbitrary point you take your profit, and begin again. It's essentially a multiple-stage parlay.

This system was conceived with the purpose of enabling one to get rich from a very small bet. If played successfully for seven consecutive bets, a $5 wager will earn $635 profit. But how could one ever anticipate a trend like that? If any readers know and write a book about it, every casino in the world will go under. I don't think I'm going to see that in *my* lifetime.

Imagine, for a moment, that you just won six consecutive bets. Would you have the guts to let it all ride? And if you did and lost, how would you feel? It would feel great *before* the last decision, when all the other players are cheering you on. But when that 7th bet goes down, don't count on their support. Your fifteen minutes of fame has come and gone. Now, you're just another schmuck who made a foolish bet.

The world's full of people who can do *that.*

The biggest problem is, when do you take a profit? If you're a bad guesser, you may never win a series.

If you're a masochist, this might be the one for you.

THE 31 SYSTEM: Like the Martingale, this one is a progression; that is, a strategy that calls for increasing the bet size until a win occurs. With the *31*, a series loss is not as devastating, but you'll *feel* that loss when it comes.

The 31 System gives you nine chances to win, but you'll need back-to-back wins at the conclusion of each series. It consists of (up to) nine bets that occur on four levels:

LEVEL 1:	1	1	1
LEVEL 2:	2	2	
LEVEL 3:	4	4	
LEVEL 4:	8	8	

FIGURE 34
The 31 System Tiers

In playing the *31 System*, you start out with a single-unit bet. If that loses, the next bet is also one unit. If once again you lose, you make one more bet at the one-unit level. Should you endure another loss, you move up to level 2 and bet two units. Until you win, keep following the diagram above.

The *31 System* is so named because 31 units are required to complete a betting series. At the $5 level, that works out to $155; at the quarter level it's $775. When you finally win (presuming the cycle hasn't been exhausted), you parlay the winning bet. If that bet succeeds, you'll show a profit for that series, regardless of where (along the chain) the wins occurred.

It sounds ingenious, for you can lose eight consecutive wagers and still end up in the black. The trick is, you've got to end up with back-to-back wins.

This system is clever in its conception, but there's one thing about it that bothers me: it doesn't work. When I look over my old minibaccarat scorecards, it's all too clear that this system would have done more harm than good. And that's where I draw the line. I'm not looking for ways to go broke.

For anyone who is not completely clear on how this system works, here are a few examples:

Let's say that one unit is $5, and you lose the first bet. The next bet is also $5, and you win. At that point you parlay your bet and win $10. You now have $20, which cost you $10 to generate. Your profit is $10.

Now let's look at where you would be if you lost the first five bets, then got your back-to-back wins. From level 1, you'd be out $15 ($5 x 3). Level 2, another $20 ($10 x 2). At the first stage of level 3, your four-unit bet wins. You parlay to eight for the follow-up and win again. You now have $80, and it cost you $55 to do it. Your profit is $25.

If you had come through with the consecutive wins at the 2nd stage of level 3, it would have cost you another four-unit bet ($20), so your profit would be reduced by that amount, leaving you with only a $5 gain. Obviously, you're better off when the first win (of two) occurs at the first—rather than the second—stage of whatever level you're on.

According to Robert Eisenstadt, who applied the 31 System to pass and don't pass craps bets in a book called *Systems That Win,* one can expect to lose a complete betting series 10.8% of the time. But he admits that his objective is *"to snatch a few victories while the gods of chance are napping."*

Doesn't sound especially solid to me.

D'ALEMBERT: This one is also called the *Pyramid.* The idea is to increase the bet by one unit after each loss and reduce by one unit after each win. Every series is supposed to earn a profit, but there are times when your bets get so big, the only sensible option is to bail out and eat the loss.

The D'Alembert was designed to be played with a notepad, where you add numbers as you lose, and cross them out as you win. This keeps you in touch with where you are in the series, but I see no need for that if you obey your loss limits.

Bottom line: there are better systems out there.

CONTRA-D'ALEMBERT: Here we have another mirror-image strategy, which, fortunately, has nothing to do with the *Iran-Contra Affair* or Honduras or any other banana republic. With the *Contra-D'Alembert,* you increase one unit when you *win,* and decrease by one when you *lose.*

One positive aspect to this system is that when you hit a losing streak, the size of your bet is quickly reduced until it bottoms out at the one-unit level, which is where you stay until the wins return. This helps cover the downside, but trouble occurs when you hit a losing streak right after a winning streak, because if you stick to the system you'll give all your gains right back to the house. Therefore, it would make sense to get in the habit of cashing out immediately after hitting numerous consecutive wins.

With that provision added, this isn't a bad system, for it allows one to exploit favorable table conditions while holding down losses. But the elimination of one demon allows another one to move to the front: should you encounter a wagering situation of wins that come in tight groups, one loss can blow away all your gains in a single stroke. For example:

Your first bet is one unit. You win and add a unit, so now you have a two-unit bet at risk. If that wins, your next wager is 3 units. Along comes your first loss and you have nothing to show for the fact that you won two of the last three decisions; all your profit was dissipated financing the wagering increases.

If such a trend were to persist, to continue would be suicide. You may never, ever win a series.

One way to circumvent this little problem would be to use a three (or more) unit bet as your base, such as $15. When your first bet wins, your next bet is $20. Should that also win, you progress to $25. Then if you lose the third bet as you did in the first example, at least you'd have a two-unit profit.

At the right table, this system can work wonders. But that's the problem with systems: you've gotta find the *right table,* and pick the *right system,* to use at the *right point in time.*

If I could do that, I wouldn't bother writing a book.

1-2-3-4 SYSTEM: The *1-2-3-4 System* is a four-stage progression that seeks to garner a win before the fourth stage of the series is reached. It's like a one-way *pyramid:* you start with a 1-unit wager, and progress to 2, 3 or 4 units—as required to win a series. Whether you win or lose the series, the idea is to regress to the one-unit level at its conclusion.

This is more of a procedure than a system, for it can be applied to even or non-even money bets, and, it doesn't necessarily pretend to show a profit at each stage. But I see it as one of the most basic procedures used by table game specialists, and regard its inclusion into the *Systems* category as a necessary part of your foundational training. What I'm saying, is that this system is the core of many viable table game procedures.

The 1-2-3-4 is not as drastic as the Martingale, for only ten units are risked throughout its four stages, as opposed to fifteen. Its strength lies in its moderation, for its *soft increases* do less potential damage to one's bankroll than the steep incline of the Martingale, and, the progression ends at the fourth stage. At a choppy table, the 1-2-3-4 is usually superior to flat bets.

But there's another way to utilize the 1-2-3-4. For bets that pay better than even money, there is a chance to show a profit at every stage of the progression. Such is the case with wagers paying 9–5 and up. Therefore, if the 1-2-3-4 was played against place bets at the craps table (for example), the 6–5, 7–5 and 9–5 returns *could* help you realize a profit at every stage.

OSCAR'S GRIND: This is the most conservative —and therefore perhaps the most viable—of all the systems shown in this chapter. Because it lacks ambition, it is the most ambitious strategy of them all.

One lousy unit. That's all you stand to win from each and every series. Not very exciting, but it does help you minimize your losses, which is 90% of professional gambling. Remember, more important than knowing how to *win* is knowing how to *not lose*. Oscar understands this.

The rules aren't *too* complicated:

1) Increase your bet by one unit after every win, *provided* it won't result in a series gain that exceeds one unit.
2) Never modify your bet size after a loss.

That's it. That's all you need to remember. Just follow those two rules and you can't miss.

Let's look at a hypothetical wagering example:

You lose your first six bets. Since your bet amount doesn't change following a loss, you are six units behind. Then you win one bet. Your next wager should be for [an increase of one] two units. If you should win that next bet as well, you go to a three-unit bet. If that one also wins, you'll be right where you started nine bets ago, even though you lost twice as many bets (6) as you won (3). But you still need a one-unit profit to end the series. Your next bet is just that: one unit. If it wins, the series is over and it's time to begin another one.

What you've just seen is, of course, an absolute best-case follow-up to a string of losses, but it was done without having to bring out any big guns. With the D'Alembert, six straight losses would put you 21 units behind, a far cry from 6.

Although this system gets high ratings, it's not perfect. There are times when Oscar takes you to the land of large bets—but you should be okay if you set up strict loss limits.

What could cause such a conservative system to fail? Well, one thing would be solitary wins surrounded by multiple losses, on a continuing basis. This keep pushing your bet levels upward, and the only remedy is consecutive wins. If you do run into that, avoid resorting to large bets to pummel your way out of a bind. Believe you me, it's been done. By me, by everybody. And the lesson we learned is that it isn't worth it to sacrifice a week's worth of gains just to (try to) salvage one lousy session.

Having said that, just let me say that of all the systems I have seen, Oscar's Grind impresses me the most ✠

SUMMARY OF
SYSTEMS IN GAMING

The game never ends when your whole world depends on the turn of a friendly card.

—The Alan Parsons Project

Like any other seasoned pro, I've seen fire and I've seen rain. I've seen losing streaks that I thought would never end. I've seen lonely times when I could not get a win. But I always thought that the perfect system was out there. Somewhere. Hidden by the trees, underneath a big stone, or maybe just too obvious to see.

Forget about it. If it existed, I would have found it by now. Believe me, I've checked every angle and analyzed every option at least eleventeen different ways. And I'm just one of many fools throughout the centuries who have tried.

Anything can and will happen at the tables. No system can cover every possibility. Some systems are better than others, but the more successful it is, the greater the chance you'll encounter a really big surprise right about the time you thought you were finally safe. That's just the nature of the beast.

To be honest, I begrudge the space I used to show you these systems, but it is necessary. You need to know these techniques because they are foundational. Sometimes I must refer to them in conveying similarities with a procedure that *is* valid.

But mainly, as an aspiring pro, you can't afford to be caught asking the question, *"What's a Martingale?"* ✠

13

GAMING PROCEDURES

Now that we've passed through the land of *systems,* we are free to move to a higher plane. *Gaming procedures* are what you'll be playing most of the time, and even though many non-pros do the same, there is no grand design to what they do. That's what makes what you're doing better: while they're immersing themselves in an ocean of cheap thrills and gluttony, you'll be walking through the stages of a master plan.

In this context, gaming *procedures* differ from gaming *systems* in that you will not be pushing yourself through a mechanical ritual. What you do will be structured, but you'll be more sensitive to the permutations of the table.

Much of the time you'll be making *surgical strikes,* which are isolated bets or progressions that are enacted only after a wagering trigger has been identified. Other times you'll jump right into the moving stream of table decisions and do your best to swim with the current. In those cases, your main objective will be to avoid being carried away by a riptide that is beyond your ability to control. But there will be times when that can't be helped. That's what makes gambling the challenge that it is ✠

PROCEDURES FOR CRAPS

Many readers will find themselves settling into one of the three recommended games as their favorite. Then again, some may be compelled to play whatever is accessible. Although there are times when I prefer roulette or minibaccarat, my majority favorite is craps, for I feel it is the most versatile of the three. So, we shall begin with procedures for the game of craps ✠

SIZING UP THE TABLE

I learned early on: the more you know, the luckier you get.

—J. R. Ewing,
from TV drama *Dallas*

Statistically, there are more *cold* than *warm* or *hot* craps tables in the world. This statement is merely an acknowledgement of the probabilities, which reveal that all six of the point numbers are more likely *not* to pass, than to pass. So, if you're looking to cop a ride on the coattails of a streaking table, you should know how to play the side that wins the most.

Becoming an inveterate don't bettor, though, ain't the answer. You may win more often, but your losses, when they come, will be more dear. And all it may take is a few good poundings to put you away for the night.

Most craps players prefer pass line wagering, but those who advocate back line wagering seem to be very faithful to their cause. Makes me wonder how much craps they *really* play, because I don't see how they could win consistently from such a one-dimensional approach.

But if one *must* play both sides to succeed, how does he know which side to pick? Surely there's more to it than simply imitating the last table result?

Indeed there is, though winning at the tables is often little more than the product of a series of trial-and-error experiments. You may start out losing, in which case you must be very cautious. Could turn out that you're at one of those weird tables that will never kick back a dime, as long as you live. So, seek another table. Eventually, you'll find one that gives you something back. So now you must ask yourself how to play it. Specifically, what's the best way to wrangle a day's pay out of this table? How can you make the most of the opportunity?

As you play, you'll learn more about the tendencies and quirks of the table. A picture will start to emerge. Sometimes the wins will come automatically, and you'll be able to bet with confidence. Other times, it will seem like you just can't get a break. That's OK. Walk away and don't look back.

There are two outward signs you should be on the lookout for: *warm* or *cold* table activity. *Warm* table activity is when the dice frequently pass, or, (place bet) numbers are rolled in abundance on the way to a line decision. *Cold* table activity is when the 7 seems to be lurking behind every corner. Most craps tables incline toward one side or the other.

As it is in life itself, if you do your homework, you are better prepared to face whatever comes. Sizing up the table, beforehand and as you play, will keep you on track. Of course, there is always the possibility that doing so will lead you straight into an ambush, but that's the exception, not the rule.

Information is all around us, all the time. Those who make use of it are the ones who stay on top ✠

BASIC LINE BETTING

Spare no expense to make everything as economical as possible.

—attributed to Samuel Goldwyn

You want to hear something amazing? I once assembled all of my old craps scorecards and did a study. What would happen, I imagined, if all I did was play basic line betting and nothing else? What if I simply imitated the last line result at the table, betting *pass* after a shooter made his point, and *don't pass* after every seven-out? Would it be possible for me to make money through such a primal exploitation of gaming trends?

The betting parameters were elementary: on an ongoing basis, imitate the most recent line decision, and quit after the first loss that follows a profitable series of wins.

It looked very promising at first. . .but then I saw the flaw: whenever the table decisions zigzag, you will do nothing but lose. No problemo. We just need to tweak it a little. I added a provision that after three consecutive losses, discontinue play at that table. Amazingly, it worked.

Did you hear me? I said it worked. On paper, it overcame the house edge and showed a profit. *Who knew* it would be so simple? Well. . .it's not. My sampling was too small to assure any measure of scientific reliability. But it helps make the point that when you're playing a bet that carries a minimal house edge, all it takes is one little streak (or two) to put you in the black. And streaks (trends) are out there, everywhere we go.

For those who seek a potential for gain with a minimum of planning and legwork, I would suggest *basic line betting.* Simply imitate the line decisions for as long as you continue to win. When you reach your win goal or when losses start to mount, go to another table, or quit for the day.

Doesn't *sound* hard, but I can see how it *would* be for quite a few readers. The biggest problem will be resisting the temptation to cover the other numbers with place bets while a line decision is in progress. All around you, you'll see and hear the other players betting and making money while you stand there with your lonely little line bet. Can you handle that?

Basic line betting was chosen as the first procedure to describe in this chapter because it is the primary staple of my wagering diet. I use it to 'tread water' at the table while pursuing another betting scheme like the *Sister System,* or placing inside numbers, or awaiting a lucrative hot or cold streak within the line bets themselves. While in the water-treading mode, my bets are frequently near the table minimum, and I often hedge during the come-outs. This involves playing *any craps* during most come-outs when betting on the *right* side, and *always* hedging the Yo (11) when betting *wrong.* If I find myself getting burned by the 7 during back line come-outs, I resort to *Odds Betting* (the subject of the next subchapter), which brings all the nonsense to an immediate halt.

In Chapter 20, the first exercises are devoted to *basic line betting* and *odds betting.* Their betting parameters, which were designed to cover all possible contingencies, are clearly spelled out. All that is required on your part is to follow the instructions and go through the motions, as shown ✠

ODDS BETTING

This is one of the most efficient procedures you can play in a casino. With *Odds Betting,* you can play both sides of the table—and exploit its most basic trends—without exposing yourself to the severe punishment that is frequently inflicted upon *wrong* bettors during the come-out phase of the game.

Odds Betting involves placing a bet on both the *pass* and the *don't pass lines* **simultaneously** at the come-out. This allows you to play the *odds* bet (with its 0% house edge) without having to go through the come-out gauntlet to get there. Once your man is on base, you put up the *odds* bet on the side of your choice. This concept was introduced by John Patrick, and is referred to as the *Patrick System* in his books on craps.

Playing *pass* and *don't pass* during the come-out may sound like betting on *red* and *black* simultaneously at the roulette table, but it's not at all the same. True, one cancels the other out, but *after* the point is established, you can play the best bet in the house as a tack-on to the foundation you've built. The only hang-up is the 12. If someone rolls a *midnight* during the come-out, your bet on *pass* loses, but the *don't pass* bet is a push. With any other craps or natural roll, the one that loses is compensated by the one that wins. Not so with the 12 (which is what creates the .92% vig of this bet). Now, you could hedge with a small bet on the 12 (which pays 30-1), but I do that only when betting large.

Once you're on base, follow the trend. If the last shooter made his point, bet *right.* If he sevened out, bet *wrong.* If you just keep duplicating what last happened, you're in position to reap the bounty of any streak that might happen along.

Some readers are sure to question why *basic line betting* is advocated if *odds betting* is so efficient. Truth to tell, *line betting* permits you to *play to the trend* more closely than *odds betting*. The latter eliminates the lows (very constructive, I agree) but it also takes out the highs. Last week, for example, it took one of the shooters at my table *nine rolls* to establish his point: 7–2–11–7–3–12–7–7–4. . . That's five naturals, three craps rolls and finally, he establishes the point. Since I was betting *right* and hedging every roll, his come-out gave me *eight* straight wins, which singlehandedly turned my session around. With odds betting, I would have just been turning over money for each of those rolls, until losing to the 12 on the sixth roll.

Odds betting can steal away profits on the *don't* side as well. If your table isn't showing a propensity for come-out sevens, you can get *even money* for your don't pass bets instead of paying the heavy penalty of laying $50 to win $25, as the case would be if the point was 4 or 10. Major difference.

But there's one more angle to consider. Career gambling isn't pretty, isn't fun, and isn't what most people imagine it is. Every so often, one *needs* a lift, a bonus, a present of some kind just to make it through the next fifteen minutes. You're not likely to get that with odds betting, which is as tasteless and bland as anything you will ever experience. With line betting, these little bonuses fall into your lap from time to time, and buddy let me tell you that they can mean a lot to someone as emotionally and spiritually deprived as a *disciplined* player of casino craps.

Bottom line: Odds betting is a fantastic last resort; a way to shield yourself from the cruel downside that comes on like a storm and hangs on for what seems like forever. But there's no need to use it unless necessary. Its sole purpose is to offer protection during the come-outs, but if you can manage without it, you'll probably save money.

And don't worry about what the dealer is going to think when he sees you betting both sides. By now, they've seen this technique enough times to take it in stride ✠

THE TWO-NUMBER DON'T

The problem with warm table strategies is that the 7 has a way of showing up just when you thought you could trust the table with some serious bets. This has to be *the most maddening trend of all*. If you're getting beat up playing *right*, one possible solution is to switch over to a back line strategy.

The *Two-Number Don't* is a wagering procedure that involves betting *don't pass,* and immediately following, **one** *don't come* bet. This helps maximize your potential for gain at a cold table by giving you more coverage, and, spreading the risk.

At a new line bet come-out, drop $10 on the *don't pass*. Let's say that 9 becomes the point, so you lay $15 odds and then drop $10 into the *don't come*. Now the shooter rolls a 4, so that bet goes behind the 4. Then you pull your odds off your basic don't pass bet and await the decision.

At a cold table, this may be the most efficient *one-size-fits-all* strategy you'll ever use. Through precision timing *and* moderation, you've conscripted the almighty seven, without the usual penalty associated with laying numbers. If the cold trend holds up and the timing doesn't blow up in your face, this technique will allow you to get an even money return while you maintain a statistical wagering advantage. That's not a bad place to be.

Most *don't come* bettors play two or more bets per come-out, while others prefer to play a continuous chain. That is precisely the trap that you would do well to avoid. The *Two-Number Don't* is a more conservative way to play, but I believe it maximizes the back line potential.

Betting the don't pass *only* has its limitations. For one thing, those bets can't win from a come-out seven like the (established) don't come bets can, which are out of sync with the line decisions. This helps you make use of *all* the sevens. Playing more than one don't come bet, however, pushes the productivity envelope, for the bets entering the come-out will at some point fall to the (line bet) seven-outs that come sooner than you'd like. In that case, they drain the profit out of the bets that *do* win. You're better off if you don't overplay the seven card.

At a cold table, you'll do nothing but win with this procedure. At most choppy tables and even some warm tables, you can also do well, for you don't necessarily need a seven-out to win. But you'll be in position to take advantage of the fact that most table decisions, in fact, *do* end with a seven-out.

Perhaps the best feature of this procedure, though, is how the two bets draw strength from each other's presence. As soon as you get your don't pass wager on board, you can add odds, which act as a shield to protect the don't come bet you are now about to make. Should the seven-out come immediately, the odds offset the loss of the don't come bet that got burned in the come-out. Once the DC bet is safely on board, however, you remove those costly odds, and enjoy the advantage you now hold: two chances to get an even money return while you retain a better-than-even-chance to win *both* those bets.

For maximum efficiency, it's best that you start out *'treading water'* with line bets until the table tips its hand. Once you have determined that a table *truly is* cold, add in the don't come phase, but keep a close watch on both bets. Put your emphasis on the ones that win, and increase your bet size as profits come in. And if you hit an extended winning streak, leave after the first loss that follows. Don't give all your gains back to the house!

Most important, don't try to make the *two-number don't* work at a warm table, thinking that the trend is bound to change. If you keep losing, get a clue. There are lots of other tables. Chances are, there's something better out there ✠

$22 INSIDE
AND OTHER PLACE BET VARIATIONS

When the table starts heating up, or, when you see a pattern where lots of numbers are rolled between come-outs, it may be time for one of the variations of *$22 Inside*.

We're talking *place* bets here, which should remain in action (in most cases) for only a short time. Their purpose is to help one capitalize on warm spells at the craps table.

$22 inside is the command to the (craps) dealer to *place* the four *inside* numbers (5, 6, 8 & 9). Statistically, those four are the most frequently-rolled numbers at the craps table—after the 7. When you cover those four, you have exactly *half* of the 36 dice combinations working for you. The only catch is that one little 7 will knock them all down.

This book advocates placing numbers in groups only when the table is sending the right signals, and *then,* only for short periods. It's a tough loss to bear, especially when one plays larger multiples of the $22 base amount we're discussing.

To play this group of wagers successfully, you need to get in the habit of calling those bets *off,* or taking them down, after you've gotten two, three, or perhaps four hits—whatever you think you can get away with. Then keep them down until the next shooter comes up to bat. If you play this group of bets, there will be many times when you'll get scorched by the 7 on the very first roll after you put them up. Playing daredevil with the seven is seldom easy, but if you can get the hang of it you'll probably discover there's some good money to be made here. Just don't forget what a precarious ledge it is upon which those sitting ducks sit.

The breakdown of the *$22 inside* wager is as follows: $5 each on the 5 & 9, and $6 each on the 6 & 8. Remember, the 6 & 8 must each be placed in $6 increments (see Chapter 8). Together, the four bets add up to $22.

Now, I hope I'm not breaking anybody's heart when I say this, but in all honesty, there shouldn't be that much call for you to ever play $22 inside *specifically,* or even a multiple thereof. Most of the time you'll have one of the four numbers covered (more efficiently) with your *pass line + odds* wagers, in which case you will decline coverage of the number that happens to be the point. If 9 was the point and you wanted coverage on the (remaining) inside numbers, for example, you'd request *$17 inside,* because that's how much the other three cost (at the $5 level). And if 8 was the point, you'd ask for *$16 inside,* because one of the $6 bets (the point of 8) would not need coverage as in the previous example. Since most players bet the pass line, dealers know exactly what you want when you ask for off-amounts like $16 or $17 inside.

As if this wasn't already confusing enough (for newcomers), we must now address the matter of *outside bets,* which happen to be personal favorites of mine.

Now, don't be blaming me for this, but it's a fact that there's some overlay between the *inside* and *outside* bets. Generally, *inside* bets mean 5, 6, 8 & 9, and usually, *outside* bets mean 4, 5, 9 & 10. See the problem? The 5 & 9 swing both ways. But it gets worse. The term *outside bets* can also mean just the pairing of the 4 & 10, so there will be times when the dealer won't be sure exactly what you want. Usually, he can figure it out from context, or your prior wagering patterns. But be prepared to tell him what you mean in specific terms if he should ask.

Why bother with *outside* bets, you may ask? Well, sometimes the table can favor those numbers, and since they (as a group) pay better than the *inside* numbers (as a group), it might serve you well to pay attention to such inclinations. Hey, it won't do you much good to cover the 6 & 8 if those numbers aren't hitting. Remember, *playing to the trend* is how you win.

Apart from letting you know about these betting options, the purpose of this lesson is to tune you in to the nomenclature you'll need to know in the various wagering situations you'll encounter. For example, if the point is 5 and you wish to cover the remaining outside numbers at the one-unit level, you toss $15 on the layout and say *"$15 outside, please."* The dealer would assume that you mean the *non-point* numbers, since there is no way to evenly divide $15 between (just) the 4 and 10.

Sometimes the table minimum itself clarifies what you want. At a $5 table, *"$20 outside"* would probably get you coverage on the four outside numbers (unless you specify otherwise). But if that table had a $10 minimum, the same request would put coverage on just the 4 and 10, because the $20 you laid down was sufficient to cover only two numbers.

Now we come to betting the place numbers *across*. At a craps table, this means either covering all six place numbers, or, covering all the place numbers *except* for the point. For this set of wagers, there is *no chance* the dealer will confuse your intent (as long as you give him the correct amount), because the two sets of figures could each be applied only one way.

There's just one more matter we need to address: *buy* bets. Whenever your bet on the 4 or 10 reaches the $25 level, it is more economical to *buy* the number than to *place* it. This was covered in Chapter 8 and is demonstrated in figures 35 and 36, but we do need to mention this now, because it affects the size of the group wager. As a general rule, for every $25 wagered on a buy bet, add $1 to cover the house commission, which you will gladly pay for the privilege of getting the better deal.

Now, before you go charging on out there putting up a wall of bets, you need a sign that the table is ripe. I generally wait until one of the inside numbers hits before putting up place bets, and they are usually added very cautiously; one or two at a time.

The real art in placing bets in groups like these lies in being sensitive to the inclinations of the table. In time, you'll learn when to *advance*, and when to *retreat* ✠

TABLE STATUS	VERBAL COMMAND

When 8 is the point:

4	5	SIX	8 (ON)	NINE	10

PLACE BETS / *PLACE B*

"$16 inside."
COVERS THE THREE NON-POINT INSIDE NUMBERS

"$20 outside."
COVERS THE FOUR OUTSIDE NUMBERS

"$26 across."
COVERS ALL NUMBERS EXCEPT THE POINT

When 9 is the point:

4	5	SIX	8	NINE (ON)	10

PLACE BETS / *PLACE BETS*

"$17 inside."
COVERS THE THREE NON-POINT INSIDE NUMBERS

"$15 outside."
COVERS THE THREE NON-POINT OUTSIDE NUMBERS

"$27 across."
COVERS ALL NUMBERS EXCEPT THE POINT

When 10 is the point:

4	5	SIX	8	NINE	10 (ON)

PLACE BETS / *PLACE BETS*

"$22 inside."
COVERS ALL INSIDE NUMBERS

"$15 outside."
COVERS THE THREE NON-POINT OUTSIDE NUMBERS

"$32 across."
COVERS ALL SIX NUMBERS

FIGURE 35
Nomenclature for Multiple Place Bets

	1 unit coverage	2 unit coverage	5 unit coverage
WHEN 6 IS THE POINT	*$16 inside* *$20 outside* *$26 across*	*$32 inside* *$40 outside* *$52 across*	*$80 inside* *$102 outside* *$132 across*
WHEN 5 IS THE POINT	*$17 inside* *$15 outside* *$27 across*	*$34 inside* *$30 outside* *$54 across*	*$85 inside* *$77 outside* *$137 across*
WHEN 4 IS THE POINT	*$22 inside* *$15 outside* *$32 across*	*$44 inside* *$30 outside* *$64 across*	*$110 inside* *$76 outside* *$162 across*

FIGURE 36
Nomenclature for Place Bets
(Different Coverage Amounts)

CLOSED PROGRESSIONS

"You caught that right on the last stage of the progression, didn't you?" said the craps dealer as he made the payoff for my successful place bet on the 5.

"Yeah." I agreed, though a little surprised at the unsolicited remark. Seldom do you get comments like that from craps dealers. But this was in 1992, at the time of the culinary workers' strike at the Frontier in Las Vegas, and during that period it seemed like a lot of strange things happened there.

Didn't matter to me. Back then, I *couldn't lose,* no matter what I did in that casino. (Looking back, it's safe for me to say that, but switching to the present tense and saying *"I can't lose in that casino"* would most certainly put the kiss of death on any winning streak of mine.)

At the time, I was playing a *closed progression* (on the 5) at one of the Frontier's warm tables, during that winning period I talked about back on page 32. The progression I played cost $55 per series, and was structured as shown:

LEVEL	BET	COST	WIN	PROFIT *(at that stage)*
1	$5	$5	$7	$7
2	$10	$15	$14	$9
3	$15	$30	$21	$6
4	$25	$55	$35	$5

FIGURE 37
Progression On The 5

Let's say that you're planning to play a progression on the 5 at two different craps tables. You are seeking out two *warm* tables (one at a time), and your win goal is $50 at each, which would get you to your *win goal* of $100 for the day. To achieve this, you're willing to risk $55 each session.

At level 1 (from Figure 37), you are risking $5 in your attempt to make $7. At level 2, your $10 wager (if successful) will recoup your previous loss, *and* return a $9 profit. At level 3, you stand to win $6 after paying for the two previous losses. At level 4, you're risking $25 more to make a series profit of $5. If four tries doesn't get it, you leave the table with $55 less than when you arrived, unless you had some wins along the way.

If your table stays warm, you are more likely to win $50 than lose the $55 session money. If not, there would be a good chance that you won close to $50 before suffering a series loss. All you're seeking is enough wins to earn $50 before leaving, which works out to between six and ten wins.

What I've just described is a four-stage progression utilizing soft increases, on a wager that pays slightly better than even money (7–5, to be exact). The bet is *placing* the number 5 at a craps table, though one might prefer placing the 9 (which has the same return), if that number seems more ubiquitous.

Now, before initiating play with this system, be sure to wait until the chosen wagering target wins before sending your boys out into the battle zone. Yes, this means you're going to miss what *would have been a win,* but doing so will undoubtedly save your ass countless times from the shooters who establish the point, and then seven-out on the next roll.

Closed progressions such as this one have their strong points, but they are far from infallible. At a warm table, they'll quickly get you to your win goal, but you could get burned if your table suddenly turns cold. This book does advocate closed progressions, but this advice applies only to those who (after experimentation) have found a way to make them work. If you're having difficulty, concentrate your efforts elsewhere ✠

THE 5/9 PROGRESSION

This is a closed progression against two numbers, but they are covered one at a time.

Right after the come-out, place either the 5 or 9. Which one you cover is determined by the point number. If 4, 5 or 6 is the point (a number from the left half of the group of boxed numbers), place the 9. If the point is 8, 9 or 10 (from the right half), bet the 5. We'll assume that we're at a $5 table that shows signs of warmth, and begin with a $10 bet—*after* we've seen a *would-be win* go by, as explained on the previous page.

Leave your place bet up for just one hit. If it wins, you can then do one of two things: take the bet down and wait until the next point is established (at which point you repeat the process), or have the dealer reduce your bet to $5. If, however, you should lose the original bet, wait until the next point is established and then proceed to the next level, as follows.

The progression is similar to a miniMartingale, but with soft increases instead of doubling up: $10–$15–$25. The cost of each cycle is $50; if you exhaust two cycles ($100) without a hit, bail out. The table is not as warm as you'd hoped.

A win at the first stage will get you $14 profit, at the second stage $11, and at the third, $10.

For those with limited bankrolls, there is a conservative variation that runs $5-$5-$10. This will result in a win structure of $7-$2-$4. Not a terrific return, but it's a sensible way to evaluate the table temperature. It costs just $20 a series, but you forfeit the option of regressing your bet after a win.

If you manage to find a warm table, you should be able to reach the $100 win goal in less than an hour (when starting out at the two-unit level as originally shown). Once you've reached that goal, move on.

Sometimes, the assigned number wins repeatedly, but the rules call for you to wait until the next come-out before putting up a new bet. There *is* a rule that can be invoked to cover that situation. After winning at the $10 level and taking the bet down, if that number is rolled again, you can use *that occurrence* to trigger a $5 follow-up bet that can stay up for repeated wins or be taken down, as you wish. You've already gotten your profit, so all you're risking is part of what you've won.

At this point, I need to make to make a generalized comment. Before playing any craps procedure, it is essential that you watch some results go by, to verify that your table has a propensity for churning out the numerical patterns you seek. Doing so will save you money, sweat and tears. For example, if you are playing a procedure that targets the 6 and 8, wait until you witness the table's ability to *produce those numbers* before commencing your attack. At the craps tables (like all the others), there are no givens. Just because the 6 and 8 combine to form 10 out of the 36 possible dice combinations is by no means a guarantee that you can catch those numbers at your table.

Never forget that.

Returning now to our main program: the toughest part of the 5/9 progression is mastering the discipline. If you have found the warm table that is recommended, then all around you the players are going to be making big scores and whooping it up, while you plod along with your solitary wager that's only up and working about two-thirds of the time.

Is that going to be a problem for you?

Just keep in mind that their wins come and go, while your gains move in one direction only:

Upward ✠

THE SISTER SYSTEM

Back in Chapter 8 (page 89) you were told about *sister numbers* as they applied to a pair of dice. The most significant are the three groupings: 4–10, 5–9 and 6–8, for they are the only numbers that may be wagered as place bets.

In all my experience playing craps, one observation I've made that seems fairly consistent is that the sister number—to any given point number—frequently comes up on the way to the line decision. I have an excellent theory on why this occurs, but as it is not very scientific, I won't go into that. The point is, I believe this is an exploitable situation.

This method is similar in some ways to the 5/9 Progression, except that you're dealing with payoffs that change according to the probability of the point number.

You wait to see what number becomes the point, then place the sister number immediately. If that bet wins, take it down and wait for a new point to be established. Then you repeat the process. If you lose that bet, wait until the next point is determined, then proceed to the next stage of the $15–$20–$20–$20 progression. Now, when covering the 6 or the 8 you have to substitute numbers divisible by 6 to conform to the 7–6 payoff. For those numbers, I go with flat $18 bets throughout the progression. And when betting on the 4 or 10 at the $20 level, you'll want to *buy* those numbers, which technically costs $21, instead of $20.

The cost of an entire series will run somewhere between $72 and $78, depending on how many times you placed the 6 or the 8, or bought the 4 or 10.

The *Sister System* may be the most viable of all the craps systems shown in this section, for it works at *all* warm tables, *many* choppy tables and *some* cold tables. And apart from my observation that sister numbers often precede line decisions, there's another reason they work: many times you'll be saved from a seven-out because your bet was taken down after you got the hit you sought. See, it doesn't matter if the line decision is yea or nay as long as you get your hit, as Figure 38 illustrates:

TABLE RESULTS	BET	WIN	PROFIT
8–12–11–6–5–5–3–7*out*	$18	+$21	+$21
9–7*out*	$15	–$15	+$6
8–6–3–11–7*out*	$24	+$28	+$34
4–11–10–5–7*out*	$15	+$27	+$61
4–3–5–7*out*	$15	–$15	+$46
10–4–7*out*	$21	+$39	+$85
9–11–3–5–8–7*out*	$15	+$21	+$106
8–6–8*win*	$18	+$21	+$127

FIGURE 38
The Sister System

Figure 38 is a reproduction of the table results that occurred at the Aztar riverboat casino in Evansville on February 21, 1996. Just about any craps players in the world would describe this table as being certifiably *cold.*

The columns to the right of these table decisions show the bet, the amount of each win or loss, and the running profit at each stage, using the $15–$20–$20–$20 progression (with $18, $21 and $24 bets spliced in as required).

Imagine that. A $127 profit at a *cold table* in just fourteen minutes, using a strategy designed for warm tables—and you never needed more than $18 of your buy-in to get there. But mind you, that's not your typical cold table.

Now, on those occasions when the shooter makes the point but the sister bet didn't win, wait until the next point is established before giving the dealer instructions for your next bet. It keeps things simpler for the dealer *and* you to just say *"Nine to the four"* (for example), so that your bet is moved from the sister of the old point (5, in that example) to the sister of the *new* point (of 10). Another reason for doing this is that the new point number might turn out to be the same as before, in which case your previous bet will also serve as the subsequent bet.

A good way to select a table for this system is to review the table results while playing other strategies, and give yourself the option of switching to this procedure if the table seems to show a knack for producing sister numbers on its way to a line decision. But do so only if you think it will improve your overall wagering performance at that table. The craps scorecard ahead in this book is designed to help you track the sister numbers.

Just so that you don't end up with a skewed picture of how well this strategy works at cold tables, below are craps results that occurred five days later in the same casino:

6-5-7*out*
7-6-7*out*
7-6-10-7*out*
5-7*out*
4-7*out*
3-10-5-2-4-5-7*out*
9-8-7*out*
7-10-7*out*
6-7*out*

FIGURE 39
Ice-Cold Dice Results

As Figure 39 clearly shows, there are tables that are *cold,* and those that are *ice-cold.* When the seven-outs come *that* fast, none of the *front line* strategies will work.

So how does one defend against those situations? There are two things you should know about that. First, don't delude yourself by thinking that you'll never lose a series. It doesn't happen often, but it happens. When it does, leave the table and start another progression at a new table. Second, I know this won't be popular with some readers, but I like to play the *Any Seven* (for $5 at the level demonstrated) whenever I lose to a lightning-quick seven-out. Sometimes, a quick seven-out precedes a *string* of quick seven-outs, and at times, playing *the Red* is all it takes to keep me in the game. If not, I'm out five bucks. Boo hoo.

Now, when you do start a new progression, you could go to the next level, which is comprised of four place bets of $24 for the 6 or 8, $25 for the 5 or 9, or (four) $26 buy bets for the 4 or 10. Just make sure you go to a fresh table, and, that you have an adequate bankroll for this.

Financing both progressions costs up to $182. I recommend a $200 buy-in, to cover (also) the cost of the *any sevens*.

If you play only this and stick to the rules, an $800 bankroll (and a daily loss limit of $200) can keep you winning for some time. But I recommend that you stay at the 15–20–20–20 level until you have proved that you can make it work.

Although I call this a progression, it's really just two tiers of flat bets, except for the slight increase from the first stage to the second. As such, it doesn't aspire to show a profit at every stage, but keeps you in the game for a good long time.

Now, don't forget, in the case of Figure 39, you would have been saved by your habit of making sure the table put out (at least) one of the desired results before proceeding to play that system. You *do* remember me saying that (back on page 181), don't you? Well, after witnessing five *would-be* losses (as Figure 39 shows), you would have abandoned your plans to play the Sister System at that table, *right?*

Whatever you do, never, ever try to *force the win*. Some tables will *not* cooperate, and there's nothing you can do about it. Find another table and start fresh ✠

MULTI-LINE

This procedure is more suitable for readers who are already familiar with the game of craps. It's not complicated, but I can see how it would *appear* to be, to a newcomer.

I've never been very fond of come bets, because I feel they are addictive, and therefore dangerous. But some years ago it came to my attention that a single come bet makes a terrific complement to line bets, when one plays both sides. The essence of *Multi-Line* is to follow the trend, imitating the most recent line bet result (pass or don't pass), then add one come bet once the point is established. Now you have three types of bets working for you, though never more than two *types* at the same time.

Then all you have to do is cater your play to the current trend. How do you do that? Analyze the effectiveness of your bets as you play. Increase or reduce certain bets. Add odds or forego the odds. Put your emphasis on the bets that win.

There are just two particulars you need to know. First, you play *come bets* only; never the *don't come*. You see, half the value of the come bet is to hedge the possibility of a seven-out right after the line bet point is established. To a come bet, it's a *come-out* 7. Second, never let more than two come bets accumulate. If you have two active come bets, hold off on putting up more until a decision against at least one of them occurs.

That's all there is to it. Please don't be fooled by my brevity in describing it, but there isn't much more to say. Just remember to keep on top of what the table is doing, and utilize common sense. If it serves your purpose to use the come bet primarily as a hedge, by all means play it that way ✠

PROCEDURES
FOR ROULETTE

You can't win if you can't find a game to play.

—the Author

During the American Revolution over two hundred years ago, British soldiers were forbidden to play dice games—under penalty of death—while serving on active duty. Though England lost that war, British influence still prevails in Canada, whose constitution forbids dice games. So, if you live or vacation in Canada, you won't be able to play craps while you're there.

As if to fill that void, minibaccarat has a higher profile there than in many of the riverboat casinos in the US, but *roulette* seems to be available wherever you may find Class III casino gambling. And when you factor in crowded playing conditions that often predominate during peak periods, you may find that roulette is the only action you can get. This is not the best of reasons for choosing a game to play, but it does help shed some light on one of the brutal realities of player-side gaming: *You can't aspire to win if you can't find a game to play.*

But I don't wish to send the wrong message. Roulette didn't earn its place among the *recommended three* strictly from default. As a game, it's more interesting than minibaccarat, and the pace is more manageable than at craps. And, there are times, you may find, when the wins come easier at the roulette table than at the others. That just might work to your advantage ✠

THE ANGEL AND
THE SLEDGEHAMMER

The *Angel* and the *Sledgehammer* is the name I've given the pair of bets illustrated in Figures 40 and 41. Between the two, all numbers on the roulette layout are covered except for the 0 and 00, which can be hedged.

The *Sledgehammer* covers a large, centralized swath of the layout, and although the bet return is only 1–2, it is one of those rare wagering types that you can ride for numerous consecutive wins if you catch a trend in its early stage. The *Angel* can also be potent when the trend moves in that direction, for it has the inverse return: 2–1. Together, they can offer a tremendous one-two punch when a table trend is predictable or repetitive.

Most of the time you're going to get a mixed bag, so please, don't be thinking this is divine information. They are a tricky pair, which can be treacherous to an unskilled player. But with a hedge, either one or the other will win, every time.

The sledgehammer does help you win more often, but realize, you must risk *four* units to win *two*. You are covering four sixlines, and only one of them can win. You automatically lose three of the four bets when you *do* win, but the one good bet returns five units. Since your original bet is intact, you end up with six units from a four-unit bet, for a profit of two. Got it?!

The sledgehammer was so named because its strength lies in massive firepower. With all those numbers going to bat for you, the odds favor you'll win at any given point in time.

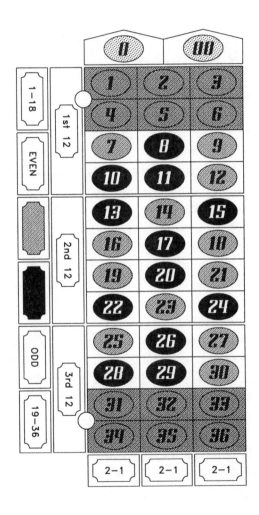

FIGURE 40
The Angel
Two-Unit Bet Returns 2–1

As for the *angel,* well, I needed a name that symbolized the opposite of brute force, which is what the sledgehammer seems to represent. I chose the word *angel,* but that bet, mind you, was just created from leftovers of the sledgehammer, the primary creation. Still, the angel has proved its worth over the years.

Most of my play on the angel and the sledgehammer comes in the form of *surgical strikes,* which are solitary bets made after a specific table trend has been identified. Such wagers are covered in depth in the next chapter. Right how, we need to take a look at the long-range procedures.

There are many sledgehammer variations, but for sit-down roulette sessions I usually play either the *majority sledge,* where I play for as long as necessary to garner a majority of wins (utilizing *press and pull* as I go), or my personal favorite, something I call the *vagabond sledge.*

The latter involves playing the two different configurations shown in Figures 42 and 43. As you play, you switch your bets from the numbers [7–30] to [1–12 & 25–36]. The former is *Sledgehammer A* and the latter is *Sledgehammer B.* Each variation covers exactly 24 numbers, which means that statistically you should win nearly 2/3 of the bets you make. But an artful dodger might be able to do even better than that.

How do you know which of these two variations to play? Well, do you see the overlapping coverage in Figures 42 and 43? Numbers [7–12] and [25–30] (labeled *hot zones*) are covered in both sledgehammer versions. This double coverage is significant. Let us say that you're playing the 7–30 group and number 15 wins. No problem. Keep doing what you're doing. But when number 8 wins on the following spin, that's your signal that the table results are moving outward (into the hot zones), which is your cue to move to the 1–12 & 25–30 groups. Keep doing that until the table results move back into (or past) the hot zones again.

This, believe it or not, helps maximize your advantage because it keeps the uncovered area of the layout much smaller than the covered area, *and it keeps it a moving target.*

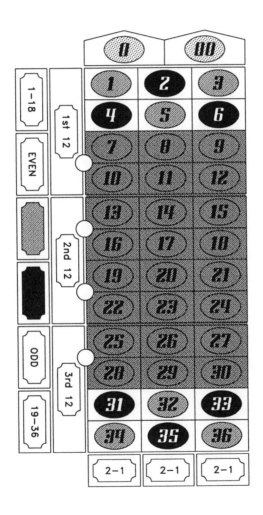

FIGURE 41
The Sledgehammer
Four-Unit Bet Returns 1–2

Does this actually work? Well, anything can happen at the tables, but it seems to help my game if I play the *sledgehammer A* when the table decisions are moving inward through the hot zones, and the *sledgehammer B* when they move outward. Some tables really *are* that cooperative.

As for the *angel*, I frequently play that as a complement to the *majority sledge* mentioned earlier. When I lose my sledge bet to an angel number, sometimes the best way to rebound is to play the angel, anticipating a back-to-back hit from the [1–6 & 31–36] grouping. It happens all the time, and pays 2–1.

Incidentally, you could create a wagering situation that is very similar to these, by playing the *dozens* (outside bets), but I prefer the inside bets because you can hedge the zeroes without having to meet the table minimum all over again ✠

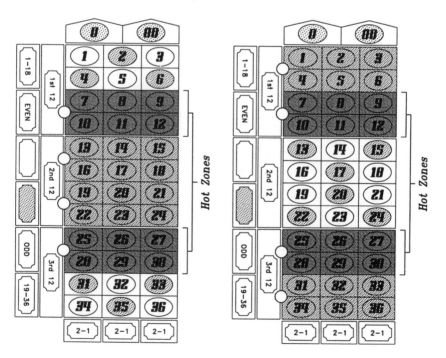

FIGURE 42
Sledgehammer A

FIGURE 43
Sledgehammer B

FIXED SPLITS

You can't expect to hit the jackpot if you don't put a few nickels in the machine.

—Flip Wilson

The young Asian man approached the roulette table and put one nickel on each of five *split* bets. He stood there, waiting, and in a few seconds the dealer placed the dolly on one of the numbers he had covered. He smiled, picked up the 17 chips the dealer had pushed his way, and then re-created the same bets he had covered before. The next spin resulted in another win, from a different area of the board than before. For the next four spins, he covered the same ten numbers (with his five *split* bets), and subsequently won two of those four.

Bottom line? He won four of six bets, each paying 18 for 5 (5–2 odds). In his case, it worked out to four $90 wins minus the $25 bet that was placed six times. That's $360 minus $150, for a $210 profit in about ten minutes.

How did he know?

What *were* those magic numbers?

I would have thought it nothing more than a fluke, but the sonuvabitch did it *again* while I was at *another* table, a couple of hours later.

How is that possible?

If you play in casinos long enough, you're going to see it all: the bearded lady, the elephant man, the second coming. But it doesn't mean a thing; a fluke is still a fluke.

I knew that, but it bugged me. In my mind, I visualized a reconstruction of his bet. I knew the 17–20 was one of the splits, and the 26–29 was another. . .

I came up with a five-chip bet, made from what I could recall of the numbers he played:

0–00, 10–13, 17–20, 26–29 and 33–36. That's two green numbers, one red and seven black. I don't know why black was favored, but I believe those were his choices.

Just as a goof, I walked up to a fresh roulette table, placed five nickels on those five splits, and won $65 when 36 red won the spin. *"I wish I knew how I did that,"* I whispered aloud, to no one in particular.

"If you knew, you'd be a millionaire," offered the player seated to my right.

My first attempt at a *lucky* win—in my entire professional career—had been successful, but I wasn't about to give any of my profit back to the house. Still, I hung around long enough to see if a second bet would have won. The next spin went to number 12, a would-be loser. I left the table.

On my way upstairs I passed another roulette table. The white ball was sitting in the number 10 slot, one of my chosen ten. *"Hmmm,"* I said, also to no one in particular.

At home, I did an analysis of a couple thousand spins from previous sessions, and found that those numbers did indeed come up more often than your average group of ten numbers. But that doesn't mean those numbers are magic. It may have been nothing more than a statistical wave.

Also for the record, my roulette analysis turned up quite a few winning streaks from that group, including one that lasted for eight consecutive spins.

What's the recommendation? Target the clusters. When the numbers from this group start hitting, play the group. If five or so spins go by and your bets aren't hitting, lay back. Usually, I play this bet in conjunction with *Mixed Media,* a procedure that's coming up in the next chapter ✠

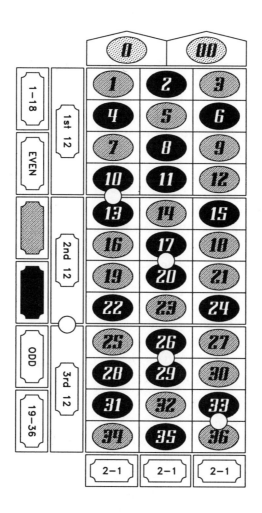

FIGURE 44
Fixed Split Locations

CHINESE ROULETTE

Back on page 48, I described a technique for even money roulette bets that involved moving your wager continuously from one betting option to another. I call this *Chinese Roulette,* because it reminds me of a *Chinese fire drill,* where a carload of people stop the car, exit, run around in circles, then re-enter and zoom away— strictly for the amusement of anyone watching.

To a casual observer, *Chinese roulette* looks like the ultimate in random guesswork, but it's actually a very systematic procedure for outside bets, which has two wagering cycles: red-even-low, and black-odd-high. Your first bet is on *red,* and if that wins, you go to the next step on the cycle and bet *even.* Then on to *low (1–18),* and then back to *red.* As long as you keep winning, stick to that cycle, but if you lose, change your next bet to the corresponding spot on the black-odd-high cycle. To clarify, let's say your first bet (red) lost. Had it won, your next bet would be even, but since you lost, you bet the equivalent spot on the other cycle, which would be odd. Once you switch cycles, stick with it until you lose, at which point you return to the previous cycle.

If you suffer chronic losses, you might try switching cycles after *two* losses instead of one.

The constant mid-course corrections of this procedure design to keep you in the game until you catch a streak. Your *win goal* is six to eight units; your loss limit is ten units.

Try this at the nickel level first. It's a good way to tread water while learning the game. If you discover that you're doing well, you might try pressing your bets to a higher level ✠

THE FAVORED FIVE

On balance, every roulette number wins once every 38 spins. That's the probability you should get from a million trials, though in the short term, the numbers won't fall perfectly into place. Some numbers will be favored and others neglected, but it will be more than a routine scattering of the distribution. Seldom will you come across a table where repeating numbers don't *continue* to repeat. The *Favored Five* was created to capitalize on this unexplainable yet rudimentary fact of gaming.

During the live session shown in Figure 45, numbers 2 and 9 collectively won *eight* out of thirty-two decisions, four times the statistical expectation. This is a good example of a *positive trend*. But how does one best exploit it?

The *Favored Five* caters to the *repeaters* at a roulette table. The first five numbers to repeat (since your arrival) are the chosen five (numbers) to bet. Your expectation is that since they repeated, they'll continue to do so.

The scorecard shown in Figure 45 was designed to facilitate the processing of table data for this procedure. Ahead, we'll take an in-depth look at the scorecards for all the recommended games, but this will give you a preview.

On the right side is a miniature roulette layout that is used to cross out each number as it wins. This will tell you immediately which numbers are repeating. As each *repeater* is identified, you write a '2' inside the dashed box as shown, then backtrack to the first occurrence of that number and enter a '1' alongside that to confirm the repeat. If the number continues to repeat, add '3', '4', or as appropriate.

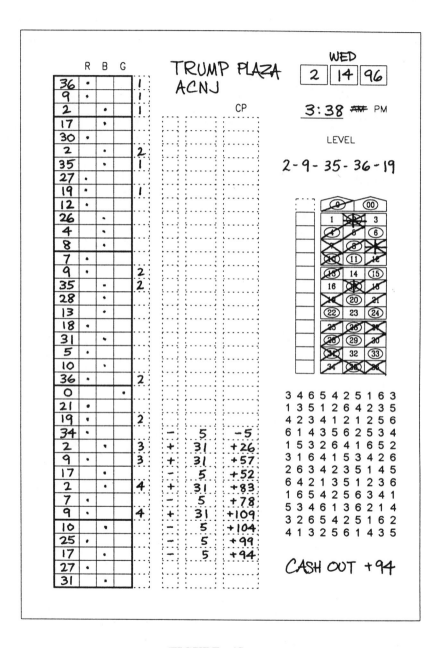

FIGURE 45
A Favored Five Scorecard

Since you are seeing this scorecard in advance of the chapter that explains how it works, let's take a moment to clarify what's going on here.

The column at the left is where you enter the table decision. On this scorecard, the first three numbers to win were 36, 9, and 2. To their right are three more columns, entitled *R, B, & G*, which stand for the color category of that decision *(Red, Black,* or *Green).* Then we come to the dashed column, which, as just explained, is where you denote the status of the five (chosen) repeating numbers. To the right of that are three more dashed columns, which are used to show whether the result was a win or loss (+ or –), the amount of that transaction, and the *Cumulative Profit.*

The first number to repeat in this example was the 2, which took place on line 6. Because that number was already crossed out on the *crossout diagram,* you knew instantly that it was a repeater. So then you backtracked to the first occurrence of that number (on line 3), and entered a '1' alongside, to confirm. The remaining four numbers were handled accordingly. Note: as you accumulate your five numbers, write them out in a string, as shown (below the date), so you'll have them to refer to.

On line 26, you accumulate your fifth repeater, which serves as your wagering trigger. Presuming you have made your buy-in, you're now ready to cover your chosen five. Do so by putting a $1 chip on each one (2, 9, 35, 36 & 19). Each chip is covering a 35–1 longshot, but collectively they pay 6–1.

Your first bet loses, so you are down five bucks. You enter that result as shown, putting a – in the *win/loss* column, a 5 in the next column, then –5 in the third. But then things start to perk up as you win the next bet and post a $31 gain, giving you a cumulative profit of $26. Then you win three of the next five decisions, which results in a profit of $109 by the 33rd line.

Please take note that from there, the wins quickly evaporated. Since trends of this nature are fleeting, we must adjust our loss limit: Quit, 1) after seven consecutive losses, or 2) after three losses that follow (any number of) consecutive wins.

Since you're pursuing a longshot trend that is scheduled to expire at any moment, you will seldom have a reason to place more than a dozen bets, which means that you may be spending more time accumulating table data, *than betting*.

But every cloud has a platinum lining. Well, not *every* cloud, but some do. At any rate, if you can get past the drudgery of this strategy, you may find your reward. The loss limit is seven straight losses, which comes to $35 at the $5 level. Not a bad downside for a procedure that needed only $10 of the buy-in to generate a profit that peaked at $109 within thirty minutes.

Now, the closest thing to a flaw in this procedure is the little matter of *timing*. Sometimes, the five numbers you choose turn out to be the wrong five. It really hurts to watch number 29 hit four times, and you weren't on it. And you can count on that to happen if you play it enough.

But, returning to the matter of the precious lining, you can usually get around the timing snag by utilizing soft increases after a losing session. If a session doesn't nab any hits, increase your total bet per spin to $10, next session. And if that doesn't help you connect, you might want to raise the stakes one more time, to $15. To do this, though, you'll have to create a *business plan* that spells out all the wagering parameters (This is covered in Chapter 18). Most important, you need to have your *session loss limits* and your *daily loss limits* etched in stone.

Now, *where to stand* and *what to do* while accumulating your five targets: until the betting begins, stand near the wheel, or any suitable spot nearby. The fact that you're noting the results will not bother any casino personnel or the clientele, though you may hear an amusing comment from time to time. Of course, if your table has a scoresign, there will be times when you can derive all five numbers from those that are posted.

Tedious though it is, the *Favored Five* is surprisingly effective. But if your timing is off, you might end up sounding like Libby, from *Sabrina The Teenage Witch*, who said (taken out of context): ***I need a trend, and I need it now!*** ✠

THE PHASE-IN

On your way to mastering the recommended games, one of the problems you're likely to face is finding an opening at a $5 table. Most casinos have them (for roulette and craps), but they fill up fast and tend to stay that way.

There's a reason for this: naked greed. The casino profits go up when they force their clientele to play at the $10 tables (and up), because these levels are outside the comfort zone of most players. And what choice do we have? If we want some action, we've got to play with the big boys.

This can pose a problem for beginners, and for those who have a dire need to get the most mileage from their bankroll. So, how do we deal with it?

Two ways. The most obvious, of course, is to make it a habit to arrive early enough to get first dibs on table space. This may be the best solution. All it requires is some planning.

Way number two is an idea that came to me while playing the *Favored Five*. My assistant had warned me against playing at that table, because the scoresign wasn't showing a tendency for *repeats*. I disregarded the advice, but as I played it became clear that I was getting beat up, bloodied, and bruised. But I also observed that the *fixed split* numbers were coming up big time. I phased in those bets and ended up doing surprisingly well.

For those who seek a $5 table but find nothing but $10s, this might be the hot tip. If the *fixed split* numbers are making their presence known, play the two strategies together. Chances are you won't go too long before hitting *something* ✠

BASIC STRATEGY: MINI-B

Since minibaccarat has only three different wagering options (unlike craps and roulette, which have dozens), there aren't a lot of procedures from which to choose.

So, what is there? Pattern play, as shown back in Chapter 9. This has built-in complexities that tend to relieve the monotony that otherwise might be difficult to bear. Sparring with the table on this basis is a real challenge. Who will win? The quiescent monolith that cannot retaliate, or you, the skilled table game specialist? Sadly, the former gets the better of most challengers.

In Chapter 9, you learned about primary and secondary table patterns, anti-pattern trends, and the reoccurring single and double. That information tells you essentially everything you need to know about *what* bet to make. But it doesn't fully cover *how much* to bet and other particulars like when to start and end the session and what your win goals and loss limits should be.

Until you are the Lord of MiniBaccarat, limit the buy-in to $100 at a $5 table or $200 at a $10 table, and quit when you've won 50–100%, or lost 75%, of your buy-in.

When do you start and end a session? Usually, I like to know what the last five decisions were before putting any money at risk, and I quit when a point is reached where I'm content with my profit, or feel a need to stem the tide of losses, or, I find that I can't make any headway. If you're not winning, there's no point in continuing to rack up commission bills.

For starting out, you might want to consider duplicating my settle-for-small-gains experiment, as described back in Chapter 11. This is, in fact, my favorite way to play the game ✠

AUXILIARY BETS

As a table game specialist, your livelihood depends on your ability to recognize a conspicuous trend at an early stage and catch a piece of it before it fades. But frequently, you'll be committed to another procedure when this observation is made, posing a dilemma: *Where doth exist the line between pursuing an aberrant trend, and abandoning one's discipline?*

Example: you're playing the *sister system* at craps, which commits you to cover just *one* place number, when you realize that everyone's rolling a lot of numbers on the way to a line decision. You want to cover some inside numbers to take advantage of this, but doing so messes up the accounting for your original strategy. And anyway, wouldn't that conflict with the discipline you're sworn to uphold?

There is a way to handle this problem: *Auxiliary Bets.* Bets that are made from a separate fund that has been assembled solely for that purpose. But this fund should be smaller than your original buy-in, and closely monitored. This is another argument in support of the idea of having an associate. Doing the accounting for this would be very difficult for someone who is in the midst of a struggle to the death, as all gaming sessions seem to be. But with assistance, the burden is manageable.

In the above example, you would make a secondary buy-in, even if you could afford them from your rack, because you want the monies to be *separate.* This fund should be no greater than 30% of your original buy-in amount. Then keep track of how these new bets are doing. If you don't see positive results, back off. It was not the opportunity you thought it was! ✠

SUMMARY OF GAMING PROCEDURES

The difference between *systems* and *procedures* (in gaming) is that the former are close-ended strategies that have a *do-or-die* mentality. They work *most* of the time, but when they fail, you're left with an expensive mess to clean up.

Gaming *procedures* do not aspire to such a lofty goal. They are like tools in one's toolbelt. For this table, you need a hammer. For that one, you need the wrench. The seasoned player succeeds because he takes the time to evaluate the table, then pick the *right* tool for the job.

Some masters of table games specialize in certain procedures, like playing the back line at craps or even money bets at roulette. In those cases, they don't need to carry many tools. But most pros like to keep their options open toward several games so they're ready for almost anything.

Although the serious players thrive upon the anomalies of gaming, they must take care not to become ensnarled in one that happens to turn against them. In this business, bull-headedness can be fatal. If the table refuses to give you the result you seek, accept the fact that that item is out of stock *at that table*. Go elsewhere. Trying to force the result is more likely to destroy you than make you rich. And you can't afford to be undone by that which brought you riches in the first place.

Make the most of what is offered. A table trend (like money) makes an excellent servant but a terrible master ✠

14

SURGICAL STRIKES

I take my luck where I find it.

—Gregory Peck, from
The World In His Arms

As I understand it, a *surgical strike* is *an offensive maneuver that endeavors to strike an enemy target with pinpoint precision.* Through coordination of timing and position, one of two warring sides hopes to hit a precise target and nothing more, and then make a quick exit before the enemy can react.

That sounds a lot like what you'll be doing in casinos, if you follow the advice of this book. Over a period of time you'll size up the table while calculating which weapon would be most effective. When your evaluation is complete, you'll send in a 'smart bomb' to hit your target. Whether your strike is successful or not, your next move is to head for the door. There's no way the table is going to lure you into prolonging the engagement.

In this book, the terms *surgical strike* and *one-shot* are synonymous. Officially, a one-shot is a solitary wager that begins and ends a session, but there is also an informal version that is comprised of a brief wagering series. In this chapter we will take a look at both interpretations ✠

THE APPLICATION OF RACETRACK WAGERING TECHNIQUES TO CASINO GAMES

To win, you have to play the odds; but sometimes it pays to play a longshot.

—the Author

At some point in my career development, I came up with a neat little trick that helped me out many times. Whenever my losses began to mount, I often resorted to *one-shots*. These were large solo wagers made randomly at table games, *after* the disposition of the table had been assessed for specific trends. These were really just *bail-out bets*.

An example would be to walk up to a craps table and look it over. If the place and come areas are loaded with chips and the players are enthusiastic, you may have found a warm table. The point is 10 and you've watched at least three rolls go by. When you can get the dealer's attention, you drop $105 on the layout and say, *"Buy the point for a hundred."*

The dealer will give the money to the boxman, then pull out four greens and stack them in the 10 box, with a *buy* button on top. At this point you're hoping that a 10 will be rolled before a 7. Only those two numbers can affect your bet.

A decision is likely in the next couple of minutes. If you win, ask the dealer to take down your bet *("Down on my buy, please")*, and he'll probably give you twelve greens. Take them to the cashier and collect your $195 profit, then take a break.

I want to emphasize that this tactic is **not** recommended to correct a losing binge, for it was conceived from a desperate need to compensate losses. It was surprisingly effective when it worked (which seemed often enough), but the price I paid for victory was a relapse in my discipline, too dear a cost. Its effectiveness, though, led to an observation.

I began to compare casino wagers with those at racetracks, and realized that casinos offer many advantages if you *pretend* you're at the track instead. (This assumes you're there for the money, not the entertainment.) Look at it this way: at the track, let's say the favorite is 7–5 odds at post time. There are ten other horses in the field, and longshots *do* occasionally win. You have one way to win and ten ways to lose.

Not very good odds for a bet that pays only slightly better than even money. The favorite is *most likely* to win, but if today happens to be a longshot day (those flukes of nature when the favorites lose, all day long), you could end up spending all night pulling harpoons out of your bottom.

At a craps table you can get the same 7–5 odds *placing* the 9, with just *one way* to lose. Or bet *against* the 9 (which pays less), but you'll still have just *one way* to lose.

Statistically, a bet on the 9 will lose more often than win, but when looked at as a one-shot deal at a fresh table, you have a 50-50 chance no matter which side you pick. But there's another matter to consider: the 15 to 30 percent house edge that goes with all racetrack wagers. Whatever that figure is at your local track, that's the percentage of your bets that will *lose* as a consequence of the "tax" imposed by the track.

In sharp contrast, the house edge for a place bet on the 9 is just 4 percent. This figure also applies to the sister number, the 5, and, the house penalty for placing the 6 or the 8 is just 1.52 percent. Under two percent!

This struck me as a much better deal, provided that a racetrack situation could be simulated in a casino. Well, it can, if you're able to grasp the concept of *Imposed Velocity.*

IMPOSED VELOCITY: As noted in the pages describing *Continuum,* the problem with casinos is that they make you play too darn fast. But, do they really?

Actually, no. That's what they *encourage,* but the pace can be whatever you want if you plan ahead. There's no need to play the way *they* want; you can opt to *impose your own playing velocity.* This is how to merge the best of both worlds.

It may help you to achieve the proper mentality by pretending, when in a casino, that you're at a racetrack instead:

You walk up to a craps table. *They're all in line. . .the flag is up, aaand, they're off!*

You reach into your pocket for a bill. *Coming around the clubhouse turn, it's. . .*

You tell the dealer your bet. . . .*on the backstretch, Asian Cat has moved into contention. . .*

The shooter throws the dice. . . .*aaaand at the top of the stretch, Asian Cat has taken the lead!*

The stickman calls, *"Number nine, winner!"* as the racetrack announcer says, *And it's number nine, Asian Cat, by two lengths, followed by the seven. . . .*

The dealer pays your bet and you head for the cashier.

The utilization of *imposed velocity* helps keep you from getting pulled in to the *continuum* the casinos rely on to guarantee their profits. *You* are the one controlling the pace of the betting activity instead of the casino.

What you now have is a simulation of racetrack conditions without the destructive 20 percent house edge. You can turn over money at a pace *you* choose, and give yourself the time you need to make an intelligent betting decision. All that's missing is watching the horses run around the track.

That's not the reason you go, is it?

But there is one more little twist. This is most effective when you add in the mentality of *Controlled Greed.*

CONTROLLED GREED: During perhaps the most compelling moment of the movie *Wall Street,* Gordon Gecko echoed the words of takeover specialist Ivan Boesky, who once proclaimed that *Greed is good.* In that context, Mr. Gecko was right, but *greed* is also the great destroyer of men who were legends, and some of the most brilliant minds in world history. It is considered a deadly sin by most everyone—myself included—but it has it's place, if it's controlled.

Controlled greed? Greed used moderately? Yep. This is just one of the many paradoxes of gaming. Nevertheless, it would be advantageous for you to introduce the concept of *controlled greed* into your style of play.

To survive as a professional gambler, one needs an excess of *ambition* and a touch of *greed.* You have to have the stomach for large bets, but also, the good sense to quit at the right moment. You must desensitize yourself to the sums of money you're turning over, while you retain the underlying knowledge of how much those chips are worth.

Controlled Greed is defined as ***a passionate desire for a sensible bet acquisition.*** In this application, *greed* is constructive, for it offers the motivation to carry you through the gratification vacuum that is part of this life.

You need a strong incentive to guide you past the temptations and the loneliness that constantly surround you. You will be in the no-man's land between *seduction* and *discipline,* and there will be no peace until you're finished for the day.

Until you've been there, you cannot begin to imagine what lies ahead. Sorry, you can't do it. You have to pay the dues and make the moves. If you're like the rest of us humans on planet earth, you're going to have to make the same mistake *ten thousand times* before you've learned enough to stay out of trouble for *one week.* Did I say *ten* thousand? I meant *twenty* thousand.

The *Partnership Imperative* will make things easier for you than it was for me, but the two of you have to stick to *all* the rules right down to the tiniest detail ✠

APPLYING THE CONCEPTS

How are these concepts of *imposed velocity* and *controlled greed* applied in real life?

You have to know what to look for, and stay focused. The first stage as you enter a casino is the *Analysis Stage*. What is the general mood? Is there enough room at the tables? Any trends in progress? You're a shopper, looking for a bargain, hidden perhaps underneath a bunch of old crates.

As the situation comes into focus, you mentally prepare for the bets you will make, including how much cash to put on the table, what to say and—most important—when to leave. At that point, your role has changed from that of a shopper, to a Marine Corps General in charge of a small war.

Your assignment is to *seize, retain, and exploit the initiative.* Before you send a single soldier (dollar) to engage your opponent (the house), you must possess a razor-sharp vision of exactly how that battle will end. You must visualize victory, and yes, defeat. You must follow through on your attack regardless the end result. This is a limited war in which no more will be risked than what you and your associate agreed to at the front end. There is *no chance* you'll be surprised or drawn into a war of attrition. You will be *out of there* in a matter of minutes.

Your goals are conservative. You're not seeking a lucky win. There are only two possible outcomes, and you have sized up the parameters of each. This is where you'll need your discipline. This is where you'll find out whether you possess the right stuff. This is where you'll discover the truth about *you* ✠

ONE-SHOTS FOR CRAPS

Whenever I buy in for a craps *session,* my objective is to win a majority of (relatively) small bets. Not so with the *one-shots.* Since they are fewer in number, more precise, and since I have more time to analyze the table, they are usually larger.

THE RANDOM 22

Moving in silently, downwind and out of sight, you've got to strike when the moment is right, without thinking.

—Pink Floyd, from
Animals

The *Random 22* is a technique every craps player should know about. It's a cluster of four separate wagers that is usually played sporadically, as an ongoing strategy. It is advisable to play this only at *warm* craps tables.

When you play *$22 Inside,* you are covering each of the four inside numbers (5, 6, 8 & 9) with one-unit place bets. Since these four can be rolled a total of 18 ways, you are covering exactly *half* of the total dice combinations. This sounds pretty good when one considers that these bets can win indefinitely.

The downside is that while you *win* your bets one at a time, you *lose* them all at once. So, anyone who plays this strategy must forever play dodge ball with the seven.

To me, that sounds kinda like playing Russian Roulette for a living; that seven is a straight shooter who *never* runs out of ammo. But at the right table, one can do amazing things with this strategy. Just remember to watch yourself.

It might help you understand this cat-and-mouse procedure if I describe my first two experiences:

My first session was at the Flamingo Hilton in Las Vegas, where I made $200 in about forty minutes playing at the two-unit level (which costs $44, not $22). I was doing my best to artfully dodge the 7 by taking my bets down after three hits per shooter, but doing so hurt more than helped. You see, the table was warm to the point that I'd have made more if I left my bets up *until the 7 took them down.* That's what the other players did, and they were doing better than me. In that case, my discipline was in fact a liability— but please, don't even *think* about using that as an argument against maintaining your discipline!

My next session was next door, at the Imperial Palace. I was at another warm table, doing quite well using my instinct to call my bets *off* and *on* at random. I was roughly $150 ahead when I got burned and lost my first $44. Then I fell into a loop where the seven came the instant I called my bets *on.* I tried a series of counting procedures to compensate, but it mattered not. The seven was *right there* every time I activated my bets.

The moral to story one is that a right bettor can do no wrong at a warm table. The moral to story two is that when the seven starts blasting your bets off the board, Get out! Get out! Get out! Now! Now! Now!

The *Random 22* is generally most effective when one limits himself to two or three hits, then pulls down all bets until the next come-out, or the next table. At the right table, you can rack up some wins pretty quick. The only problem is, those tables aren't all that abundant in the world ✠

THE RANDOM BUY

Attain the unattainable.

—Alfred Tennyson

There was only one player at the table, and his point was 10. Even though the situation didn't meet my usual criterion for betting, I decided to risk $52 on a hunch. I took two greens and two whites from my pocket, put them on the layout near the dealer and said, *"Buy the point for fifty."* In less than two minutes I had won $100. As I was wondering what to do next, the shooter came out on a 4. I decided to invest in him one more time, regressing my bet to $25 (+$1 for the commission). He made that point as well.

For the third point that I was there to see, he came out on 9. My original instinct was to place the point for a quarter, but a little voice inside my head told me that since it was easy for the shooter to make the two hardest points, 4 and 10, it might be difficult for him to make an easier point like the 9. I held back, but stuck around long enough to see the result. After two more rolls, he sevened out. My bottom line was a net gain of $147 in just under five minutes —from an initial investment of $52.

This happened a few years ago at the Resorts in Atlantic City. What I did was *buy the 10,* and later, the 4. I prefer to take that kind of risk only at warm tables, but sometimes one can maintain an above-average performance strictly from instinct.

So, what you should really be seeking is a *lively* craps table where the point is 4 or 10. And the more excited the players seem to be, the more eager you should be to *buy the point,* **if** you can manage to squeeze in.

If, however, the players seem disinterested and bored, you're better off avoiding that table altogether. And if you're wondering, I don't recommend laying the point. Just keep on walking. When you're in the *Random Buy* mode, you're looking for a hot chance on a 2–1 bet or no bet at all.

Now, technically, this bet doesn't pay 2–1 because a 5 percent commission is levied by the house. There are times, though, when you pay less than that through rounding.

Figure 46 shows some common *buy bets*, which are advisable only against the numbers 4 and/or 10:

BET	COMMISSION	TOTAL BET	WIN	PROFIT
$ 20	$1 (5%)	$ 21	$ 40	$ 39
$ 25	$1 (4%)	$ 26	$ 50	$ 49
$ 35	$1 (2.9%)	$ 36	$ 70	$ 69
$ 50	$2 (4%)	$ 52	$100	$ 98
$100	$5 (5%)	$105	$200	$195

FIGURE 46
Buying the 4 or 10

Note that when buying the 4 or 10 for $25, you pay only a 4% commission. When buying for $35, you pay less than 3%. This is called the miracle of numerical rounding. Casinos, in an attempt to make that wager more attractive to the public, allow the 5% figure to be rounded *downward*.

Now, I don't want to paint too rosy a picture here. The hard truth is this isn't an easy bet to win. If that wasn't the case, the boxman wouldn't accept your bet so gleefully. You see, the man isn't stupid. He knows that for every 4 or 10 that wins, two will lose. That's the probability, Jack.

Nevertheless, if you restrict your play to when the table is exhibiting signs of warmth, there's a chance you can beat the odds. I've never tried doing so, but I suspect that one could make a living specializing in *one-shots* like these ✠

THE RANDOM LAY

Everything in life, it seems, is a trade-off. If it tastes good, it's probably bad for your system. In matters of love, you often have to choose between a stunning appearance and a loving heart. If you like living in a city that offers everything you could want, you must endure a higher crime rate.

The same rules apply in gaming. If you seek a greater quantity of wins, you must settle for a low return. Such is the case for those who prefer to *back the seven* at craps. The odds are on their side, but they get beat up pretty bad when they lose.

If you happen to sidle up to a craps table that has only a handful of grim-looking players whose chip racks are nearly empty and some of them are betting the back line, chances are pretty good you've found a *cold table*. One way to handle that situation is to lay the point immediately, then continue to do so as long as you keep winning. Using the base level *lay bet* cost figures shown in Figure 23 (on page 106), you just might be able to squeeze out five or ten (or more) consecutive victories.

Riding a wave of consecutive wins is not too hard to learn. The real art lies in reading the table signs beforehand. One thing that has helped me immeasurably in the past is to ask the closest player how the table's running. The answer I get often surprises me. When it does, I hold back as I await evidence to either confirm or deny that appraisal. Of course, table trends can change directions in a heartbeat, especially at craps.

While you continue to win, lay each new point until you lose. Then, hold back or reduce your bet as you await the next outcome. If you lose again, it's time to take a hike ✠

THE SIX/NO SIX

This is the horseplayer's special, and it can be applied to either the six or the eight. At a craps table, placing the six gets you 6–5, a notch above even money. Laying the same number returns 4–5, a notch below. Which one of these payoffs you'll seek depends on the latest result, at that table or the one before. All you do is follow the trend, duplicating whichever of the two bets would have been most recently successful.

The *Six / No Six* can be played as a one-shot wager or as an ongoing strategy. If played as the latter, this will comprise your primary strategy and your wagers will be working continuously. Meaning, your bets will be oblivious to the come-outs that occur as you play.

Because you'll be imitating the most recent result toward the number and your bets always work, you'll be able to take advantage of midgame streaks *and* come-out sevens. But if you win because of a seven, remember to replace that bet immediately, because the dealer assumes your bet is a one-time deal—even when you give him explicit instructions. Stay on top of things. If you don't, you could lose a chance to exploit three or four consecutive come-out sevens. Each of those could represent a winning bet, and that string could occur in fifteen seconds.

The *Six / No Six* should be played with flat bets (bet amounts that remain constant). After two losses, you can choose to do the opposite of what you were doing, but if you lose a total of four bets, it's time to call it a wrap at that table.

This procedure is a miniature landscape of this book's overall strategy, which is to *exploit the trends of gaming* ✠

THE ANY SEVEN PARLAY

Back in Chapter 8 (page 117), you learned of the *Any Seven Parlay.* This procedure was designed to capitalize upon longshot opportunities that routinely occur at the craps tables, and it earns a delicious 20–1 return.

In that chapter, I was making the point that seven is the most likely of all numbers (at craps) to be rolled *consecutively,* and, that streaks of three, four or five sevens in a row are not really all that unusual. In fact, I have seen streaks of *six* consecutive sevens on quite a few occasions. Would you mind if I fantasize for a moment and project how much I could have made from one of those streaks, if I could have anticipated such an event, had acted upon it, and was not constrained by table maximums?

For this projection, we'll assume that six consecutive sevens were rolled at our table, and I used the first of those sevens as the wagering trigger, parlaying everything at each step:

LEVEL	BET	WIN	PROFIT
1	$5	$25	$20
2	$25	$125	$120
3	$125	$625	$620
4	$625	$3125	$3120
5	$3125	$15,625	$15,620

FIGURE 47
The Any Seven Parlay
(Carried To An Extreme)

This five-stage parlay would return $15,620 from a $5 bet, in about one minute. On that basis, you could lose the first 3000 bets before winning, and still show a profit. This is mere speculation, mind you, for the table maximum would prevent you from making that bet. The point is, *the circumstances* for making such a wager exist in casinos every day.

Now that you have seen the extreme, let's take a look at the *Any Seven Parlay* as it was designed for this manual. Your focus will be on the triple sevens, and the betting scheme will look similar to the first two lines of Figure 47. But we need to tweak the figures a little to help mitigate the downside.

Using any (come-out) seven as your trigger, you're going to start out with a $5 bet on *Any Seven*. If that loses, well, you're out five bucks. If it wins, however, instead of parlaying the whole $25, tell the stickman you want to *press it to $20*. That makes use of the underlying concept of the *RE Parlay* (page 141), where you recoup your original bet after winning the first stage of the parlay. This will keep you in the game for a good long time.

So, if the first two stages are successful, you'll clear a cool $100 from the *any seven parlay*. But it needn't stop there. Let's say you have invested (and lost) $25 in this procedure. Now, to get to that place, you've probably had a few where the first stage won, in which case you were just turning over money. Meaning, every bit of that $25 was lost because *neither* of the two stages took hold. At any rate, after losing that amount, I would suggest that you move up to a new betting tier of *$10* instead of $5. Be prepared to invest as much as $50 (five *complete* losses) at that level, before going to the next tier (of $15).

There are four tiers in this progression (please see page 250), which costs $250 and gives you twenty chances to hit back-to-back sevens. If you don't catch it in twenty tries, you'll have to write off the series as a loss. Since I've never exhausted a series, I think the possibility of that is remote, as long as you stay on top of things and don't miss your cue.

That's the key. It's a fast-moving game ✠

THE SELECTIVE SHOOTER

And the earth becomes my throne
I adapt to the unknown
Under wandering stars I've grown
By myself but not alone.

—Metallica, from
Wherever I May Roam

Alongside S.R. 160, about 20 miles southwest of Las Vegas, a man with a scraggly beard was going about his morning routine. He put on a pair of jeans and a plaid shirt, and after finishing his coffee, doused the fire and rolled up his sleeping bag. Then he put his few possessions in the hiding place under a shelf-like rock, and headed for the road with his thumb out.

It was five minutes before the first car came by, a late model Buick that whizzed right past, but shortly after that a blue pickup came by and stopped. Without a word, Lars opened the door, got in, and the truck sped off.

He told the driver he was going to the Flamingo Hilton, which turned out to be convenient. All he had was $32 in his pocket, but that was all he needed. He got out of the pickup in front of the casino and walked through the south entrance. After carefully choosing a place at a craps table, he laid a twenty on the felt, saying *"Three reds and five whites, please."*

He picked a spot to the left of the shooter, so he'd be next in line to shoot. When the dice came to him, he put a $5 chip on the pass line. He went on to make four points, then cashed out with a $64 profit, and left the casino.

Outside the casino he took in a breath of fresh air and stood there, first looking south, then north. Slowly, deliberately, he made his way to the Barbary Coast, next door. He bought in at another craps table, and like before, waited until the dice came to him before placing a bet. It took him only two minutes to wrangle a $38 profit, putting him over $100 ahead for the day.

He then went to Tony Romas on Sahara Avenue for a meal of baby back ribs, then bought a pair of jeans and a carton of cigarettes before taking a cab back to his desert home.

After paying the fare, he had $32 in his pocket.

The *Selective Shooter* is a procedure for craps that involves backing only *yourself* at the tables. As an option, you may find it advantageous to include your partner into the loop, but be aware: doing so may work *for* or *against* you.

Your objective is to get the dice as quickly as possible (at any given table), and wager your own roll only. Whether you pick a table with no players, or try to squeeze in at an active table to the left of the shooter (so that you'll be next in line to receive the dice), it matters not, as long as you customize your play to the type of results you expect to get in that situation. For example, some feel that inactive tables tend to produce more seven-outs than the ones where they squeeze in, so they might want to cater their betting toward that expectation. As they say, *if it improves your win rate, it can't be a bad thing to do.*

In playing the *SS*, there is one question that will be foremost in your thoughts: *"Is today a pass or don't pass day?"* Generally, I find it easier to answer *that* question than to try to gauge the table temperature. The reason for this, strange as it may sound, is that my abilities as a shooter frequently coincide with my moods. If I'm feeling confident and optimistic, it's a *for-sure* that I'll roll more numbers than when I'm upset. You may not understand how moods can affect table results, and I don't either. But when your income depends on maintaining your success rate, you tend to accept, rather than question, your good fortune.

To me, the *SS* is the last refuge for those who need to win and have nowhere else to turn. If I was in a *must-win* situation (like the homeless man who was just described), the *SS* is exactly what I'd want to play.

But you need to start out with small bets, until you get a feel for what kind of day you're going to have. After you've racked up some results from your own shoots, you might be in a good position to project your day's strategy. Each direction (*do* or *don't*) has its advantages, so don't try to induce a win from one side or the other. Accept whatever the table chooses to give you. Go with the flow, wherever that may lead.

If it ends up being a *pass* day, you could easily make a good day's pay in just ten minutes if you can roll fifteen or more numbers while backing yourself. And if you feel like a *loser,* you can actually profit from that as well; you might be able to cash in on a prodigious gathering of seven-outs *that you induced.*

In order to find the ideal conditions for doing this, it may be necessary for you to plan your visits for those times when the table conditions favor the player (that is, many tables to choose from). Certain times of day are better suited for this, and sometimes even the weather can factor itself into things.

Although the *SS* usually works well for me, I must caution you against overconfidence in your betting direction. There have been times when I would start out making more passes than not, and then suddenly my game just bottoms out, and I can't make a point for the next *ten* line bets. Had I been betting *right* the whole time, I would have been slaughtered. Fortunately, my mood changes when I start losing, and if I bet (the back line) so as to match that mood, I generally come out okay.

It takes more effort and more legwork to play the *SS* than to strap oneself in to a table and play the game like everyone else, but I find that the rewards justify that expenditure. When winning at casino table games is the only way one has to put food on the table, he doesn't usually mind putting out a little extra effort—if that's what it takes to succeed, and survive ✠

ONE-SHOTS FOR ROULETTE

Truth to tell, most of my action at roulette tables comes in the form of one-shots. This is because I'm not terribly fond of dealing with those pesky zeroes, which are a real nuisance to hedge when you're playing a sit-down session for small stakes.

Since my *one-shots* are typically larger than my session bets, it's easier meeting the table minimum with my hedge.

In this section we will look at some of the techniques used by those who specialize in one-shots for roulette ✠

THE RANDOM ANGEL

In the previous chapter we talked about the *Angel,* which is an inside roulette bet on the first and last sixlines, paying 2–1. Oops. Right away, I see a young man in the back row with his hand up. He wants to know why one should play *those* sixlines, instead of two contiguous sixlines, or any of the six outside 2–1 bets, which would certainly be more convenient.

My answer, regretfully, is not very scientific: I've tried every other combination, and I lose with them. I can't explain why this group of numbers behaves differently, but as I said two pages back, when one must win to survive, he tends not to question his success. Bottom line: this group of numbers seems to work best.

In playing the *Random Angel,* there are two different wagering triggers to look for:

1) An *Angel* number (1–6 or 31–36) won the most recent table decision, *but not the one before that,* or
2) An *Angel* number *hasn't won* the last four decisions.

You can specialize in just one of these two wagering triggers or make use of both. Option number 1 goes after the *positive trends* while number 2 targets the *negative trends.* My success rate is higher on the latter, but it doesn't come up as often.

Once you've spotted your trigger, lay your chips on the first and last sixlines. Hedging the 0–00 split for perhaps 5% of the total outlay is optional. Examples: at the nickel level (a $10 total bet), I don't bother with a hedge. At the quarter level (a $50 bet), I may put $3 on the zeroes, just for protection.

Now, if my bet wins, I get $100 for my $50 bet and I'm *gone* from that table. If it loses, I usually give the table one more chance and repeat the bet, but no matter what happens, that will be my last bet at that table for the time being.

So, the range of possibilities is: you have one chance to win $100, another to win $50, and one to lose $100. A win at stage 1 returns 2–1 and a win at stage 2 earns the equivalent of even money (when you factor in the loss at stage 1).

When playing the Random Angel, I prefer to do so with chips that are in my pocket, as opposed to making a buy-in on the spot. Reason, I don't want to affect the existing momentum of the game. If the dealer has to take the time to negotiate a buy-in, the natural flow of the game is interrupted, which may torpedo the result that I seek. Call me superstitious, but I think I do better if I can slip my bet in without making waves.

Though I admit it's a hassle having to reach across the table to both ends of the layout, experience has taught me that I'm better off if I make the effort. One thing I've learned in this life is that there are a lot of *Angels* in the world ✠

THE RANDOM SLEDGE

Can't have a *Random Angel* without a *Sledge* equivalent. The latter is one of my favorite betting schemes, for there are days when I can't seem to lose while playing it. But don't be misled. I go to great lengths to find the perfect table, and even then I seldom hang around for more than one or two hits.

The *Random Sledge* is nothing more than the *sledgehammer* inside bet for roulette (as described in Chapter 13) played in short bursts, moving from table to table in an attempt to circumnavigate losses. With this procedure, it's best that you take your money and run after one or two hits—if you were fortunate enough to win in the first place.

You may be able to successfully extend your stay at a table if you play the *Vagabond Sledge* (also in Chapter 13). This involves shifting your coverage from *Sledgehammer A* to *Sledgehammer B* as you play, which keeps your area of vulnerability (the uncovered section of the layout) a moving target. But very, very seldom do I ever play any sledgehammer version without a hedge on the zeroes. Reason, this is an expensive bet. Foregoing the hedge is what I call penny-wise and pound-foolish.

The main thing to look out for when playing this bet, though, is other players using value chips *inside*. If this is the case, you're going to have to take time out to convert your chips to table chips, or forget about playing at that table. Remember, you don't want to upset the existing momentum of the game.

A final word: there are times when it's hard to win with this betting procedure. But in the hands of a skilled user, I believe the *random sledgehammer* can be very effective ✠

THE RANDOM Z

The *Random Z* bet is one of the products of a 5000-spin databank of live results I created in the 1980*s*. Close scrutiny of those results revealed a higher rate of back-to-back hits in a certain section of the layout, and to this day I find that the bet I created to exploit this quirk still seems to work. It's probably just one of those fourteen-year trends that will soon fade.

Sorry, but I really don't have a better explanation. Maybe it doesn't matter which numbers you cover. At any rate, the bet of which I speak is essentially the combining of two *quad* bets (shown in Figure 48), which pay 7–2 when paired up. I call it the Z bet because it takes on the shape of a crude "Z".

Officially, I am unable to make the claim that any section of the roulette layout is superior to another, else my credibility in this business may go down in flames. *(The odds on that are also 7–2.)* Therefore, I will promote this bet by virtue of its 7–2 return, which makes it similar to the odds found at a racetrack. All the same, I suggest the placement that covers the numbers shown, as a means of standardizing the wager.

The *Random Z* is one of my signature bets; that is, something I'm prone to play whenever I see the betting trigger on a scoresign. I utilize a 1–2–3–4 progression (that often spans a period of days). When a number from this group has just won the latest decision, I place a bet on each of the two quads, for up to two times at the same table. If I lose again, I give the next table two chances at the next level. Starting with nickel bets, a progression gives you eight chances to win and runs $200. But you should know, very seldom have I lost a progression of the *Random Z* ✠

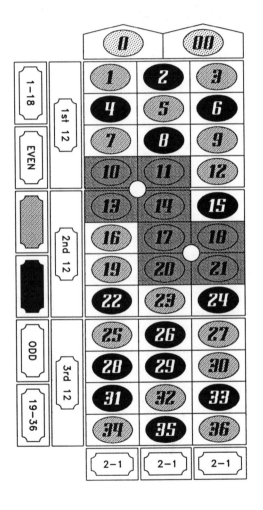

FIGURE 48
The Z Bet
(2-chip bet pays 7–2)

EXPLOITING THE ZEROES

One man's meat is another man's poison.

—Oswald Dykes

To most roulette players, the zeroes are as welcome as the AntiChrist at a church social. To others they're merely a nuisance, like a telemarketer, or a swarm of gnats.

Then there are those who adore the zeroes.

If you have a plan; if you're waiting (for them) with the net, the zeroes can be a welcome sight. I've passed many a roulette table that showed five or more zeroes on its scoresign. That's five chances out of twenty to hit a 17–1 longshot. That's some serious money we're talking about. But the operative question is: how do you catch a trend like that?

Actually, they'll *come to you* if you know how to play them. This is where an assistant is invaluable. Have him or her commence (or prompt *you* to begin) a separate betting series when the zeroes start hitting—which lasts for six consecutive bets, or until you win, whichever comes first.

Mind you, this is advised only for those who have the bankroll to see it through, for that bet on the 0-00 may have to meet the table minimum by itself, which means your series will probably begin with $5 bets, and move upward from there.

Typically, each six-bet series utilizes flat bets, but your bets increase when you go to the next series, which is triggered by every occurrence of a 0 or 00 result. Chapter 20 gives you the specifics you need to play this procedure ✠

MIXED MEDIA

When playing roulette, most of my time is spent awaiting my wagering trigger. If I wanted to play the *Random Angel* for an extended period, for example, the only time I would bet is after an angel number appeared, or had not appeared for the last four spins. But what to do in the meantime? One might feel silly standing there like a statue, waiting to place a bet.

You could resort to *one-shots*, but some situations don't lend themselves well to this. Riverboat cruises come to mind, because *there*, the player has limited mobility and less tables to choose from. That being the case, what do you do?

The answer is to play *Mixed Media* bets. These are secondary wagers that have been assembled for the purpose of holding your place at the table while awaiting a specific event, and, affording you the possibility of supplemental income.

There are times, of course, when these secondary bets do more harm than good, but they are designed to offset losses from your mainstay bets, and they may even lead to something that is very profitable indeed. But the main benefit in using *mixed media* comes from relieving the monotony of intermittent play. . .which might otherwise be almost unbearable. And that can go a long way toward helping you hang onto your discipline.

So what is *mixed media* composed of? Ideally, a collection of even money bets that complements *your* style of play, and, that you have used with some success. You could limit yourself to just one or two bet types, or allow yourself to choose between a dozen or more, if you can think up that many. One such collection that I like is configured as shown in Figure 49:

PRIMARY: *The Random Angel (for example)*

SECONDARY: RS   *(Reoccurring Single)*
                     RD   *(Reoccurring Double)*
                     ZZ   *(Zigzag, also known as P4)*
                     ST   *(Streaks: P1's, P2's and P3's)*
                     PT   *(Pattern Bets: P5's & up)*
                     GTR   *(Go To Red)*
                     NB   *(No Bet)*

FIGURE 49
A Mixed Media Collection

The abbreviations that accompany the above were created to identify (on your scorecard) the type of bet you made. The roulette scorecard, as you will see, was designed to show the win or loss amount of each bet, but when playing secondary bets, you need to show what you did so your performance can be evaluated later on. This information should be entered on the same line that shows your bet result, wherever you can find space.

To clarify the above, the RS*s* and RD*s* are your *reoccurring* varieties, as noted in Chapter 9. The ZZ*s* and ST*s* are from the *Five Primary Patterns,* also from Chapter 9. PT*s* are *pattern bets,* typically P5*s* through P10*s*. For those, just follow the prevailing pattern of the moment.

The last two were created as last resorts, when all else fails. *GTR* stands for *Go To Red,* which is only a tiny notch above tossing a coin to derive your choice, but at least it's consistent. You might be surprised how effective it can be at times. Finally, we have *NB,* which stands for *No Bet.* Most roulette dealers will let you slide through an occasional spin without betting, as long as you don't abuse the privilege.

There are times that I use the *mixed media* assortment of bets for my primary wagers, as I roam the casinos looking for a hot bet. In those cases I usually specialize in just one or two of the options, like the *reoccurring single* and *double* ✠

THE RANDOM PLAYER BET

In some ways, minibaccarat exists in a category all by itself. It doesn't have nearly the amount of betting options as roulette or craps, the table minimums are usually higher, and when you do find a game, it often has no players at all, or it's booked solid. This is unfortunate, because the ideal condition is a table that is half-full. But if you do find a suitable table, the only *one-shot* endorsed in this book is the *Random Player Bet*.

There was a time, years ago, when I always bet on Bank for my minibaccarat *one-shots*. After all, Bank was *supposed* to win most of the time. Problem was, I always seemed to *lose* those bets. These days, my one-shots go on Player.

The *Random Player* bet is a single bet, on Player, that starts and ends a session at a minibaccarat table.

What are the advantages?

Let's say that you normally buy in for $100 and shoot for a $50 profit. With a *Random Player* bet for $25, you stand to make half that amount in ten seconds. You won't always win, but the outcome of *any* session is an unknown, isn't it? It's quick and dirty. No tedious grind, no commission to pay.

What's the wagering trigger?

There are two ways to play this bet. One is to bet at random, whenever you chance upon a minibaccarat table with an open seat. The other (which I prefer) is to bet on Player *only* when you come across a table with (at least four) players who are betting on Player *unanimously*. Such is likely to be a table that is *trend-heavy*, and, in the midst of an overpowering *Player* trend. Few things in gaming (or life itself) are surer than that ✠

THE SIGNATURE BET

A real man makes his own luck.

—Billy Zane, from the
1997 movie, *Titanic*

Back on page 225 I used the term *signature bet* in describing how I play the *Random Z*. I'd like to take a moment to clarify the term, as it is used in this book.

Signature bets are like pet wagers, which are played randomly yet regularly. Ideally, the performance of these wagers should be tracked (with the *statistics scorecard,* coming up), because in my experience, groups of random bet results usually start to concur with the statistical probabilities after, perhaps, thirty or forty trials. So, if my records show that these bets are overperforming, I prepare myself for the inevitable compensatory losing streak. And if they're underperforming, I get ready to harvest some wins. I have the edge, because I have an idea what to expect.

One example of a signature bet would be to bet the 3rd Dozen roulette bet whenever you pass a table where a number from that group has just won the last decision. Personally, I prefer the Angel when going for a 2–1 payoff, but I suggest the 3rd Dozen because it's easier to reach, and you don't (usually) have to worry about the problem of other players using value chips.

A friend of mine bets $5 on the 11 at the craps table whenever an 11 is rolled, expecting a double hit. Another friend always bets the hard 8, when (and only when) 8 is the point.

These are just some examples. Whatever you choose for *your* signature bet, make it wild, make it bold, make it *fun* ✠

SUMMARY OF SURGICAL STRIKES

Circle and pounce.

—the Author

It would be nice if life were such that a person could make an honest living specializing in a single gaming procedure or technique. If that was possible, though, it would have been discovered long ago, and then there would be no need (or demand) for books such as the one you're holding.

As I've been saying all along, you've got to take some time to size up the table. Once you think you've got it pegged, send in a battalion of your best men. If you do your homework, you should win more of these battles than you lose.

The name I give for this mentality is *Circle and Pounce*. Like a hawk flying high above the trees, you circle the landscape in search of prey. You spot a chipmunk in an open field, which looks like an easy hit. . .but should you bother with something so small? *Yes,* you decide. Then you pounce.

Circle and pounce, circle and pounce. That's how you make a living, as a player, in casinos.

Sometimes it's advantageous to play a session; sometimes it's better to hit and run. Whatever you decide, try to keep your forays brief, because the longer you stay at the tables, the more the house edge will wear you down.

Bet quickly, and bold. That's how you win ✠

15

TIMING AND TEMPERATURE

Returning now to the subject of *inanimate object behavior,* we shall take a look at *table temperature.*

Technically, there is no such thing as a *hot* or *cold* table at craps or any other casino game. The tables are inanimate objects and the results thereupon are purely random. Therefore, every table decision is independent of all others.

While it is true that the dice have no memory, no capacity for cognitive thought and no sense of time or place, table results often follow a path that *appears to be* consistent or predictable. But as convincing as it may be, an abnormal table trend is merely a random occurrence and nothing more.

Was it coincidence that eight shooters out of nine sevened out *by the fourth roll,* as seen back on page 184? Was that just a freak of nature? Indeed. The dice did not *react* to any of the previous decisions, and the table itself exerted no influence whatsoever upon those results. But we call it a *cold table,* because of the need we have to give a name to the phenomenon.

That's all. Tables are never *hot, cold, warm* or *choppy.* These descriptions apply strictly to the *trends* occurring at a given table, at a given point in time.

TABLE TYPES:
PRELIMINARY DESCRIPTION

My experience has allowed me to identify five different types of craps tables, which of course refers to the playing conditions at the tables and not the tables themselves:

1) *The Hot Table:* The most lucrative table. The numbers pass, and many auxiliary numbers are rolled.

2) *The Warm Table:* Also very favorable for *right bettors.* The dice pass more often than not, and many auxiliary (place) numbers are rolled along the way.

3) *The Repeat Table:* At such table, patterns are repeated. Single numbers; groups of numbers; patterns in general. A good money-maker if you tune into it.

4) *The Cold Table:* At this type of table, the overwhelming majority of shooters can't make a single point. Lucrative for those playing the back line.

5) *The Choppy Table:* The most unpredictable (and therefore the worst) table you will ever encounter, for there is no consistent pattern to exploit. Unfortunately, it is also the most common of all the table types.

Following, are the specifics of each:

THE HOT TABLE

What It Is: The *Hot Table* is the most sought-after table type of all. Five-figure incomes can easily be made in an hour from a hundred-dollar buy-in, if one bets aggressively with the shooter who *refuses to die.* Except for the very end, all the sevens show up during his come-outs, so he continues to roll the dice, make points and help everyone at the table benefit handsomely.

How To Identify It: Four ways. First, it's from where all the yelling and cheering (in any casino) originates. Second, the table layout will be lit up like a Christmas tree with place and come bets. Third, look at the chip rack directly in front of the shooter. If you see *stripes* in his columns of chips, that means the chips are coming in so fast he hasn't time to organize them. Fourth, *everyone's* racks should be loaded with chips.

How To Exploit It: Finding an opening isn't likely to be easy. If you *are* lucky enough to squeeze in and you think the shooter will last a while longer, you might want to lay a couple bills on the table and tell the dealer *"$162 across; buy bets on the four and the ten".* But be prepared for the possibility that you'll lose every dime of it in a *St. Louis second.*

If you do start catching some wins, press up the winning numbers one at a time in ten dollar increments (or so) until you've won enough to cover your investment. Then you may wish to go for larger gains. Occasionally, tell the dealer *"Same bet"* for five or six hits, as a hedge against the possibility that the seven will take all your bets down on the next roll.

There are more efficient ways to exploit such a table, but this is a simplified strategy that works ✠

THE WARM TABLE

What It Is: The virtue in a *Warm Table* lies in the scarcity of times you'll hear the phrase *"Seven-out, line away."* Most shooters at such a table hold the dice for several minutes, which is a long time in craps terms. How many points they make is not really the issue. This table type is best known for all the place numbers rolled on the way to a line bet decision.

How To Identify It: Most (if not all) players at the table are happy and enthusiastic, and the numbered boxes on the layout are loaded with place and come bets.

How To Exploit It: A conservative approach would be to toss the dealer a green and say *"$22 Inside."* This will cover the four inside numbers (5, 6, 8 & 9), which have a greater chance of being rolled than any number except the seven. Collectively, these four numbers give you 18 (out of the 36) ways to win.

You might wish to take down your bets after getting three, four or five hits and then wait for the next come-out to resume your betting, or you could leave them up until the seven comes along and makes the decision for you. Then replace those bets at the new come-out.

If the 4 or 10 seem to be coming up quite a lot, you may opt to take some of your profits and cover one of them or both. Just be cautious. Having bets on all six place numbers is, in my experience, tempting fate in a wanton and reckless manner.

If you wish to play more aggressively, you can bet larger, or make it a habit to cover all six numbers. Just don't forget about the seven that's always waiting in the weeds ✠

THE REPEAT TABLE

What It Is: From time to time, you are likely to encounter the *Repeat Table,* where table decisions fall into a repetitious pattern. The more attuned you are to the *possibility* of this occurrence, the greater the chance you will reap its reward.

How To Identify It: A *Repeat Table* manifests its magic in a number of ways. A pattern of two passes, two don'ts, two passes, two don'ts. Tables where field numbers are rolled in long strings, or a seven is rolled at every come-out. Tables where the number 9 passes whenever it's the point. Or, shooter after shooter rolls two numbers and then sevens out. Cold tables, tables where numbers come in pairs, or tables where every shooter makes his first point. These are all *Repeat Tables.*

How To Exploit It: It is vitally important that you get into the habit of notating the decisions at every casino game you play. This will help you see what's really going on. When a table is producing repetitive patterns, you'll become aware of it faster if you've been tracking its results. As soon as you've identified an ongoing trend, follow the leader. But it's not a *monkey see, monkey do.* You must envision the big picture; *see* the big picture; become an inseparable part of the big picture.

Let me remind you once again that to do all this, you need a partner. The action at the craps tables is usually too fast for one person to notate, place bets, *and* evaluate. To do the job right, you really do need assistance.

In Chapter 16 you'll learn about *customized scorecards* for the recommended games, which help you and your associate organize the incoming data from the table ✠

THE COLD TABLE

What It Is: The most enduring *Cold Table* I ever witnessed was at the Showboat in Atlantic City. It started out as a warm table but the trend changed. I was a bit late in picking up on the new direction, but I made out fine.

As cold tables go, this one was a plum. No one ever rolled a seven at the come-outs, though there were some elevens. The dice circled the table once, and every shooter went down with a crash. Normally when that happens the players start to leave, but it was Friday night, and all the tables were packed. None of the players at that table wanted to leave for fear of being shut out, but no one wanted to play the back line, either. They were there to party it up or die. So the players kept losing and I kept winning. *This has to end sometime,* I thought.

The dice went around the table again, but no one could make a point. As the dice was on its third trip, some working-class hero busted the trend and hit a point. Having cashed in on over twenty consecutive wins, I colored out.

That's what you call a *cold table.*

How To Identify It: Usually, the tables with fewer players. The mood is subdued, the chip racks are barren, and there are not a lot of chips on the layout. Some of the players betting the back line is also a tipoff.

How To Exploit It: As long as you don't get burned by the sevens at the come-out, play don't pass and take odds. If it helps your game, expanding to a *two-number don't* might maximize your potential for gain. And if the sevens show up during the primary come-outs, you can revert to *odds betting* ✠

THE CHOPPY TABLE

What It Is: The worst table you'll encounter. Also the most common table type there is. It's your worst nightmare and your most dreaded daytrip rolled into one. Whatever you do, this table will do the opposite. Until a recognizable pattern emerges, there is virtually *no chance* for you to win.

The choppiness of course pertains to the line bet results. The pass line will win some, but you never know when to expect what. Most of the time, the dice won't pass, but betting the back line is not (usually) the answer.

How To Identify It: It's that cursed place where nobody wins, no one has any fun, and the players are disinterested.

How To Exploit It: Very difficult. The hot tip is to keep your bets small until the table starts showing signs that it is heading in a certain direction. Or, find another table.

What makes this type difficult to exploit is its uncanny ability to do the opposite of the bet you choose. It's tough to convert that kind of energy into something positive ✠

SUMMARY OF TABLE TYPES

*What you don't know **can** hurt you.*

—ITT Tech Commercial

Success as a craps player requires an awareness of the table types *and* the ability to anticipate changes in the table patterns. When the sands are shifting around, you must pay special attention to all the particulars of that new direction, so that you lose no time adjusting your sights.

The sooner you can identify the emerging trend, the sooner you'll reach your daily *win goal.*

Every game in the casino has built-in snares you can't control, so your best move is to specialize in the exploitation of the one thing *they* can't control:

Gaming trends.

Aberrations of chance.

Flukes and anomalies.

Unexplainable phenomenæ. . .

. . .occurring every minute in a casino. Sooner or later, the cards, dice or wheel will tip its hand, exposing a numerical pattern that holds up for the next fourteen decisions.

This is where you step in and take control, for the beast has fallen into deep slumber. Understand, there's not a moment to lose. He could wake up at any moment ✠

THE SIX SIGNS
OF AN IMMINENT SEVEN

You are at a warm craps table playing pass line with odds, and you have a couple of place bets up. You're doing pretty well, but suddenly the stickman is tapped on the shoulder. . .and your blood begins to run cold.

"Danger! Danger!" In your mind, red lights are flashing, a siren is sounding and you hear the loudspeaker: *"Attention, please: This is a red alert. The stickman has just been replaced at craps table number nine."*

There is not a second to lose. You pull up your odds bet while telling the dealer *"Off on my place bets"*, then toss a nickel to the stickman, saying *"$5 Big Red."*

The new stickman pushes the dice to the shooter, who wipes out on the very next roll.

The loss of your pass line wager was unavoidable, for that bet can't be removed, but you saved your odds and place bets, and even made a profit with your big red bet. And all this was possible only because of your (recently acquired) awareness of *the six signs of an imminent seven:*

1) *One or both dice accidentally go off the table.*
2) *A new stickman comes to replace the present one.*
3) *You see a seven anywhere on the dice, at any time.*
4) *Two Craps numbers are rolled consecutively.*
5) *Your place bets have not had a hit for five rolls.*
6) *The game is delayed because of a dispute.*

Am I saying that the dice *react* to the above?

Of course not. But if you pretend that they *will* react every time one of those six occurs, you'll save money.

Maybe it's the fact that the 7 is so ubiquitous, any excuse to pull up your bets is bound to help. Maybe it's something cosmic. I can't explain why doing this will save you money, but I'm sure that in time you **WILL** come to agree with me. At any rate, here is what I advise in each respective situation:

1) *One or both dice go off the table:* Call your (pass line odds or place) bets off for three rolls. About half the time, I expect to see a seven during that period.

2) *A shift change for the stickman:* Call your bets off for one or two rolls. After that, you may be okay.

3) *You see a 7 on the dice:* It matters not *where* you saw it or for how long; call your bets *off* for three rolls.

4) *Two Craps numbers (2, 3 or 12) are rolled consecutively:* Two Craps numbers tells me that the 7 is getting ready to pounce. Place bets *off* for one or two rolls.

5) *Place bets haven't hit for five rolls:* If your place bets aren't hitting, take them down. Doing so will probably save you money. This rule is a little different from the other four, because you react to the *lack of* an event.

6) *The game is delayed because of a dispute:* Any protracted delay will *cool down* the dice, but take special heed if bad vibes are beginning to circulate. Place bets *off* for two rolls.

I wish I could give you a scientific reason for doing these things, for telling you this doesn't help my credibility. Especially in light of the fact that if these signs *aren't* bringing sevens, *they may be ignored.* But experience has taught me that it is usually a good idea to heed these signals.

You really don't need a reason. If it saves you money, it can't be a bad thing to do. And any rule that gets you to pull your bets up periodically will probably work in your favor ✠

DICE FIXING

I fix my dice so that the threes are in a V position. Thus, the dice do not show a seven on any side.

> —Frank Scoblete, from page 24,
> *Beat The Craps Out Of The Casinos*

I never pick up the dice so that the numbers on top or the side facing me add up to a number I don't want.

> —Lyle Stuart, from page 161,
> *Winning At Casino Gambling*

When the dice hit the far wall of the table, all the fixing in the world won't help you, for they will just bounce around in an uncontrolled pattern.

> —John Patrick, from page 35,
> *John Patrick's Craps*

The three quotes above pretty much run the full spectrum of opinions on the subject of *Dice Fixing,* which means setting the dice in a fixed position prior to the roll. One guy favors a very exact position, the next is concerned with only two sides, and the third assures us that fixing is a complete waste of time.

Who do we believe? Surely, one of these three opinions is more correct than the others, but which?

Just lately, I've noticed that dice fixing has become the vogue. Used to be, the *fixers* would get hassled by the boxmen, but the casinos are more tolerant these days. Now that the trend has been firmly implanted in the national soil, maybe they consider *resistance to be futile,* as they say in deep space.

Regarding the three opinions expressed on the previous page, who can say if any one of those is superior? Certainly not me. My personal preference is Frank Scoblete's V positioning, for I believe that it helps my game when betting *right.* But no one can prove what *would* have happened if another position were chosen, for a dice roll cannot be finitely duplicated.

To help you decide, let me present a few *facts.*

In my experience, many shooters have a tendency to roll the sister number immediately after establishing the point. Well, prior to that roll, the stickman probably forwarded the dice to him with the point number facing up. Guess what number is on the bottom? The sister number.

In my experience, I can *induce the seven,* often within three rolls, *if* the table is cold to begin with. Of course, if I could do this at any table, I'd own half the continent. But the (theoretical) fact remains, my percentages (to induce a seven) improve when I fix the dice to form a seven on top, *if I'm at a cold table.*

In my experience, the craps shooters who end up having the longest rolls almost *always* turn out to be dice fixers. When I'm at a warm table and I see the shooter fixing the dice, I tend to have a bit more confidence in his staying power.

I doubt that men of science will ever prove or disprove a causative link between *dice positioning* and *dice result,* so your best bet is to do what feels right. A couple tips, though:

1) Make sure both dice hit the far wall. The boxman will insist on this, but more importantly, failure to do so has a tendency to bring on an immediate seven-out.

2) Try to avoid hitting any chips or a player's hand. If the dice take a bad or unplanned bounce, this also seems to prompt a seven, quite reliably. You'll see ✠

16

CUSTOMIZED SCORECARDS

Choice is nothing without knowledge.

—United Health Care of Ohio

Fact is, those who play professionally do not use scorecards like the ones you're about to see. But I'm going to try to convince you that you can't succeed without them!

If you don't mind going through *what they went through,* you can forget about the scorecards. The trouble is, it took them years of bitter strife and a truckload of money to get there. Wouldn't you rather take the shortcut?

Customized Scorecards help you to see the big picture, and to evaluate your performance after the fact. Every sliver of data you acquire in this way brings you closer to your goal of becoming an accomplished veteran of the games.

Even if you specialize in *one-shots* and seldom participate in extended (sit-down) sessions, the scorecards can help you sort out the statistics as they accrue. When your wagering data is compared to the probabilities, you might be able to piece together a realistic projection of what the future will hold ✠

THE CRAPS SCORECARD

Having observed that I was notating every dice result at his craps table, the boxman (with a chuckle) called me a *dice counter*. But my habit didn't bother him in the least.

At a different casino, the boxman asked me what number would be rolled next. *"Six,"* I said. Then the shooter sevened out. *"I was close,"* I insisted.

These are the exceptions. Most of the time, no one seems to notice my habit of notating the table decisions. Not the customers, not the casino personnel. So much the better.

Figure 50 on the facing page shows a customized scorecard for craps. Think of it as an itinerary map, for it helps you see where you're going and what you need to do.

The top section is for time and place particulars. In the space at the top left, write the **CASINO** and its location. Moving from left to right, the three rectangles are for the **MONTH, DATE** and **YEAR**. To the right of that fill in the **TIME** the session began and then cross out the **AM** or **PM** that *doesn't* apply. **LEVEL** pertains to where you parked. Fill this out as soon as you park, denoting the aisle number or parking level, if applicable. After a really *good* or really *bad* day, you'll be glad you remembered to do so!

Just below that area, the boxes with the numbers inside are to help you keep track of your *Any Seven Parlays*. This is explained in more detail on page 249.

SN stands for *Sister Number*. Check the box if the *sister* was rolled on the way to a line decision. **PT** is to be checked if the point was made. The space in the middle is for the table results, and the boxes at the right are for showing gains and losses.

AZTAR
~~EVANSVILLE~~

| | WED | | | | | LEVEL |
| 2 | 7 | 96 | 2:12 | ~~AM~~ PM | | |

LINE

A7 ~~5~~ ~~8~~ 5 : 5 : 5   15 : 15 : 15 : 15 : 15   25 : 25 : 25 : 25 : 25   A
       10 : 10 : 10 : 10 : 10   20 : 20 : 20 : 20 : 20   30 : 30 : 30 : 30 : 30

SN PT

SISTER SYSTEM

SN	PT			LINE
✗	::	11 6 5 2 5 3 10 9 8 7out		1
✗	::	9 5 10 10 7out	+3.0	2
::	✗	8 4 (DD) 8H W	+1.7	3
✗	✗	9 5 8 (DD) 9W	+5.2	4
::	✗	3 6 6W	+6.2	5
::	::	3 11 3 8 7out	+3.1	6
✗	::	6 3 8 10 8 10 11 4 10 2 7out	+7.5	7
✗	::	6 8 7out	+10.5	8
✗	::	5 6 9 12 6 8 7out	+13.5	9
::	::	12 8 3 9 4 9 11 9 11 7out	+15.5	10
::	✗	5 5W	+13.9	11
::	::	7 2 9 8 8 10 4 4 (DD) 7out	+9.6	12
::	✗	7 5 4 8 6 5W	+7.4	13
✗	::	11 2 11 8 6 5 7out	+12.3	14
::	::	12 6 2 7out	+10.5	15
✗	✗	6 5 9 8 6W	+14.0	16
::	::	10 5 7out	+12.5	17
✗	::	8 6 4 (DD) 5 10 6 10 7out	+16.0	18
✗	::	10 11 8 8 6 4 2 3 7out	+18.7	19
::	::	4 7out CASH OUT 3:02	+17.2	20

FIGURE 50
The Craps Scorecard

The *Craps Scorecard* has been painstakingly designed to show all the relevant data that accumulates as you play. This incarnation, which is the most efficient of all those I've tested through the years, can help you spot wagering opportunities and keep track of where you're at in your series or progression.

Figure 50 is a completed version of Figure 59 in the back of this book, which is intended to serve as a master for printing up your own scorecard pads. It is shown at full scale, which will result in a finished product that measures 4" x 6" when trimmed just inside the peripheral border. Have the printer bind them into pads of 50 sheets for convenience.

This scorecard shows the table results from a live session at the Aztar riverboat casino in Evansville, Indiana. After watching the first shooter roll the sister number (to the point) just before sevening out, I opted to play the *Sister System*, along with *Odds Betting* for my secondary strategy.

For the *Sister System*, I went with a progression that ran $15–$25–$35 for the numbers 4, 5, 9 and 10. Corresponding bets for 6 or 8 are $18–$30–$42. For *Odds Betting*, I chose $10 bets with single odds. I bought in for $200 and vowed to leave if I exhausted a *Sister System* series, and would discontinue *Odds Betting* after two or three (consecutive) losses, depending on how things went.

I put $10 on the pass line and another $10 on the don't pass, then threw a buck to the stickman to hedge the 12. The shooter rolled a 9, so I laid $15 for my odds, then placed the 5 for $15 and won $21 almost immediately. After that I pulled up my place bet and won again three rolls later when the seven-out came along. That added $9 ($10 minus the $1 hedge) to my $21, raising my win total to $30 at the end of line 2.

On line 3, the shooter came out on 8, then rolled a 4, then one of his dice flew off the table. Please note the **DD** on line 3, right after the roll of 4. That stands for *Die Down*, which is something I like to note on my scorecard, for such occurrence is often followed by an immediate seven-out.

But not in this case. In fact, the opposite occurred on both lines 3 and 4. Instead of sevening out after the dice went down, the shooter made the point on the following roll. This is contrary to what I usually expect, but one must always be prepared for the unexpected. If you look ahead to line 12, however, you'll see that *that* **DD** occurrence *did* precede a seven-out.

After 50 minutes, I left the table with a $172 profit. $156 of that was from the *Sister System,* and the other $16 profit was from *Odds Betting,* which I discontinued on line 13 after suffering three consecutive losses.

Notes: All of the come-out craps and naturals forced me to keep replacing my hedge (thereby spending more), but the come-out 12 rolled on line 10 paid for those. Of course, I didn't cash in on the other come-out 12 on line 15, because my line bets (and hedges) had been discontinued by that time.

Above line 1 is *line A,* which shows the two *Any Seven Parlay* bets that I made, denoted by the diagonal lines that crossed out two of the "5" boxes. That area (denoted *A 7)* shows the progression I recommend when playing the Any Seven Parlay: Five bets at the $5 level, five at the $10 level and so on. Please see Figure 51 on the next page for the statistics of the progression, which gives you twenty chances to generate a profit ranging from $80 to $250, depending on where the win occurs. There are four tiers in this progression, but I've never needed to go past the third. The cost for all twenty bets—should you somehow lose every one—is $250. But as long as you don't miss your cue, the chance of you exhausting a whole progression is pretty slim.

Getting back to Figure 50, my (two) **A7** bets were triggered by the come-out sevens rolled on lines 12 & 13. Both were losses, so that series would have been carried over to my next session. If someone *had* rolled triple sevens during a come-out, I would have made either $100 or $95 (See Figure 51) from that auxiliary bet, and completed the series.

One more thing. The **8H** that appears on line 3 means that that 8 was rolled the hard way ✠

By the way, the $5–$10–$15–$20 tiers of this progression are derived from the 1–2–3–4 System, as shown in Chapter 12.

BET	COST	WIN	PROFIT *(At that stage)*
$5	$5	$100	$100
$5	$10	$100	$95
$5	$15	$100	$90
$5	$20	$100	$85
$5	$25	$100	$80
$10	$35	$200	$175
$10	$45	$200	$165
$10	$55	$200	$155
$10	$65	$200	$145
$10	$75	$200	$135
$15	$90	$300	$225
$15	$105	$300	$210
$15	$120	$300	$195
$15	$135	$300	$180
$15	$150	$300	$165
$20	$170	$400	$250
$20	$190	$400	$230
$20	$210	$400	$210
$20	$230	$400	$190
$20	$250	$400	$170

FIGURE 51
Any Seven Parlay
Statistics

THE ROULETTE SCORECARD

The *Roulette Scorecard* is a bit fancier than the one you've just seen for craps, but you need something special to offset the relatively high vig of roulette. As before, an unmarked original is offered as a reproducible master ahead in this book.

The space in the middle at the top is for the name of the casino and its location. To the right of that goes the date, time and parking level, as shown a few pages back. Just below that is a small diagram of a roulette layout, which can be used for crossing out the winning numbers as they accrue. The information you gather from that alone can be useful in a variety of ways.

On the left side are a number of columns, some of which are outlined with solid lines, and some with dashed lines. From left to right, the first column is for the table result (the number that won). The next three are entitled *R, B & G*, which stand for *Red, Black* and *Green*. The idea is to mark the appropriate box after the table result is known, as shown in Figure 52. Thereupon, the *B* box is checked with a small dot to denote Black numbers; the *R* denotes Red numbers, and the *G* represents the 0 and 00. This information duplicates what is shown on the scoresign, and can help you see table patterns. Attached to those four columns is a dashed column that is used to show the wagering categories, which can vary depending on the strategy that's used at the time. In the Figure 52 session I chose to play *Fixed Splits* (as shown in Chapter 13) on a continuing basis, while awaiting wagering opportunities for the *Random Angel*. I was using the dashed column to identify the *Angel* table results, to help me see the pattern as it related to that betting category as the game proceeded.

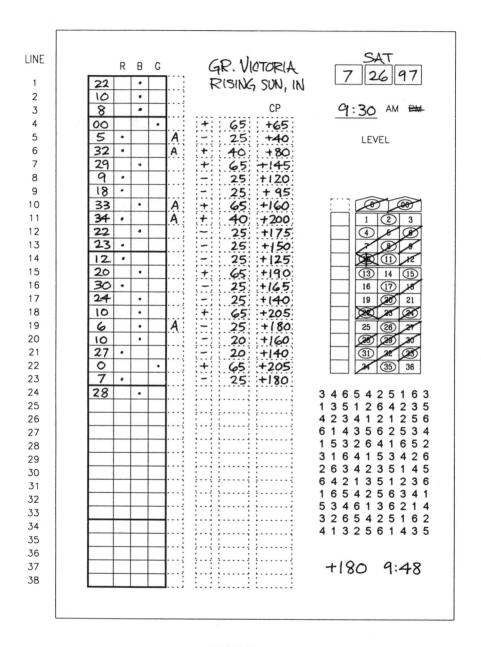

FIGURE 52
The Roulette Scorecard

To the right of the columns just described is a group of three free-standing columns that are outlined with short dashes. The first is to denote wins (+) or losses (–), as the case may be. This allows you to see how you're doing in general—which can be very helpful —for you can lose that awareness in the heat of battle. The next column is to show exactly *how much* money was won or lost (if any) during that table decision. The third column is marked *CP*, which stands for *Cumulative Profit*. If you have time to do so, it's a good idea to maintain a monetary status report.

The dimensions on this scorecard are intended to be 4" x 6" (same as the *craps scorecard*) when trimmed just inside the border. There are 38 rows, which correspond to the quantity of bettable numbers at American roulette. Please note that a bold line appears beneath the third row and every ten rows thereafter, which is meant to bestow a sense of how many decisions have occurred. The first three table results are the minimum I generally need to see before venturing a wager, which is why the first bold line appears after the third row, and this is also why the three 'financial status report' columns don't begin until after that row.

Finally, in the lower right corner, you'll find a group of 120 randomized numbers. These are sometimes used to help me make betting choices for roulette, and craps. If I'm seeking a 5–1 roulette payoff, they help me to select which sixline to play, spin after spin. If I select them in groups of two, I am then pursuing a 2–1 return. In groups of three, an even-money return, etc. At a craps table, they can help me make a line bet choice. Even numbers mean bet the pass line; odd numbers mean bet the back line. As I move through the list (from left to right), the numbers are crossed out so that I don't lose my place.

Figure 52 shows a live session that took place at the Grand Victoria (riverboat) casino in Rising Sun, Indiana. I bought in at 9:30 am on July 26, 1997, and cashed out eighteen minutes later. After witnessing a *Fixed Split* number win the next-to-last decision, I opted to play flat bets against the ten *Fixed Split* numbers while playing the *Random Angel* sporadically.

The line-by-line betting activity was as follows:

Line 4: The 00 won, which is one of the *Fixed Split* numbers that was covered. An immediate win of $65.

Line 5: Number 5 (an *Angel* number) won, cueing me to bet the *Angel* on the next spin. The Fixed Split bet lost, costing me $25 and knocking my *CP* down to +$40.

Line 6: The *Angel* bet paid off, giving me a profit of $40 and pushing my *CP* to +$80. Note: the fixed splits bet is discontinued whenever I am cued to bet the Angel.

Line 7: Having completed the Angel betting series, I return to the fixed splits bet and win $65. *CP* is now +$145.

Line 8: My $25 bet on the fixed splits does not win.

Line 9: Another fixed split loss. *CP* now stands at +$95.

Line 10: A fixed split winner and an Angel number as well, prompting an *Angel* bet on the next spin. *CP* is +$160.

And so on.

Now, back on page 251, I said that this scorecard duplicates the information on the casino score*sign*. Some readers may wonder what is served from this duplication. Three things:

1) Casinos are frequently *so* crowded that you can't see the scoresign when a quick decision is needed. This information must be at your fingertips *at all times*.

2) Scoresigns *do* occasionally post the wrong number. You need *accurate* data in the casino, and, for later analysis.

3) You can use the space for other even money wagers such as *even & odd* or *high & low* (instead of *red & black*).

Getting back to the randomized numbers in the right corner, the best way to use them is, with imagination! Why, there must be fifty ways they could be used to help you make a wagering choice. But then, you may ask: *how is betting from randomized numbers any better than random guessing?*

As long as you stick to the pattern and use a controlled betting procedure, there will be *structure* in what you do. And *that* is one of the key components of *discipline* ✠

THE MINI-B SCORECARD

Now that you've seen the scorecards for craps and roulette, the *minibaccarat scorecard* should not be too hard to figure out. The upper area of Figure 53 is for time and location, etc, as before. The three dashed columns are for (+) or (–), win or loss amount, and cumulative profit, as for roulette. The *P* and *B* at the top of the two main columns, of course, stand for *Player* and *Bank*. The only explanation needed, I imagine, is for the boxes marked *P* and *A* that run alongside the main columns. These are to categorize the table decisions as *Pattern (P)* or *AntiPattern (A)*. Sometimes it helps to know that while playing.

As stated earlier, I will often use the scorecards supplied by the casinos when playing minibaccarat, but Figure 53 shows the customized scorecard as it was used for a brief session at Bally's in Atlantic City in November 1996. Notice that I parked at the Sands, a block away from Bally's.

The *P & A* boxes show the history of the table in terms of its recent trends, and aspire to keep you tuned to the *big picture*, but remember, not every table result is a *P* or *A*. A fair percentage will of course be *neutrals* (See Chapter 9). For the Figure 53 session, I did not utilize these columns because I was focusing primarily on *reoccurring singles* and *doubles*.

After paying the $15 commission and a $5 tip, my cashout was +$80 for 19 minutes of work. I left at that time because—try as I might—I wasn't getting any *'traction'* at that table.

Unless you really like these minibaccarat scorecards, you may be ahead to use the ones offered in the casinos for the time being. But someday you may appreciate this option ✠

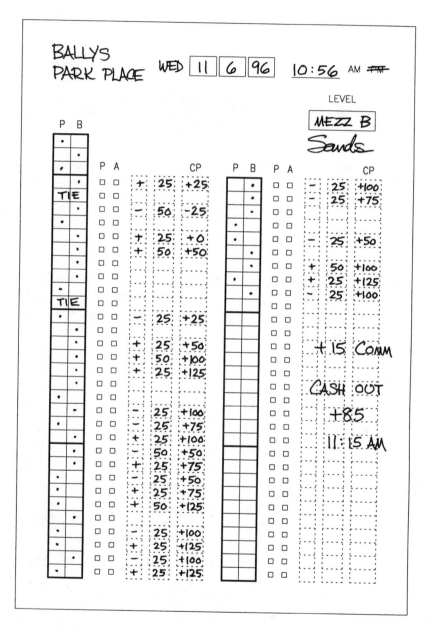

FIGURE 53
The MiniBaccarat Scorecard

THE STATISTICS
SCORECARD

Finally, we come to the *statistics scorecard,* which was first recommended on page 231, as a vehicle for tracking signature bets. Also, there are times when I like to know the scheme of things in terms of my overall win and loss ratios, and this is just the ticket for getting that information.

Figure 54 shows a completed *statistics scorecard.* The idea here is to review your primary scorecards and notate the wins and losses—on *this* scorecard—in the same order they occurred. This will help you keep tabs on that elusive *big picture.*

To illustrate, let's presume that you had been having rotten luck with your 2–1 bets, and had lost the last ten in a row. Well, if you play regularly, your deficit is accruing. If you continue to play, you're bound to hit a *compensatory* winning streak at some point, and you may be able to maximize that opportunity when it comes, *if you're waiting for it.* Now, don't be counting on the law of averages to set everything right before you bed down every night, but this data can provide valuable insights.

When I go on extended trips—especially overseas—I like to keep tabs on how I'm doing. If for some reason I'm getting caught in some snare whenever I visit French casinos, for example, I want to know about it. Recognizing the problem is halfway to solving it, as they say at *BP ProCare.*

The small *W* to the left of the dashed columns stands for *Wins,* and *L* signifies *Losses.* Since 1–1 and 2–1 bets are staples for me, they have permanent places in the boxes at the left. The remaining boxes can be filled in to suit the need ✠

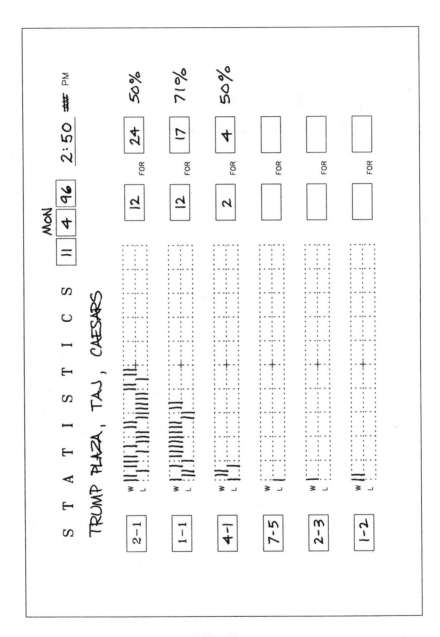

FIGURE 54
The Statistics Scorecard

SUMMARY OF
GAMING SCORECARDS

The official position of this manual is that without scorecards to assist you, you're subjecting yourself to unnecessary hardships. With them, table trends leap from the page and head straight for your pocketbook. With them, your performance at the tables is a matter of record that can be evaluated at your leisure. With them, you're cruising around in a sleek, new Jaguar XK8 while the rest of the world is peddling a trike.

All four scorecards are designed for a finished size of 4" x 6", which is non-intrusive and inconspicuous, yet large enough to hold a generous amount of data. To make them even more efficient, it is recommended that you have the different types printed in different (pastel) colors, so you can find each one quickly. The color scheme I use is as follows:

Craps: *White* (plain copy bond)
Roulette: *Lavender* or *Grey*
Minibaccarat: *Coral Reef* (peach)
Statistics: *Sea Spray* (light blue)

These paper grades are (or should be) available at *Kinko's Copies,* which is a national photocopy/office services chain. Some of these are a bit pricey (being resume quality), but I think it's well worth it to help keep these 'betting aids' organized while you're in the casinos and at home.

When you get these printed up, it wouldn't hurt to tell the printer that you'd like all four groups to be trimmed to the exact same size. (Makes them easier to carry.)

The strength in these scorecards lies in the permanence of the data they record, their portability, and their versatility. For virtually any betting scheme you wish to employ, there is a scorecard that's suitable for that application.

There are times when it is advantageous for you and your partner to keep separate records of the same game, so it might be a good idea to carry extras. As an example, I sometimes keep track of the *procedural bets* (for a chosen strategy), while my assistant or partner records *auxiliary bets* on a separate scorecard. This is not a bad idea.

To recap the four scorecard types:

The ***Craps Scorecard*** gives you an overview of table trends, line bet direction and how you're doing monetarily. Unlike other players at the table, you have all the pertinent data about what the table *and you* are doing, at your fingertips.

The ***Roulette Scorecard*** is the Maserati of the bunch, but you need something extra to offset the high vig that accompanies the game of roulette. This scorecard design rises admirably to the occasion.

The ***Minibaccarat Scorecard*** is only marginally more efficient than those supplied at the tables. Still, you might decide that it's worth its weight for the *consistency* it provides, as Player is always on the left, and Bank on the right.

The ***Statistics Scorecard*** gives you a sense of perspective in terms of the collective betting activities. Are you holding your own or underperforming? This scorecard offers unique insights into the history of your performance.

Together, these scorecards help you organize the table data. In the movie *Wall Street*, Michael Douglas had it right when he said that *"Information is a valuable commodity."* ✠

17

THE PSYCHOLOGY OF PROFESSIONAL PLAY

This is the chapter that takes you into the mindset of those who specialize in table game play. How do they do what they do? How do they look at life? What are they like? *What is it they know that gives them their edge?* ✠

SEEING THE BIG PICTURE

Sometimes you have to look back in order to move forward.

—from *Star Trek Voyager*

All of the successful table game specialists I've known have three things in common:

1) They are very focused on their specific goal.
2) No one else is doing what they're doing.
3) They are always attuned to the *big picture*.

Which big picture?

Seeing the big picture is part perception, and part attitude. It's how you see the *games* you play, the *numbers* they generate, and the *statistics* spawned from those numbers. Sometimes, the difference between success and failure lies in how one perceives that endless string of table decisions.

Most players have little or no regard for the big picture when they're in a casino. They stroll up to a table, make their buy-in and take their best shot. Their goal is to catch a hot streak, get lucky, make some easy money. They aren't looking for the big picture and it never occurs to them to do so.

They don't see it. The casinos win.

Seeing the big picture *means visualizing all your sessions as part of a connected chain.* Information acquired from yesterday's session can help you gauge the odds of the bet you're contemplating today. This, in fact, is the whole point of the *statistics scorecard*, of which you've just learned.

Seeing the big picture *means not obsessing over the vigorish of a bet when table evidence overwhelmingly favors the occurrence.* Occasionally, at racetracks *and* casinos, a 4–1 bet is more sure than one paying even money. Are you gonna pass on a bargain like that? If you've spotted a winner, *go for it!*

The trick, is to listen to what's in your head:

Hmmm, I haven't seen back-to-back sevens for a long time. Hmmm, 00 doesn't seem to be hitting today.

When things you normally anticipate don't occur on schedule, make a mental note. The stage is being set. The odds are changing. You can benefit from this.

In your daily routine, your objectives are really no different from that of any other professional working in the field of finance. Just like them, you're turning over money, using your expertise to seek a profit as you do so. Your job is harder, because you're much closer to the firing line. . .but just like them, you must always keep the big picture in your sights ✠

NICKEL MIDNIGHT

Like an athlete who can smell victory, he pays no heed to the
punishment he absorbs.

—Margaret A. McGurk,
reviewing *Donnie Brasco*

There was not even six inches between me and the player to
my right, but the young African American insisted on squeezing in.
My neighbor didn't complain, so I also let it go. The new player
stood there fidgeting with a bunch of reds and greens in his hand.
Then he spied my scorecard.

"Any twos come up lately?"

Looking at my card, I responded, *"Yeah, there was one just*
three rolls back."

"What about twelves? You seen any twelves come up in the
last forty rolls?"

Again I checked the card and saw none since beginning the
sheet, nearly forty rolls back. I told him so.

Immediately, he pulled a nickel from his hand and tossed it
toward the stickman. *"Nickel midnight,"* he said.

His one-roller on the twelve did not win. He repeated the bet,
again and again, taking no heed to his losses. Finally he won, eleven
rolls into the bargain.

"One forty-five and down; move it to the two," he said. The
stickman moved his nickel to the 2, and the dealer put $145 in chips
on the layout in front of him.

Five rolls later he won another $145 on the 2.

"Move it to the 12?" asked the stickman. He nodded.

After losing the next twenty rolls—during which time two 2*s* came up (but no 12*s*)—he left the table. The tally was two wins and thirty-five losses against a longshot that paid 29–1, for a net gain of $115 in about thirty minutes. But had he quit after the second win, his profit would have been $215.

He fit the description noted on page 261: focused on his goal, doing something different, tuned in to the big picture.

I had often considered going after the 2 or 12, but wasn't sure how to proceed. Witnessing his betting scheme opened my eyes. The dude had put some thought into it, and made some choices. Then he had the guts to follow through on his plan.

Up to that time, what kept *me* away from chasing longshots like that was intimidation. I thought I'd be a nuisance with my bet requests every five or ten seconds. I thought I'd look like a fool when I kept losing and losing.

It's not like that at all. The stickman is there to help you. After *Nickel Midnight* had placed his second consecutive bet, the stickman was there with his hand out, waiting to catch the chip for the next one. The bettor didn't have to say a word; the repeating bet was understood. And another thing: he sure didn't look like a fool when he got paid $145 for his $5 bet.

Seeing the big picture means seeing beyond the rain. Putting some trust in the fact that the oasis is out there. Visualizing victory in spite of the long odds.

Is this strategy viable? That's for you to decide. I don't play it, but I think it could work. If you try something like this, though, the most important things to consider are your win and loss limits. You can't go out there and bet upward to infinity, because some tables won't cooperate with the procedure. If the dude had set a win goal of *two* wins, he'd have done much better, but doing so may have hurt him in a previous session.

Who can say?

Seeing the big picture means looking at the whole instead of the fragments. Use your imagination, be creative, and never forget that *eventually,* every dog has his day ✠

THE PROFESSIONAL'S OUTLOOK

To whatever extent possible, a seasoned professional places his bets when the conditions for winning are ideal. But. . .how does one do that? How can anyone anticipate a table game decision with any degree of certainty?

If you've been paying attention, you should have some idea how it's done. For example:

After a shooter rolls three (or more) come-out sevens, the hot tip is to lay the point.

If you've just arrived at a minibaccarat table and everyone is betting Player, only an idiot would bet Bank.

When 00 has won two of the last seven spins, don't even think about a large outside bet without hedging the zeroes.

If the dealer at your blackjack table is hot, don't expect that to change anytime soon.

After conceiving the *Sister System,* I tested it with live bets, and bombed out **Big**. Why? I forgot to confirm the *presence of that trend.* Before betting on that expectation, I should have waited until seeing **at least one** would-be win.

You wouldn't spend a whole morning fishing in a lake that wasn't stocked, would you? Well, don't set your sights on a target *whose existence has not been confirmed.*

Having the discipline to await the right table conditions is what separates the amateurs from the pros ✠

BATTLING BACK

Above all, challenge yourself. You may well be surprised at what strengths you have, what you can accomplish.

—Cecil M. Springer

If I was called upon to name *one* reason for my longevity in this field, it would most definitely be my talent for *battling back*. That is, my ability to salvage a losing session.

Very seldom do I hit a winning streak right off the bat, which means that most of the time, I start out in the hole. And when that happens, I pretty much forget about trying to win. All my thoughts are focused on *getting back to zero*.

Accomplishing this is never easy. You lose $200 in just fifteen minutes, and now you're going to have to spend the next hour and a half getting it back. When you succeed in doing that, *then* you can start thinking about looking for ways to win.

Perhaps it will work out differently for you, but as I see it, the only way you're going to have a chance to make it in this field is to specialize in *battling back*. Learn how to dig yourself out of a hole. Squeeze out a win against the odds. Defy Mother Nature, gravity, and all the laws of physics.

Hey, you can do it. It's not easy, but it's doable. All you need do is remember the lesson from way back on page 8:

*Before you can learn to win, you must learn how to **not lose**.*

In this line of work, there is no greater truth ✠

FOURTEEN QUESTIONS

One thing that frustrated me in my early years of gambling was the inability to find answers to the questions—*about professional gamblers*—that I wanted to know most of all. And while there is certainly no shortage of books that talk about gambling *today,* none of them venture to take you *inside the head* of a real professional. This section is an attempt to supply those answers:

What did it take to succeed?
How hard was it to get there?
Did it change your perspective in life?
What strategies work best for you?
How many hours a day do you work?
How many days a week?
Has your career helped or hurt romance?
How do you maintain your discipline?
What do you do on your days off?
What was your biggest win?
Your biggest loss?
How often do you have a losing day?
Do you regret choosing that career?
What's it like to live that life?

These are the questions that mattered to me. I'll be speaking for myself, of course, but I'd be willing to bet that somewhere in here, you're going to learn something ✠

What did it take to succeed? Many, many false starts, expensive mistakes, elaborate gimmicks, patchwork solutions, blue summers, black winters, unbearable pain, calamity, insanity and sheer amazement, the good, bad and ugly, the agony and ecstasy, blood, sweat & tears, conspiring with the angels, dancing with the devil and shooting for the moon.

And the second week was even tougher.

Mastering the discipline is the key, but *that's* like participating in a twisted experiment of some angst-ridden, demented little caesar who dwells in a dark castle far away from probing eyes.

Please bear in mind, readers, that the point of saying these things is to help *you* avoid the same runaround that I went through. I've laid out the path for you. All you have to do is follow the rules and stay focused on your objectives. You and your associate will, together, keep each other on the path.

How hard was it to get there? You know the saying, *One step forward, twelve steps back?*

In bookstores, you can find books where people *claim* to have had terrific success playing a certain system for twenty years, as if saying it proved the point. That's not the way it is at all. The pros don't just *arrive*, then exist in that plane forever. It's an up and down thing. At times they lose their bankroll, and when they do, they're dead in the water.

Yeah, I know. You've seen *Maverick*, about the gambler who had no difficulty raising $50,000 to enter a poker contest for a goof. And that was way back in the 1800*s* when that amount was worth *five million* in today's dollars. And you may have seen other shows with similar storylines.

Therefore, all professional gamblers *today* must have a lear jet, a fleet of limos, a private island in the Bahamas, a castle in France and a harem of lusty mistresses. *Right.*

Truth: some of the pros I know are just getting by. For me, reaching (and remaining at) the professional level was assuredly the toughest thing I've ever done.

Did it change your perspective in life? You might say that, for I seem to have picked up the habit of assigning *odds* to just about everything:

I'm gonna be pretty busy that day. There's only about a fifteen percent chance I can make it.

Just thought you should know, there's a 100% chance that I'm not going to wear it.

Seven to two I finish before you.

But that's *me*. Might not happen to you.

What strategies work best for you? At craps, my favorites are the *Sister System, Selective Shooter, Line Betting* and the *Two-Number Don't*. At roulette, I like the *Angel & Sledge, Fixed Splits* and the *Favored Five*. At miniB, I keep my sessions short, like the *settle-for-small-gains approach* shown in Chapter 11. But I hate to single out procedures, as if at the expense of others. A lot depends on what's working that day.

For example, if I start out the day at the roulette tables and they're all timed to explode in my face, I switch gears and put my focus on craps. And vice versa. That's why most pros specialize in more than one game. If one is beating you up, you can often get a reprieve from the other.

How many hours a day do you work? This of course depends on where I am and what I'm doing. Two or three hours is generally my limit, but I have been known to put in a few six- and seven-hour days when pursuing an ambitious income goal. But I *never* do that in a single shift.

How many days a week? Again, it depends. Since I don't really enjoy gambling, it is often difficult for me to push myself to do so unless I have a specific need. That need often derives from my writing.

When in a money-raising mode, I work seven days a week. But remember, that's only for a few hours a day.

Has your career helped or hurt romance?
As a rule, women don't like gamblers, but that's because 99% of all gamblers are losers. As this book tries to point out, this doesn't have to be the case, but until you're winning consistently, my guess is that it's going to hurt you.

How do you maintain your discipline? When I enter a casino, I acknowledge that I'm entering the piranha tank. Then I glance at my elbow to see if the flesh is still there. I do this to remind myself of the difficulties I face.

In Chapter 11, *The Reality Check* offers some input on how to maintain the right mental attitude, like reminding yourself what's at stake. Life as a pawn in someone else's game, or the realization of all your dreams? Which do you prefer?

Another way to keep things in perspective is to think about what you're doing in terms of the hourly rate you're pulling down. $50 or $100 an hour (though modest in gambling terms) is not too shabby when compared against business salaries.

Remember above all, *life turns on a dime.* So does *discipline.* Sometimes the littlest things mean so much. Mistakes will be made, but swallow the loss and move on.

How do I maintain my discipline? Any which way I can. It's a never-ending dance to the sweet and bitter end.

What do you do on your days off? Depends on where I am. If I'm in Las Vegas, I might go to Hoover Dam, or Lake Mead, or Mt. Charleston. In Lake Tahoe, I might settle for a drive around the lake. In Atlantic City, sometimes I hang out with the fishermen in Brigantine, or go to the beach. In the Bahamas I sail, or do the tourist thing. In France I like to tour the countryside in a rental, then maybe cross the border into Italy to check out the Dolomitic Alps, or Venice, or Rome.

What was your biggest win? $2140, made at a hot craps table at the Flamingo Hilton in 1993.

Your biggest loss? $2700, in a three-hour period in Atlantic City. But the memory of that loss served as a powerful incentive to avoid that mistake in the future.

How often do you have a losing day? On a good week, about once every two weeks. When it *does* happen, I make it a point to watch myself more carefully during subsequent sessions, in an effort to avoid compounding the damage. I never know if—somewhere deep inside—I might still be reacting to the loss in a way that could do further harm.

When the losses come, you have to take them in stride. If I sense that my mood is compromised, I try to avoid gambling until my disposition improves.

Do you regret choosing that career? I think of myself as a writer more than a gambler. And it is my opinion that you're better off choosing something else for your livelihood. Nobody in their right mind would want to do this their whole life! It's fine for *raising money,* but having done so, focus your energy on something meaningful. As Martin Sheen said to his son in the movie Wall Street: *"Build something; create. . .instead of living off the buying and selling of others."*

Personally, I have no regrets about my involvement in this field, for it has certainly made life more interesting. As I see it, this is the path that was intended for me. But clearly, man was not meant to live this way for extended periods of time. If you don't understand this now, I think you'll know what I mean after you spend some time in the trenches.

What's it like to live that life? Indescribable. And yet, I am going to try to describe it in the following subchapter, entitled *A Day In The Life.*

I'm not going to be able to cover *every* little detail—else I wouldn't hold your interest, but I think this will help you form a picture of the way it is, or can be ✠

A DAY IN THE LIFE

I read the news today, oh boy. . .about a lucky man who made the grade. . .

—John Lennon, from
A Day In The Life

I open my eyes and look to the left. The digital clock on the dresser says 9:06. I raise my head and turn to the right. Outside the window I see the boardwalk, and beyond that the Atlantic Ocean. It's a beautiful fall day.

It's my eighth day in Atlantic City. From my bed, I grab a 3x5 index card and look at it:

			(CUMULATIVE)
MON	9–5	+140	+140
TUE	9–6	+442	+582
WED	9–7	+464	+1046
THU	9–8	+204	+1250
FRI	9–9	+514	+1764
SAT	9–10	+360	+2124
SUN	9–11	+190	+2314

Average Daily Win: $330

Today is the 12th of September, the first day of my second week in Atlantic City. My first week's earnings reflect that I had had a fairly good week. I'll go out again today, but not tomorrow. I don't usually gamble on the 13th.

After cleaning up, I put on my jeans and one of my two-pocket shirts. The latter is a must: I use the pockets for scorecards, notes, chewing gum, whatever. This keeps my hands free.

Every morning I go out and purchase my copy of *The Press* (Atlantic City's newspaper) from a machine. Doing so gives me a chance to get a little exercise and take in the boardwalk ambience. On this morning, however, I had to go five blocks before coming to a machine that wasn't sold out.

At 10:00 I'm having a $3.95 breakfast in one of those dives right on the boardwalk. For a few bucks more, I could have had a fantastic meal at the Showboat or Resorts buffet, but some days I like to keep things simple.

10:30 am: I'm back in my hotel room, sitting on the bed and clipping out newspaper articles about casinos. I prefer not to play on a full stomach, so I take my time reading the paper. Since my partner is in Canada, I'm solo this week.

11:15 am: I'm on my way out the door once again. I picked the Sands as my starting point for the day. Upon arrival, I see that only two craps tables are active, and there's no room at either one. I'm on my way out when I happen to notice someone walking away —which provides an opening.

"Change only," I say to the dealer as I lay three bills on the table, *"no action in the come."* I put the chips in my rack and write down the casino, the time and the date on my scorecard, then I take a moment to check out the players.

"How's the table running?" I ask the gentleman to my left, an older man with thick white hair. He had about $60 in his tray and a $5 pass line bet with double odds.

He glances at me and grunts, *"Cold."*

"Seven-out, line away, Eight was," announces the stickman as the dealers scoop up the losing bets.

After watching another line decision, I decide on my strategy: the *Sister System* for my primary bets and the *Two-Number Don't* for my secondaries.

After about thirty minutes, I left the table and collected my $120 profit at the cashier window. Then I took a seat at one of the console slot machines next to the cashier and completed filling out my scorecard.

I glance at my watch as I attempt to get past all the *waddlers* (obese, middle-aged ladies who exist solely to obstruct casino foot traffic) near the front entrance, and finally break free. It is 12:10. Outside, I cross the street and enter the Claridge.

I get a drink of water and then check out the gaming area. Immediately my attention is drawn to a craps table in the center of the room, where the players are excited. To someone like myself, it sounded like an *opportunity*.

To my delight, I learn the point is 4. There's no time to lose. I peel a bill from the wad of money in my hip pocket, then pull a five out of my wallet. Squeezing in, I wait for an appropriate moment, then lay the $105 on the table and say, *"Buy the point for $100."* The dealer converts my money to four greens (which he puts inside the *"4"* box) and one red, which is used to pay the commission. Then the boxman passes a *buy* button to the dealer, who sets it atop the stack of greens.

Within ninety seconds the shooter makes the point, and my $100 *buy* bet wins $200. *"Take down my buy,"* I tell the dealer, and he pushes twelve greens in front of me. As I start to head for the cashier, I notice that the boxman *(who for some reason was wearing a college varsity sweater)* is watching me like a hawk. Very odd. They don't usually (seem to) pay much attention to me on those occasions that I make a *Random Buy*.

After getting my money from the cashier, I take a seat at a slot machine on the south wall and update my daily earnings record: $315 profit, and it's 12:21 pm. It is just a little more than an hour from the time my workday began.

Outside, I continue my southward trek and head for Bally's Park Place, just across the street. After giving a buck to one of the panhandlers, I enter through the side door and take the escalator up to the casino.

Three craps tables are open: a $5 and a $10 table that are filled with players, and a $25 table where the crew waits for a customer. There's no room at the two active tables, and I'm not in the mood to warm up the high-minimum table.

Walking past the minibaccarat area, I'm little surprised to see that every seat is filled at both active tables. Looks like some Asians who may have been traveling together, perhaps on a junket. They seem to be enjoying themselves. I didn't bother to check out the roulette. At the time, I was seeking a good game of craps, and it was not to be found at Bally's.

I leave Bally's through the boardwalk entrance and make my way toward Caesars. It's a hot September day, and the beach is packed with sunbathers. Seagulls and terns fly overhead making their bird sounds as I weave through the vacationers mingling about. Not a moment too soon I arrive at the air-conditioned comfort of Caesars. I go through the first set of doors, past the guard and then through the second doorway.

I need a drink of water. That's one thing you should know about all the moving about you're likely to do: sometimes you're never in one place long enough to cop a free drink. Not that they were ever free for me anyway. I never let my server leave with less than a dollar gaming token for a tip.

It's 1:37 pm, and I have just made another $114 playing the *Sister System* at a table (at Caesars) that was fairly cooperative. I'm now $429 ahead and done (working) for the day. I head up to the Ocean One Pier, across the boardwalk from Caesars, and make a beeline for *Gourmet Burger,* where I get a cheesburger platter with extra cheddar. After finishing that, I go to the French bakery on the other side of the food court and get a palm cake.

My original plan was to go to Trump Plaza after Caesars, but since I had reached my daily win goal, I decide instead to rent a rolling chair to take me back to my hotel.

After taking a nap and watching some TV, I meet a friend in Brigantine, and later we have dinner at the Showboat.

A day in the life ✠

FINDING A WAY TO WIN

It was Tuesday, January 28, 1997, and my associate Sharon and I were nearing our win goal. All we needed to win was another $125 to reach our objective of $400.

The roulette tables had been kinder to us than the craps, so we were on our way to take advantage of that when we stopped for a moment at a craps table we had visited earlier. I started to move away, but Sharon grabbed my arm.

"That's the same shooter that had that good roll when we were here before," she exclaimed.

"You're right," I replied. *"Do you think he'll do it again?"* That turned out to be a rhetorical question, though it took a moment for me to realize it. I pulled some quarters out of my pocket and placed them on the layout, telling the dealer *"$110 Inside, please."* But it wasn't in time to catch the win as the shooter made the point (8) in the same stroke. It was now a new come-out, so I dropped a green on the pass line and then tossed a nickel to the stickman, saying, *"Five dollars Any Craps, please."* The shooter rolled a 10, which was unfortunate. That's the point number that tripped him up and ended his shoot last time. Still, I figured he'd be good for the old *three hits and down* before sevening out. His next roll was a 6, and I collected $35. Then came a 9 and I won $35 again. After that he rolled an 8, good for another $35. Then one of the dies went off the table.

That's okay. I had already taken my place bets down. I stood there, watching my pass line bet (with no odds), lying there like a sitting duck. The shooter rolled a 4, then sevened out. My net gain was $75, still $50 shy of our goal.

We went to a roulette table. It looked ripe for a *Sledge* bet, so I put down four quarters, plus a nickel hedge on the 0-00 *split*. Along comes a 6. Bummer. A $105 loss, right off the bat. Welllll, maybe I can get a reprieve from an *Angel*. I put a quarter on the first and last sixlines, forgoing the hedge this time. Up comes 35, a winner. That put me even with the roulette table (except for the $5 hedge). I followed up with the *Vagabond Sledge, Version B*, and won $45 when number 7 won.

At that point we were $40 ahead at that table, and just $10 away from our win goal. I was wondering if I should invoke the *Settle For 90* rule, when I glanced at the scoresign and realized that the table was showing signs of a classic *Reoccurring Single*. I put a quarter on black and won when the 13 came up. Having reached our objective, we left the casino.

To reach that goal, we played, in a 20-minute period:

1) *Pass line at craps with an Any Craps hedge.*
2) *$110 Inside at craps.*
3) *The sledgehammer at roulette with a 0-00 hedge.*
4) *The angel at roulette, unhedged.*
5) *The sledgehammer, version B, with a 0-00 hedge, and*
6) *A reoccurring single roulette bet, on black.*

This is called *finding a way to win.* This is how it's done. Every day, you have a new war to fight. Every day, you need a new set of tactics. You've got to kick and scratch and claw your way to every shred of profit you get.

Stay focused.

Dance the dance.

Gamble To Win ✠

PART III

PUTTING IT ALL TOGETHER

18

GETTING STARTED

Go slow, and expect setbacks.

—Paul Reiser, from
Mad About You

In many types of business enterprises, *getting started* is often the biggest hurdle to overcome. This is especially true in the field of professional gambling.

One such hurdle is the fact that you have not yet built up a monetary reserve, but this is not something money alone can solve. Even if you can *get* the money, it wasn't *won money*. It is more dear to you, for you know how hard you worked to get it, and you haven't the confidence that comes from knowing that you got it by beating the casinos.

Because of this, you have to do things differently on the front end than you would once you had found your stride. You are not immune to losses caused by flukes. They're going to hurt you, and could cause you to change your game plan.

The best way to prepare yourself for your debut on the grand casino stage is to practice with your partner, over and over again, all the bets and moves you expect to be making when you finally do make it to a casino.

After printing up your scorecards, get yourself a roulette and craps layout at a gaming supplies store (or make your own) and play, play, play. Record each result as you would in a casino and practice until you think you've mastered the moves. And remember, whatever speed at which you choose to play (at home) will probably be exceeded in a live situation.

When your (artificial) gaming table produces patterns that cause losses, quit—just as you would in real life. Move away from the table and spend a few minutes doing something else. When you do return, resume play with a fresh buy-in, and if you're playing craps, a fresh pair of dice as well.

Is it necessary to use fresh dice after a 'losing' session? Is it necessary to take a break? Yes & yes. To be truly prepared, you need to go through the motions as you would in real life. If putting out that effort is too much for you, then it's time to acknowledge that a career in gaming is not for you.

When you do make it to a casino, your focus should be on what you can learn from the experience more than how much you can make. Also, keep your visit short (no more than 2 hours), and don't plan on going back for a few days. You need to take some time to analyze the results, rate the performance of your strategy, and evaluate *your own* performance.

Accept the fact that mistakes will be made. Try to uncover the reasons they occurred, and think about how you might avoid them in the future. But after you've mastered *those* mistakes, be assured that new ones will move to the front.

Acclimating yourself to your new career will be an ongoing process of making isolated visits to casinos, then returning home to make an assessment of that experience. Little by little, you will start getting to know the wily ways of the beast. At some point you will feel ready to take him on, one on one. Your bets will then be larger, and you'll be more aggressive than before.

What you have to do will take time. As George Harrison said in his song, *Set On You:*

It's gonna take time; a whole lot of patience and time ✠

THE THREE TASKS

Don't let what you can't do interfere with what you can.

—John Wooden

It would be great if you could go on out there and make six figures a year immediately, but clearly, that's not going to happen. First, you must prove yourself worthy by completing your initiation into this profession. And there's only one way to accomplish that. You must perform *The Three Tasks:*

1) *Successful* completion of the tests in Chapter 19.
2) *Successful* completion of the exercises in Chapter 20, and
3) Building your own bankroll, as shown in *this* chapter.

Why do I put you through all this? For your own protection more than anything else. To do otherwise would be irresponsible on my part, for there's a *universe* of things that can go wrong in your quest to beat the casinos at the games *they've* been using to beat *millions* of players, for *hundreds* of years.

You *know* that's not going to be easy, don't you?

The first two of *The Three Tasks* are ahead in this book, so you should not be concerned with them until you get there. But the third one is in this chapter, and it's the most important one of all. This one will save you from *gambling away a fortune*, because you must *earn* the right to continue the quest. Someday, you just might appreciate how much that's worth ✠

BUILDING A BANKROLL I
THE FOUR STAGES

Develop a PHD attitude: Poor, Hungry and Driven; the kind of attitude that will drive you to learn more and be better.

—Rick Pitino, From
Success Is A Choice

After you have successfully completed the exercises and tests in chapters 19 and 20, you will be free to undertake the daunting task of *building a bankroll.* Be forewarned, though: this is a project that has to take place in stages.

How many stages? Probably four or more, depending on the *income goals* you set for yourself. At the first stage, you will try to make $50 a day (average) for fifteen days. For this, you will have a daily loss limit of $125, derived from a $1250 fund that has been set up as your operating bankroll. If you lose your $1250, you must stop what you're doing, read this book again, and after waiting 30 days you may try once more. Should you exhaust your bankroll *again,* it is the recommendation of this book that you STOP and admit that you are not suited for this career. And please be advised, *any gambling that falls outside the scope of the recommendations of this book is strictly your responsibility.*

Sorry, but making a living playing casino games is a serious, dangerous business. If you get off to such a bad start, you're going to have to book passage on the *reality express* before you blow a ton of money, and then come looking to hold someone liable, in a court of law, *for **your** lack of discipline!*

Remember, the casinos are masters of illusion. They can make you think you're winning while they siphon the money right out of your pocket, all day long. If you choose to play this perilous game, you'd better have some *protection*.

What I've just described, however, is the worst-case scenario. If you apply yourself and really *try* to stick to the rules, it would be, well, *impossible* for you to lose your daily loss limit *twenty times,* without showing *any* income at all.

See what I'm saying?

The stages of *Building A Bankroll* are as follows:

BUILDING A BANKROLL PARAMETERS

STAGE ONE

DAILY WIN GOAL: *$50*
DAILY LOSS LIMIT: *$125*
TOTAL WIN GOAL: *$750* *(Fifteen winning sessions of $50 each)*
   NOTE: *When reaching Total Win Goal, proceed to Stage Two*

STAGE TWO

DAILY WIN GOAL: *$75*
DAILY LOSS LIMIT: *$175*
TOTAL WIN GOAL: *$1125* *(Fifteen winning sessions of $75 each)*
   NOTE: *When reaching Total Win Goal, proceed to Stage Three*

STAGE THREE

DAILY WIN GOAL: *$100*
DAILY LOSS LIMIT: *$250*
TOTAL WIN GOAL: *$1500* *(Fifteen winning sessions of $100 each)*
   NOTE: *When reaching Total Win Goal, proceed to Stage Four*

STAGE FOUR

All parameters to be of the player's choosing, though
they should conform to the *proportions* shown above.

FIGURE 55
The Stages of Building A Bankroll

Now, let's review the parameters of Figure 55. You start out with a bankroll of $1250, which fund your *efforts* to earn $50 a day. Once you have made the $50, stop. Under no circumstances should you try to earn more *in the course of that day*. Doing it this way will accustom you to the regimen.

As you attempt to build your bankroll, there will be days when when you find yourself deep in a hole. While you're in *Stage One,* you must be sure not to let yourself lose more than $125 per day. If this means carrying only $125 plus expenses each day (to ensure compliance), then by all means do so.

As you gain experience, you will learn to quit *before* reaching your $125 loss limit, because things aren't going well and you'll have the good sense to quit. You'll do this because you know that it takes roughly *three* winning days to compensate *one* losing day, and you'll do anything to mitigate the burden.

It may be a long, long time before you can exit the first stage and go for larger gains, but you must stick to the program. This is the only way. If you do make it to *Stage Two,* the $750 you earned pushed your bankroll to $2250, which is more than enough to cover ten $175 losses as you seek earnings of $75 a day. And if you make it to *Stage Three,* your earnings will enable you to afford the higher loss-limit-fund that's necessary at that level.

At the end of the three stages, you should have earned $3325, which will allow you to return your original bankroll of $1250 to the bank, or wherever you'd like. It is recommended that you continue playing at the *Stage Three* level ($100/day) until you have earned at least $10,000. Believe me, maintaining your hold on that level of earnings is tougher than one might imagine.

Whenever you fail at any stage, you are more or less demoted to the previous stage, where you work your way back up, as before. What this does is *pace* the activity, to keep you from losing too much, too soon.

Stage Four should be self-explanatory. Increase your income goals gradually as your bankroll and abilities grow, using the same formula you utilized to get there ✠

BUILDING A BANKROLL II
THE FIVE RULES

Success seems to be largely a matter of hanging on after the others have let go.

—William Feather

In the previous subchapter we established the operating range for building your bankroll: to start out, a win goal of $50 a day with a daily loss limit of $125, which is to come from a $1250 bankroll. These amounts should help one stay out of trouble, by limiting his playing time.

The *bankroll building phase* follows the *introductory phase* (described on page 282), where you make isolated forays to the casinos to acclimate yourself to live gaming. Throughout all your visits to casinos, however, there are some operating guidelines that you must try to keep in mind:

RULE 1: *When the tables give you a hard time, settle for whatever you can get.* Don't fight too hard, because you are not (yet) a good match for such a wily adversary. Think of yourself as a thief, stealing valuables from the dragon's lair. Be thankful you got out of there alive.

RULE 2: *Your goals are modest. You're not seeking a big score.* Starting out, all you're going to do is test the water with a few $5 bets to see if you can get a nibble. If every chip you toss out sinks straight to the bottom, this is not a good sign. Pull up your stakes and move to another table.

What you're attempting to do is like jumping onto a speeding train. At first, all you seek is to hang on and keep up with the flow of things. When you start getting consistent returns, you'll know you're keeping pace with the table, for the moment. From there, try to get a feel for its direction and destination.

RULE 3: *When a well-defined trend presents itself, move in slowly for the kill.* This is why you came: to catch the table whose trend is so pitifully obvious. A craps table where some lucky shooter rolls forty-five numbers, or one where ten consecutive shooters seven out. Either one is a gold mine to a seasoned player. When you find such a gem, start out conservatively, then use your winnings to finance bet increases.

RULE 4: *When that inevitable losing jag arrives, don't let yourself be swayed by other temptations.* If you're not doing well at craps, try roulette or minibaccarat (as long as you don't exceed your loss limit). If that doesn't help, stop and acknowledge that this just isn't your day to win. Hey, we all have days like that. But most important, *don't* use your losses as an excuse to head for the blackjack tables (for example), because you were desperate to find a game *where you could win.*

RULE 5: *Remember, if you maintain your discipline, you cannot fail in the long run.* This is really all it comes down to: *Can you hang onto your discipline?* If you can, you will succeed. If you don't, you'll fail. That's it.

What this means, in specific terms, is that you must never lose your cool. Never respond to the anger you may feel. And never think you're unbeatable. Hold back when you're losing; press your advantage when you're winning.

Well, there they are. The five rules. This isn't *everything* you need to know to succeed, but if you're able to remember these five, you'll be way ahead of the pack ✠

BUILDING A BANKROLL III
EIGHT DAYS OF EVIDENCE

We strain hardest for things which are almost but not quite within our reach.

—Frederick W. Faber

In trying to teach the art of building a bankroll, I put myself into the same situation I'd expect *you* to go through. The following notes show my progress at the $100/day level, which is *Stage Three*. This shows what *you* may be doing, except that you can stop for the day when you've earned *half* of what I had to earn (for as long as you remain in the first stage).

For these sessions, I opted to specialize in craps, with a little roulette added in. I don't apologize for my favoritism toward craps; it's the only game where tables have *temperature*.

DAY ONE: The first day, I chose Hyatt's Grand Victoria riverboat in southeastern Indiana as the destination, for it was the logical choice by virtue of its location and size. I took Diane, a friend of mine, to play the role of my *assistant-in-training*. She had been to a casino only three times in her life.

Having decided to try the *Selective Shooter* (with her and me as the lone shooters), our first task was to find a suitable table, but we found one without too much difficulty. The shooter (who was to my immediate right) rolled three numbers and then made the point, 9. He came out on a 9 again and rolled ten more numbers before sevening out.

The dice came to me and I rolled a come-out 7. Not the best sign, but, you never know. Then I rolled 5–6–7out.

Since I always start the day betting *right* (when playing *SS*), I was now $12 in the hole. The dice went to Diane, who came out on 6, rolled an 11, then made the point. At the new come-out she rolled another 6, and then 4–9–10–8–8–10–3–8–5–8–4–5–3–8–5–4 before making the 6 once again. For her third come-out she rolled a 5, then came right back with another 5.

On her fourth point attempt, she rolled a natural 7, a natural 11, then another 5. That was followed by all the four horn numbers (11–12–3–2), and finally, a seven-out. Bottom line? She rolled 31 numbers, and I had already surpassed my $100 win goal through pass line bets and placing some inside numbers. We exited the boat one minute before it left the port (while still loading for the cruise). Our net gain was $110 in 19 minutes.

Some readers who are experienced craps players will surely accuse me of cheating to get that win. You see, legend has it that virgin shooters, especially women, *usually* have a good roll. There are exceptions to every rule, of course, but I admit that the very possibility was in the back of my mind.

Conversely, I stunk—as you saw—but that's the way it goes sometimes. Please be assured, being a pro is no guarantee that you can roll lots of numbers.

DAY TWO: Back at the Grand Vic (and again with Diane), I returned to the craps tables, but neither of us could get the kind of streak going that we capitalized on the day before. We decided to strap ourselves in and bet on the others at the table like everyone else, but after 40 minutes I was $91 in the hole. Feeling unlucky at craps, I ventured over to one of the roulette tables and played a few sledgehammers. I wasn't having an easy time there, either, though I did manage to win $12.

We then found a fresh craps table and started betting only on ourselves. Forty-two minutes later we left the table with a $100 profit. That put me just $21 ahead for the day, but it was time for me to quit. When the wins are *that* hard to come by, anything that even *resembles* a profit feels like a big score.

DAY THREE: It doesn't take a genius to make money at a hot table, so I won't dwell on the $145 that was made on the third day at the Grand Victoria.

DAY FOUR: On the fourth day, at the Argosy riverboat (a few miles upriver), the first table I hit was relentlessly choppy. Try as I might, I couldn't battle all the way out of the hole I'd dug. This happens about 70% of the time, and you find yourself asking, *What in the world am I doing here? How can I possibly expect to make a living doing this?*

Even after you've been playing as long as I have, this is what goes through your head. When these thoughts do start preying upon your mind, moving to another table is usually your best move. The difference can be like night and day.

After finding myself $125 in the hole, I walked to the table right next to the one I'd just come from, and asked an elderly man who was playing the back line if it was a cold table. *"You don't see many players here, do you?"* was his answer. Music to my ears. I started playing the don't.

The table was cold like he said, and it took me only 40 minutes to cash out with $308, made from the $75 I brought to the table. After tipping the crew $8, I left the casino with $100 profit.

DAY FIVE: On *Day Five*, I won $137 on the strength of my own shooting, plus that of a friend who I talked into joining me. The money was made in two brief sessions, where I was betting right and placing some numbers.

My first loss came on *Day Six*. After fighting the good fight, I ended up with a $131 loss. Could have been worse.

My profits for the seventh and eighth days were $93 and $60. Yes, it's true that I stopped before reaching my win goal, but I deferred to *Rule #1* from page 287, both days, which advises that you settle for whatever you can get when the going gets tough. Let me tell you, that is some good advice ✠

THE BUSINESS PLAN
THE SEVEN STAGES

Do it! Move it! Make it happen! No one ever sat their way to success.

—H. Jackson Browne, Sr.

How can a book on professional gambling be what it claims, you ask—when it's read by millions of people? Won't the casinos incorporate countermeasures?

I imagine they would, if this book offered a *one-size-fits-all* approach. . .but that's not the plan. The idea is to show you how to create a strategy that is customized to *your* needs. And to do that, you must put together a *Business Plan.*

In forming a business plan, your first task is to think about what you've learned about systems and procedures, and select one that you think you can stick to. That is the first of the seven stages, as noted below in Figure 56:

1) **The Selection Stage** *(Where you choose a strategy)*
2) **The Collection Stage** *(Building a databank of table data)*
3) **The Computation Stage** *(Performing trials on paper)*
4) **The Rehearsal Stage** *(Practice sessions with a partner)*
5) **The Live Trial Stage** *(Limited casino play at low levels)*
6) **The Evaluation Stage** *(Analysis of that performance)*
7) **The Live Betting Stage** *(Live gaming sessions in a casino)*

FIGURE 56
The Seven Stages of the
Business Plan

THE SEVEN STAGES:

1) *The Selection Stage:* First, you need to select a procedure or strategy that you think you can handle. In doing so, ask yourself what appeals to you. Do you think you'd prefer playing favorites, where you win often but at a meager price? Or, maybe you'd like to become a longshot specialist. Try to pick something at which you think you could excel.

Once you've settled on the type of bet return you'd prefer, your next step is to choose one of the three recommended games (craps, roulette and minibaccarat) as your dominant. Keep in mind that there may be limitations in your situation that could hinder your ability to specialize in your top choice. For example, that game may not be available in your area.

The following shows some procedural options:

CRAPS:

Basic Line/Odds Betting
The Sister System
The Two-Number Don't

The Selective Shooter
Closed Progressions
The Random 22

ROULETTE:

The Random Angel
Sledgehammer variations
Fixed Splits

The Favored Five
Chinese Roulette
Mixed Media

FIGURE 57
Gaming Options
For Craps And Roulette

For minibaccarat, there are less options because the game is so basic, but you could specialize in certain "P" patterns (like the P4s), saving your primary bets for when such patterns begin to emerge. Or, you might like to imitate my *settle-for-small-gains experiment*, playing basic *pattern* and *anti-pattern*.

Then there are strategies from other books, which you may find to be valid when squeezed through the *business plan* strainer. One that comes to mind is John Patrick's *Ricochet,* as shown in his book, *Advanced Craps.* Incidentally, I think his books would be the best source for *alternative* procedures.

2) **The Collection Stage:** At some point you will need to accumulate a databank of live table game results, so that you can perform trials on paper to validate or nullify the chosen strategies. Toward that end, *system tester* books are commercially available, but you must not rely on these exclusively. You need to mix in some *recent* results from the area where you plan to play. Reason? Trends are, by nature, complex and strange. Some appear to favor certain localities or timeframes. Your databank should be as *recent* and *accurate* as realistically possible.

Once you have accumulated data from perhaps 30 or 40 live gaming sessions, transfer the data to duplicate scorecards and make paste-ups on sheets of paper, then get several sets of copies of these scorecard groupings. This will allow you to *crunch the numbers* without tainting the original documentation.

3) **The Computation Stage.** After you get your scorecards printed up, fill them up with table data that you collected in casinos. Then you make a projection of the chosen strategy *against* those numbers, by playing a theoretical game. Cover the results and then expose the lines, one by one, *after* you've made your theoretical bet. Your mission is to find a procedure that makes money *on paper* the majority of the time.

In doing this, I must warn you against drawing a premature conclusion. You might find something that works (on paper) at 15 tables, and think you've struck gold. But if you check it against 15 more, you might find very different results.

And there's one more little catch. Never forget, that making money *on paper* is much easier than making it for real. This does, however, help you to see what to expect.

4) *The Rehearsal Stage.* When you feel you've locked onto something solid, you need to rehearse your act with your partner. Done properly, this will simulate live gaming conditions (in which you are compelled to make wagering choices against table decisions that are unknown in advance). For this, it wouldn't hurt to scramble the order of the scorecards to reduce the possibilty that you might have subconsciously memorized some of the sequences.

Be forewarned that any group of table game results will lose its effectiveness once you've been exposed to it X number of times. (You'll know the precise number when you get there).

When you can do nothing but win during these rehearsals, and it wasn't because you knew what was coming (from memorization), you'll be ready for stage 5.

5) *The Live Trial Stage.* This is where you get down in the trenches and do it—in a tentative sort of way. You'll be playing live table games in a casino, but your objective is the accumulation of information more than money. Specifically, you need to know how you perform in the midst of a live wagering situation, and how well your strategies are working.

6) *The Evaluation Stage.* Having jumped into the lion's den, you now need to stand back and look at what happened, from afar. Is your strategy holding up? If not, are the problems correctable? Are *you* holding up? Did you maintain your discipline throughout your experience? How do you feel about doing that for a living? Do you think you'll be able to stand it? These, and more, are the kinds of questions you'll need to address.

7) *The Live Betting Stage.* This is where it all leads. When you reach this stage, there are no more excuses and no more alibis. Your homework is done, and you're ready to go out there and kick some butt. Just remember, *anything can happen in the short run,* so don't let the tables deceive you into thinking that what you're doing is terrible, or terrific. Give it time ✠

THE NEED FOR A PARTNER

All great truths begin as blasphemies.

—Bernard Shaw

In Chapter 3, you were told that a partner or assistant was a prerequisite to success as a professional gambler. Now, the time has come for me to try to convince you that this is one of the greatest *truths* you'll find in this book.

When you're at the tables, there are a lot of questions going through your head. *What trend is dominating the table activity right now? Is it consistent with earlier trends? Is the table turning cold? Are you winning at that table? In general? How much are you ahead or behind?* These are just a few.

That's a lot of information to process. Do you think you can keep up with all that? Remember, you're a shark, trying to snatch the prize before the other sharks *get to you.* You've got to be faster and sharper than *they* are, every time.

This is one of many reasons you need a *presence* at your side. While you're in the trenches scrapping with the house, he can let you know when there's some late-breaking information (which you wouldn't have noticed in the heat of battle). He can keep an eye on you to make sure you don't forsake your discipline and blow a fortune in fifteen minutes. He will be your offensive and defensive coordinator, your protector, your guardian angel.

And when you've got company, you've got a *sounding board.* Someone to respond to observations that would've gone unspoken, and perceptions that wouldn't have come to light.

To make it happen, you **NEED** assistance ✠

FINDING AND TRAINING A PARTNER

There are only two ways I know to find a partner to assist you in the casinos: you could hire someone (through a newspaper ad), or recruit a friend. But you're certainly free to explore other ways, if you can think of any that'll work.

If at all possible, you would probably be ahead if you can take the *recruit-a-friend* route. That's what I did whenever I needed an assistant, though I admit that I never found that perfect association that men of business dream about. You know, like Elton John and Bernie Taupin, Rodgers and Hammerstein, or Bevis and Butthead. Still, the ones I found served the purpose.

The other route (hiring a stranger) can get pretty complicated, especially if you live in California. Bureaucrats seem to be very free in their use of red tape out there. Your best bet, I imagine, is to try to locate someone who will work part-time, on an informal basis. You may be able to sell him on the glamour aspect of having a job working in a casino.

However you choose to tackle the issue, you should probably supply your new associate with a copy of this book, and ask that he read it. That would represent *phase one* of his training period. When he gets past that, you should sit down with him and discuss the details of what will be expected, and what kind of compensation to which he may be entitled. Of course, you'll need to have put some thought into this, so you won't be at a loss to answer any questions he may have.

Phase one of the recruiting process should help you gauge the candidate's level of interest, which can make or break the hiring commitment on either side. If he likes what he reads (in *this* book), he is more likely to be flexible in his compensation requirements. And if he can't relate to this type of enterprise, that should become evident pretty quick. Then both sides can move on. My advice is: hold out for one who shows genuine interest, *without* showing signs of compulsive tendencies. What you *don't* need is someone who *can't wait* to *"get down and gamble!"*

If you are unable to finance the employment costs, you might have to hold out for someone who's willing to come in as a partner (as opposed to an assistant). In that case, each side is responsible for *half* of the total operating expenses, which wouldn't cost any more than going solo. Or you could form an *unequal partnership,* where one side does more or spends more in exchange for more authority or a greater share of the profits.

The one imperative in all this is: the chemistry has to be right. You must have a good rapport with your associate, and be able to communicate freely. Without that much (as a minimum), you're sailing a rudderless vessel. And I don't think that's going to take you very far.

In my experience, trying to keep a newly-hired assistant in line is like trying to rope four steers simultaneously. Remember, casino games move at a very fast pace. They're not going to stop the game just to wait for the two of you to catch up. So don't plan on making money while you're in the midst of the training period. An associate only becomes useful after you've gone through weeks, or months, of training and experience in the field.

Please don't be discouraged by this requirement. There's a lot you can do while you're advertising for an associate. Perform trials on paper. Learn the procedures and the payoffs. Put together your business plan. Get the scorecards printed up. When you finish that, step up your efforts to find someone, if you must. Just remember: you can't do it without help.

Maybe some day, but not today ✠

BANKROLL SAFEGUARDS

Man does not live long enough to profit from his faults.

—La Bruyère

In a recent episode of the television sitcom *Suddenly Susan,* Susan's boss gambled away his Porsche, betting that his friend from out of town couldn't toss a poker chip into a beer glass, in one try. Later, he gambled away the company he owned.

In the movie *Lost In America,* Julie Hagerty gambled away $800,000 in a single night at a roulette table in Las Vegas (while her husband slept). That money was all they had to support the two of them for the rest of their lives.

In *Honeymoon In Las Vegas,* Nicolas Cage was one bet away from calling it quits in a poker game, when James Caan suckered him into raising the stakes, which quickly resulted in Cage owing $50,000, an amount he could not repay.

This is why gamblers toss and turn at night. They know that *in just a few minutes,* they *could* lose everything that took them a whole lifetime to build. Scary? You bet.

Is there nothing you can do to protect yourself against this possibility? Must you live your *whole life* with this guillotine blade dangling over your head?

This is why you have *Bankroll Safeguards: initiatives that restrict your ability to get to your own money.* Measures that *you* incorporate to keep you from draining all your bank accounts in a fit of rage, should you suffer a *bodacious* lapse in your discipline. As I've said, you have the capacity to do this.

In considering the types of safeguards you'll need, you must project yourself into a crisis where you're forced to raise as much money as possible, as quickly as possible. Someone dear to you has just been kidnapped, and you need to get your hands on a lot of cash as fast as you can. Exactly how much could you raise in 24 hours, and how would you do it?

Include anything that could be liquidated within that period. Stocks, bonds, CDs, bank accounts, petty cash, and all the credit you could possibly get. Put all these figures on paper and then add them up. What's the total? Whatever it is, *that's how much you're liable to lose in one day if you don't take the time to assemble your own set of bankroll safeguards.*

Some years ago I renounced the use of credit, except for two revolving charge cards that are very seldom used. All my primary transactions are in cash, because that keeps me in touch with how much I'm spending, minute by minute. And when the wad of bills gets too big, I take the time to convert them to larger bills, or into high-value gaming chips. At all major casinos you can get tokens that are worth $5000 or more, which are very portable and instantly redeemable at the issuing casino 24 hours a day.

It shouldn't be too hard to incorporate your own safeguards, but you should take care of this before doing any serious gambling. For starters, avoid high-stakes poker games, because verbal bets are assumed to be binding. This is where people can lose things like cars and even houses—in a single bet.

Also, you may wish to consider making changes in how you pay for things. If you're currently using a lot of credit, it might be a good idea to start weaning yourself away from that. Of course, you should probably keep one or two credit cards for reservations or renting a car when traveling. But give yourself only as much spending power as what you think you can stand to lose in one day. And if your bank won't work with you to adjust your withdrawal allowances, consider switching banks.

Your end goal is to be where you can't raise more money in one day *than you can comfortably afford to lose* ✠

SUMMARY OF GETTING STARTED

Perhaps by now it is clear that a career in *player-side gaming* is not the glittery, glamorous proposition you once imagined it was. Having finished this book, however, the journey from here comes down to just three things: passing the tests, doing the exercises, and building a bankroll.

The latter of those three may well be the toughest task you'll ever face in your life, but you must pass through that gauntlet to earn the right to take a stab at this career. Please remember, this requirement is for *your* protection.

Those of you who have a computer may wish to purchase a casino game software package to help you perform trials, but don't rely too heavily on these. Live results are better.

I hope I've succeeded in impressing you with the importance of having an associate. Apart from what I've said, an associate can help you simulate live gaming (in your home), with the two of you taking turns playing the roles of *player* and *dealer*. This creates an atmosphere that feels authentic, and helps you to see *the other side*. And when you get to a casino and need to take some time to analyze a table trend, having someone to talk to while you stand there makes your presence less conspicuous.

Another matter not to be taken lightly is *Bankroll Safeguards*. It is almost a sparkling white certainty that some day, the long arm of *compulsion* will seek you out and whip you like a dog. When it comes, you had better be prepared ✠

19

95 QUESTIONS
THE FIRST TASK

The difference between failure and success often lies in doing a thing nearly right, or doing it exactly right.

—American expression

Of all that you've read so far, how much have you retained? How well do you know the material?

The point of the following section is to give you a sense of what you've learned. The arrangement of the questions follows the sequence of the book, to help you seek the answers—in the unlikely event that you don't know everything.

To take this test, write the question numbers *on a separate sheet of paper,* then fill in the call letters (A, B or C, etc.) that correspond to the answers you choose. ***Do not write in this book,*** for you must re-take this test in its entirety until you can correctly answer 85 of the 95 questions. (It may be necessary to re-take this test several times.)

Only when you have achieved a passing grade may you move on to the next step, the exercises in Chapter 20. And, uh, be careful. Some of the questions are a little tricky.

[The answers to all questions are on page 316]

TEST QUESTIONS
*Pick the choice that is **most correct** for each question:*

CHAPTER 1

1) *Of the three basic requirements to succeed on a professional level, which is said to be the most important?*

 ☐ A) Money
 ☐ B) Strategy
 ☐ C) Discipline

2) *What correlation was made between hitchhiking and the Law of Averages?*

 ☐ A) Every win is like a free ride.
 ☐ B) Given time, the desired result is inevitable.
 ☐ C) Never put unconditional trust in an expectation.

3) *Before you can learn how to win, you must learn:*

 ☐ A) How to play the game.
 ☐ B) How to win *the big ones.*
 ☐ C) How to *not lose.*

4) *Why were craps, roulette and minibaccarat chosen as recommended games?*

 ☐ A) They are one-dimensional games.
 ☐ B) They have bets with *'bet opposites.'*
 ☐ C) The pace of those games is easier to endure.

5) *The 'House Edge' is:*

 ☐ A) The mathematical advantage built in to casino payoffs.
 ☐ B) The difference between the *payoff* and the *bet return.*
 ☐ C) The 'home field advantage' enjoyed by all casinos.

6) *What is the 'Dagwood Edge'?*

 ☐ A) The advantage of being well-rested before going to a casino.
 ☐ B) *"Keep the game moving until the preferred side wins."*
 ☐ C) The inverse of the *House Edge.*

CHAPTER 2

7) *According to this book, 'Compulsion' works against you when:*

 ☐ A) You're losing at the tables.
 ☐ B) You're winning at the tables.
 ☐ C) Both of the above.

8) *What is 'Continuum', as defined in this book?*

☐ A) The impulse to make a foolish bet.
☐ B) The lack of time to react to an endless chain of betting opportunities.
☐ C) The inability to stop playing until you're out of chips.

9) *A 5–2 bet returns less than:*

☐ A) 2–1 odds.
☐ B) 3–1 odds.
☐ C) 9–5 odds.

10) *According to this book, which of the following is more destructive?*

☐ A) Compulsion
☐ B) Continuum
☐ C) House edge

CHAPTER 3

11) *What best describes the 'Synchronization Imperative'?*

☐ A) The need for lawyers, guns, and money.
☐ B) The need to have your house in order before doing any gambling.
☐ C) The need to synchronize *time, money, access to casinos,* and *strategy.*

12) *What is the 'Partnership Imperative'?*

☐ A) The need for a partner or assistant.
☐ B) The need for an apprenticeship period.
☐ C) The need for a partner who likes to gamble.

13) *Why is it important to have assistance in the casinos?*

☐ A) For moral and monetary support.
☐ B) To stay detached from the intoxicating effects of gambling.
☐ C) To flag down the cocktail waitress.

14) *Professional gamblers who last the longest are those who:*

☐ A) Have an extraordinary sense of timing.
☐ B) Have the uncanny ability to *win the big ones.*
☐ C) Have conservative income goals.

15) *When entering a casino, it is best that you:*

☐ A) Flash a lot of cash to let them know you mean business.
☐ B) Are well-dressed, and in the company of an attractive woman.
☐ C) Maintain a low profile throughout the visit.

CHAPTER 4

16) *Streaks of an even money proposition winning ten or more decisions:*

☐ A) Are not uncommon.
☐ B) Are extremely rare.
☐ C) Never happen.

17) *When unusual patterns emerge at the tables, you should:*

☐ A) Leave the table immediately.
☐ B) Disregard the occurrence.
☐ C) Try to exploit the abnormality.

18) *What is the Random Walk?*

☐ A) A wagering technique.
☐ B) A study of probabilities.
☐ C) A condition found at table games.
☐ D) None of the above.

19) *When customizing your play to what the table offers, you should:*

☐ A) React to the latest result.
☐ B) React to the overall group.
☐ C) Plan ahead, don't react.

20) *In this book, Positive Trends are defined as:*

☐ A) Gaming events that occur in clusters.
☐ B) Extended winning streaks.
☐ C) Favorable table conditions.
☐ D) None of the above.

21) *Negative Trends are defined as:*

☐ A) Normal event sequences.
☐ B) Prolonged absences of certain gaming events.
☐ C) Adverse playing conditions.
☐ D) None of the above.

CHAPTER 6

22) *The vigorish for most bets at American roulette is:*

☐ A) 2.63%.
☐ B) 5.26%.
☐ C) 7.89%.

23) *Outside roulette bets return:*

☐ A) Even money.
☐ B) 1–1.
☐ C) 2–1.
☐ D) All of the above.

24) *The one roulette bet that has a higher vig than the others is:*

☐ A) The fiveline bet.
☐ B) The sixline bet.
☐ C) Straight-up bets.

25) *Value chips are also referred to as:*

☐ A) Table chips.
☐ B) Generic chips.
☐ C) House chips.
☐ D) Colored chips.

26) *At a roulette table, the Chip Minimum:*

☐ A) Can never exceed the table minimum.
☐ B) Is always greater than the table minimum.
☐ C) Means the same thing as the table minimum.

27) *Which types of chips can't be removed from the roulette table?*

☐ A) Colored chips.
☐ B) Generic chips.
☐ C) Value chips.

28) *What is the 'Wagering Mandate'?*

☐ A) The specified minimum bet at a table.
☐ B) *"Seats are for players only."*
☐ C) *"You can't win if you don't play."*

29) *Hedge Bets are:*

☐ A) Large, solitary wagers.
☐ B) Small backup bets to protect a primary wager.
☐ C) Bets made at the table minimum to hold your seat.

30) *Hedge Bets are non-existent at:*

☐ A) Craps
☐ B) Minibaccarat
☐ C) Roulette

31) *What is the 'Magic Downside Number'?*

☐ A) The point where the odds change in a string of table decisions.
☐ B) The most consecutive losses possible from an even money proposition.
☐ C) A trip to nowhere.

32) *What might hinder your ability to place a spontaneous bet at roulette?*

☐ A) Other players using value chips.
☐ B) No room at the table.
☐ C) Both of the above.
☐ D) None of the above.

33) *The only place where half your even-money bet is returned if 0 or 00 wins is:*

☐ A) Atlantic City casinos.
☐ B) Casinos in Nevada.
☐ C) Some riverboat casinos.
☐ D) All of the above.
☐ E) None of the above.

CHAPTER 7

34) *At minibaccarat:*

☐ A) Each player is dealt two cards, subject to a third-card draw.
☐ B) Each player is dealt two cards for *Player* and two more for *Bank*.
☐ C) All decisions are rendered from a community hand.

35) *At minibaccarat, a bet on Bank is:*

☐ A) Betting *with* the house.
☐ B) Betting *against* the house.
☐ C) Neither of the above.

36) *The vigorish for the two primary minibaccarat bets are:*

☐ A) 1.17% and 1.36%.
☐ B) 1.28%.
☐ C) Both are over 1.50%.
☐ D) None of the above.

37) *At conventional minibaccarat, a 5% house commission is levied against:*

☐ A) All *Bank* wagers.
☐ B) All *Bank* wagers *that win.*
☐ C) All bets on *Player.*
☐ D) All wagers.

38) *If Bank has an original point count of 6, and then draws a Jack:*

    □ A) *Bank's* final point count will be 6.
    □ B) *Bank's* final point count will be 16.
    □ C) *Bank's* hand will bust.

CHAPTER 8

39) *At a craps table with several players, the shooter forfeits the dice when:*

    □ A) A 7 is rolled.
    □ B) A *craps* number (2, 3 or 12) is rolled.
    □ C) He (or she) sevens out.

40) *On a pair of dice, Sister Numbers are:*

    □ A) Different numbers which have the same probability.
    □ B) The number on the underside of whatever number faces UP.
    □ C) Both of the above.

41) *Back Line Bettors:*

    □ A) Prefer to play at warm tables.
    □ B) Are betting that the shooter will seven out.
    □ C) Both of the above.

42) *In effect, Come bets are identical to:*

    □ A) Place bets
    □ B) Pass line bets
    □ C) Field bets

43) *The payoff for placing the nine is:*

    □ A) 3–2.
    □ B) The same as for *placing the five.*
    □ C) Both of the above.

44) *Of those listed, which type of bet may not be removed at any time?*

    □ A) Pass line bets
    □ B) Place bets
    □ C) Field bets

45) *Which bet types appear on Nevada layouts but not those in Atlantic City?*

    □ A) Big 6 and Big 8 bets.
    □ B) World bets.
    □ C) Hop bets.

46) *What is the vigorish for the Any Seven bet?*

    □ A) 9.09%.
    □ B) 11.1%.
    □ C) 16.67%.
    □ D) None of the above.

CHAPTER 9

47) *What best describes a P4 even money pattern?*

    □ A) A zigzag pattern.
    □ B) A streak that starts on one side and continues on the other.
    □ C) A random pattern.
    □ D) None of the above.

48) *How do 'Pattern' results differ from 'AntiPattern' results?*

    □ A) *Pattern* sequences are more structured.
    □ B) *Pattern* sequences are considered to be more plentiful.
    □ C) Both of the above.

49) *What is an 'Encompassing Trend'?*

    □ A) A table trend that has no identifiable pattern.
    □ B) A collection of smaller trends, which form a larger picture.
    □ C) A table trend that is in a state of change.

50) *Which of the following describes a 'Reoccurring Double'?*

    □ A) An ongoing pattern of multiple wins on one side of a two-sided bet.
    □ B) The same as above, but occurring (instead) on both sides.
    □ C) Either of the above.
    □ D) None of the above.

CHAPTER 10

51) *What is 'Press and Pull'?*

    □ A) Fluctuating the bet size, in an attempt to maximize gains.
    □ B) *Press* up your bet size as you win, and *Pull* back a profit intermittently.
    □ C) Both of the above.

52) *Which of the following best characterizes a Parlay?*

    □ A) A series of continuous wins.
    □ B) Adding the proceeds of a winning bet to a subsequent bet.
    □ C) Reducing the bet size after a win.
    □ D) None of the above.

CHAPTER 11

53) *Why are Loss Limits important?*

    ☐ A) They help mitigate the downside.
    ☐ B) They keep you from chasing your losses.
    ☐ C) Both of the above.

54) *Why are 'Win Goals' important?*

    ☐ A) They help keep your expectations realistic.
    ☐ B) They help keep you from giving your gains back to the house.
    ☐ C) Both of the above.

55) *What is the 'Settle For 90' rule?*

    ☐ A) Don't obsess over winning an arbitrary figure.
    ☐ B) At the two unit level, never try to win more than $90 per session.
    ☐ C) Never play at any table for longer than ninety minutes.

CHAPTER 12

56) *What is the operative principle of the 'Martingale' system?*

    ☐ A) When you lose, start doubling your bet each time until you win.
    ☐ B) Increase your bet by one unit after a loss; decrease by one after a win.
    ☐ C) Increase the bet size by one unit after each win.
    ☐ D) None of the above.

57) *What must happen to conclude a successful series of the '31' system?*

    ☐ A) You must risk 31 units.
    ☐ B) You must get back-to-back wins.
    ☐ C) You must reach the fourth level.
    ☐ D) None of the above.

58) *Which of the following names apply to the 'D'Alembert' system?*

    ☐ A) The *Pyramid.*
    ☐ B) The *Cancellation System.*
    ☐ C) The *Labouchère.*
    ☐ D) None of the above.

59) *Which is a distinguishing feature of 'Oscar's Grind'?*

    ☐ A) Increase your bet size by one unit after a win.
    ☐ B) Never modify your bet size after a loss.
    ☐ C) Both of the above.
    ☐ D) None of the above.

CHAPTER 13

60) *The author considers 'Procedures' superior to 'Systems' because they:*

　□ A) Pay no heed to the permutations of the table.
　□ B) Exploit current trends rather than step through a mechanical ritual.
　□ C) Have a *do-or-die* mentality.

61) *In this book, 'Basic Line Betting' involves:*

　□ A) Betting the pass line.
　□ B) Betting the don't pass.
　□ C) Either of the above.

62) *In this book, 'Odds Betting' involves:*

　□ A) Taking or laying odds for line bets.
　□ B) Playing pass and don't pass simultaneously at the come-out.
　□ C) Both of the above.

63) *The verbal command 'Twenty-six across' covers:*

　□ A) All six point numbers.
　□ B) All numbers *except* the point.
　□ C) All inside numbers.

64) *What is a 'Closed Progression'?*

　□ A) A betting series that has a fixed upward limit.
　□ B) A progression that must end with back-to-back wins to succeed.
　□ C) Neither of the above.

65) *What is the strength of the 'Sister System'?*

　□ A) It helps pace the wagering activity.
　□ B) It has the potential to work at all types of craps tables.
　□ C) One is less vulnerable to a seven-out than other *right* bettors.
　□ D) All of the above.

66) *What is the strength of 'Multi-Line'?*

　□ A) It maximizes the come-out advantage for line and come bets.
　□ B) It has the potential to work at all types and temperatures of tables.
　□ C) Both of the above.

67) *What numbers do the 'Angel' bet (for roulette) cover?*

　□ A) 1 thru 6 and 31 thru 36.
　□ B) 1 thru 12 and 24 thru 36.

68) *What are 'Auxiliary Bets', as defined in this book?*

   ☐ A) Bets that aren't part of the primary betting scheme.
   ☐ B) Bets made from a separate fund that allow you to pursue a trend.
   ☐ C) Both of the above.
   ☐ D) None of the above.

CHAPTER 14

69) *Placing numbers at a craps table beats racetrack wagering because:*

   ☐ A) The vigs at craps tables are much lower than those at racetracks.
   ☐ B) Equivalent bets have a higher win rate at craps tables.
   ☐ C) Racetrack favorites seldom win more than 30% of the time.

70) *How does one control the pace of betting activity in casinos?*

   ☐ A) By playing isolated wagers to space out the betting activity.
   ☐ B) By keeping conversation to a minimum.
   ☐ C) By playing simultaneous wagers.

71) *How is 'Controlled Greed' defined in this book?*

   ☐ A) The ability to control the momentum of the game.
   ☐ B) A passionate desire for a sensible bet acquisition.
   ☐ C) A rapacious desire for wealth and power.
   ☐ D) None of the above.

72) *In the applicable context, why is 'Controlled Greed' constructive?*

   ☐ A) It's the only way one can maintain control in a casino.
   ☐ B) *Greed* is an advanced form of *Ambition.*
   ☐ C) A strong incentive is needed to counter the *'gratification vacuum.'*

73) *What is said to be the first stage, as you enter a casino?*

   ☐ A) The *Analysis Stage.*
   ☐ B) The *Dry Bet Stage.*
   ☐ C) The *Adversarial Stage.*
   ☐ D) None of the above.

74) *What is the 'Selective Shooter', as defined in this book?*

   ☐ A) Betting on selected shooters only, at a craps table.
   ☐ B) Betting on other shooters, but not yourself.
   ☐ C) Betting only on *your* (and/or your associate's) dice rolls.
   ☐ D) Someone who specializes in shooting dice for others.
   ☐ E) None of the above.

75) *What is the 'Random Angel'?*

    ☐ A) A period at a table when it seems you can do no wrong.

    ☐ B) A pair of bets made on the first and last roulette sixlines.

    ☐ C) An inside roulette bet that pays even money.

    ☐ D) None of the above.

76) *What is this book's definition of 'Mixed Media'?*

    ☐ A) A selected assortment of casino table games.

    ☐ B) A set group of six bets, used primarily for secondary bets.

    ☐ C) A group of wagers of your choosing, used primarily for secondary bets.

    ☐ D) None of the above.

77) *What is the 'Random Player' bet?*

    ☐ A) A solitary wager at one of the three recommended games.

    ☐ B) A solitary wager on *Player,* at a minibaccarat table.

    ☐ C) A random selection betting scheme.

    ☐ D) None of the above.

CHAPTER 15

78) *What is the difference between a 'Cold' table and a 'Choppy' table?*

    ☐ A) The two are indistinguishable.

    ☐ B) The patterns are less structured at a *'Cold'* table.

    ☐ C) *'Choppy'* tables are more common.

79) *The dice are more likely to 'pass' at a:*

    ☐ A) Warm table.

    ☐ B) Choppy table.

    ☐ C) Cold table.

80) *Which of the following is **not** one of the 'six signs of an imminent seven'?*

    ☐ A) A new stickman comes to replace the present one.

    ☐ B) The game is delayed because of a dispute.

    ☐ C) Players at the table are starting to get rowdy.

    ☐ D) Two *Craps* rolls (2, 3 or 12) are rolled consecutively.

81) *According to the author, 'Dice Fixing' is:*

    ☐ A) Illegal in most casinos.

    ☐ B) A matter of personal preference.

    ☐ C) A complete waste of time.

    ☐ D) Allowed in most casinos, as long as you don't get caught.

CHAPTER 17

82) *What is a 'Nickel Midnight'?*

    ☐ A) A Horn bet.
    ☐ B) A $5 bet on the 12 at a craps table.
    ☐ C) A casino incentive for late-night bettors.

83) *If a shooter rolls three or more come-out sevens, your best bet is to:*

    ☐ A) Lay the point.
    ☐ B) Play pass line with double odds.
    ☐ C) Bet Hi-Lo for the next two rolls.

CHAPTER 18

84) *Why is it difficult to get started in a career as a professional gambler?*

    ☐ A) You're not working with *won money,* so your losses are more dear.
    ☐ B) You don't yet have the confidence of a proven winner.
    ☐ C) Your mission is complex; it takes time to get it right.
    ☐ D) All of the above.

85) *What are the 'Three Tasks' you must perform before starting this career?*

    ☐ A) Slay the two-headed dragon, rid the planet of crime and fly to the moon.
    ☐ B) Learn how to play craps, roulette and minibaccarat.
    ☐ C) Pass this test, do the exercises ahead, and build your own bankroll.

86) *From 'Building A Bankroll II', the first of the five rules states that "When the tables give you a hard time. . ."*

    ☐ A) Press your bets up so you can force the win.
    ☐ B) Settle for whatever you can get.
    ☐ C) Leave the casino.

87) *What is the first of the 'Seven Stages of the Business Plan'?*

    ☐ A) The Collection Stage.
    ☐ B) The Computation Stage.
    ☐ C) The Selection Stage.

88) *Why are 'Bankroll Safeguards' important?*

    ☐ A) To keep you from gambling away a fortune in a single night.
    ☐ B) To protect you from the consequences of a huge lapse of discipline.
    ☐ C) To keep your own compulsive tendencies from seizing control of every fiber of your being, and squashing you, totally, like a bug.
    ☐ D) All of the above.

CHAPTER 21 (AHEAD IN THIS BOOK)

89) *Why do casinos offer 'Comps' to certain players?*

    □ A) To induce them to stay *there*, where it is assumed they will lose.
    □ B) Because they're *special*, and deserve to be treated as such.
    □ C) Because they are stockholders in the parent company.
    □ D) In exchange for sexual favors.

90) *While 'on duty', professional gamblers:*

    □ A) Spread out the cash and drink up a storm.
    □ B) Are allowed to "lose control" once in a while.
    □ C) Try to be inconspicuous, and do not drink.

91) *According to the author, casino towns (especially near the casinos) are:*

    □ A) Generally safe and secure.
    □ B) More dangerous than other towns with comparable demographics.
    □ C) The same as any other town of its size.

92) *Are 'rigged games' prevalent in American casinos today?*

    □ A) Yes.
    □ B) No.
    □ C) Maybe.

GENERAL

93) *Which of the following bet types carry a 5% house commission?*

    □ A) Lay bets (craps)
    □ B) Buy bets (craps)
    □ C) Bank bets (minibaccarat)
    □ D) All of the above.

94) *Which game carries the highest vigs for its mainstay bets?*

    □ A) Craps
    □ B) Roulette
    □ C) Minibaccarat

95) *What is the overall philosophy of this book?*

    □ A) Cater your play to the results the table is naturally disposed to give.
    □ B) Hold back when losing; press your advantage when winning.
    □ C) Always keep your eye on the big picture.
    □ D) Maintain a low profile at all times.
    □ E) All of the above.

TEST ANSWERS

Failure is success if we learn from it.

—Malcom Forbes

1) C	25) B	49) B	73) A
2) B	26) A	50) C	74) C
3) C	27) A	51) C	75) B
4) B	28) B	52) B	76) C
5) A	29) B	53) C	77) B
6) B	30) B	54) C	78) C
7) C	31) C	55) A	79) A
8) B	32) C	56) A	80) C
9) B	33) A	57) B	81) B
10) A	34) C	58) A	82) B
11) C	35) C	59) C	83) A
12) A	36) A	60) B	84) D
13) B	37) B	61) C	85) C
14) C	38) A	62) C	86) B
15) C	39) C	63) B	87) C
16) A	40) C	64) A	88) D
17) C	41) B	65) D	89) A
18) B	42) B	66) C	90) C
19) B	43) B	67) A	91) A
20) A	44) A	68) C	92) B
21) B	45) A	69) A	93) D
22) B	46) C	70) A	94) B
23) D	47) A	71) B	95) E
24) A	48) C	72) C	

20

GAMING EXERCISES
THE SECOND TASK

Opportunities are usually disguised as hard work, so most people don't recognize them.

—Ann Landers

Throughout this book there are references to *"the exercises ahead that show the betting parameters"* for selected procedures. This is where you'll find that information. Most exercises, though, are shown at the base ($5) level, the most common table minimum. So if you can get to Las Vegas where the minimums are lower, or if you wish to bet at higher levels at some point in the future, you'll have to make adjustments in the figures.

The first exercises involve *basic line betting* and *odds betting*. These procedures were chosen to introduce this chapter because they are at the heart of professional gambling, as practiced by most serious players I know. Also, they represent the best ways to *tread water* with low-level bets while awaiting a wagering opportunity, primarily because they carry the lowest vigorish that can be found at any game offered in a casino.

Please be advised, however, that for some of these exercises, success is measured not just in what you *do,* but also in what you have the discipline to *not do* ✠

EXERCISE 1:
BASIC LINE BETTING

Using the betting parameters shown below as a guide, play a live session for 30 minutes, or until you reach the specified *loss limit* or *win goal*—whichever comes first.

This session is to take place at a casino craps table that has other players present, and a $5 table minimum.

BETTING PARAMETERS

PROCEDURE: *BASIC LINE BETTING*

TABLE GAME: *CRAPS*

BETTING LEVEL: *$5 (As shown below):*
- Bet $5 for all basic pass line and don't pass (wins $5)
- Bet $5 when **taking odds** for the 6 or 8 (wins $6)
- Bet $6 when **taking odds** for the 5 or 9 (wins $9)
- Bet $5 when **taking odds** for the 4 or 10 (wins $10)
- Bet $6 when **laying odds** against the 6 or 8 (wins $5)
- Bet $9 when **laying odds** against the 5 or 9 (wins $6)
- Bet $10 when **laying odds** against the 4 or 10 (wins $5)

HOW TO BET: *Imitate the last line bet result, as shown:*
- If the last shooter made the point, bet **pass line**; if the last shooter sevened out, bet **don't pass**. Continue on that basis.
- Wins or losses to come-out craps or naturals should not influence the betting choice. Use only the final point decisions to make that determination.

WHEN TO BET: *First roll of new come-out; repeat for other come-outs, for a period not to exceed 35 minutes (includes 5 grace minutes).*

HEDGING: *Any Craps for pass line, and Yo for don't pass are optional.*

SESSION BUY-IN: *$100*

SESSION LOSS LIMIT: *$75*

SESSION WIN GOAL: *$50*

Are we clear on what to do? Let's review.

In a casino, we're going to seek out an *active* craps table that has a $5 table minimum. The first thing to do is to look for the red placard near the dealer, which denotes a $5 table. If you've found one and a game is in progress, drop your $100 buy-in on the layout and say, *"Change only."* But check to make sure the dice aren't about to fly as you do so.

While waiting for your chips, observe the game, but in no case should you bet until a line decision has been rendered and a new come-out is underway. Then, if the shooter made that point, your first bet will be $5 on the *pass line*. If he sevened out, you'll be putting your nickel on the *don't pass*.

At this point, any one of several things may happen. If you're betting the pass line, you could win from a come-out *natural,* or lose your bet to a *craps* roll, or the shooter may establish the point. If you're betting don't pass, you may also win, lose, or witness the establishment of the point in much the same way, or you might end up with a *push,* if a 12 is rolled. Whatever happens, enjoy the wins or eat the losses until the point is established, then *take* or *lay* odds, depending on the side you're betting. If you reach your loss limit in the midst of a series of transactions, however, that should supersede all other considerations.

Continue playing on that basis, imitating the most recent line bet result and adding your odds as you go, until one of four things happens:

1) You reach your loss limit of $75.
2) You reach your win goal of $50.
3) You wish to stop for any (legitimate) reason.
4) The 30 minutes of playing time is up *(to which five grace minutes may be added, as noted).*

That's all there is to it. For those who lack table experience, however, it wouldn't hurt to play some practice sessions at home before going to live bets in a casino.

EXERCISE 2:
LINE BETTING/ODDS BETTING

This exercise is identical to Exercise 1, except that you revert to *Odds Betting* whenever you suffer two come-out losses (losses to a *craps* roll while playing pass line, or to a *natural* 7 or 11 while playing don't pass).

With *odds betting,* you put a chip on the pass line and the don't pass *simultaneously* at the come-out. Then, after the point is established, *take* or *lay* odds as follows: if the last shooter made his point, *take* odds (add an odds bet to your *pass line* bet), and if he sevened out, *lay* odds (against your *don't pass* bet). But go to *odds betting* only if you lost your line bet to a *craps* or *natural* roll *twice* during the same come-out.

The difference between *Line Betting* and *Odds Betting* lies in how the bet responds to the come-out phase. With line betting, you can benefit from a string of come-out *naturals* when betting *right,* but the same thing will burn your butt when betting *wrong.* Odds betting keeps you oblivious to these fluctuations, *except* for when the 12 comes along, which is the only occurrence that causes a loss to one side *that isn't compensated by a win on the other side.* But this shouldn't pose a major problem.

All other betting parameters for this exercise are the same as before, except for the (optional) hedging for the *odds betting* mode. For that, the only hedge that is suitable would be a $1 bet on the 12 during the come-outs, but this doesn't make a lot of sense when betting at the nickel level.

When my bets exceed three units, I always hedge the 12 when odds betting. But for smaller wagers, it's hardly worth the effort. You'll see what I mean when you get caught in a come-out loop that goes 7–7–11–3–3–etc. It's a nuisance tossing out a chip for the midnight every five seconds.

Remember, switch over to *odds betting* only if the need arises. And there's a pretty fair chance that the table conditions won't warrant that need.

EXERCISE 3:
THE SISTER SYSTEM

Before playing the *Sister System* with live bets in a casino, it is recommended that you practice at the two-unit level with dry bets, and review the material on the *Sister System* (in Chapter 13), and on *place* bets (Chapter 8).

This is a *sporadic* wagering procedure, which means you'll be going for long stretches between bets, at times. Part of the test is how well you handle the monotony, and whether you can resist the temptation to place other bets.

BETTING PARAMETERS

PROCEDURE: *THE SISTER SYSTEM*

TABLE GAME: *CRAPS*

BETTING LEVEL: *TWO UNIT* FLAT BETS, *as shown:*
- *Bet $10 when placing the 4, 5, 9 or 10*
- *Bet $12 when placing the 6 or 8*

HOW TO BET: *After the point is established, place the sister number.*
- *If your bet wins, take down the bet immediately, then repeat the process at the next come-out.*
- *If your bet loses, wait for the next come-out, then cover the new sister number.*
- *If your bet does not win or lose, have the dealer move your bet to the new sister number (if necessary)* **after** *the new come-out.*

WHEN TO BET: *As soon as the point is determined, but take it down immediately after winning. Do not start, however, until you have witnessed at least one* **would-be win.**

LOSS LIMIT: *$75*

WIN GOAL: *$50*

DURATION OF PLAY: *30 TO 45 MINUTES*

EXERCISE 4:
THE SELECTIVE SHOOTER

For this one you'll be moving from table to table, betting only on your own rolls. To do this, you'll need a casino with favorable playing conditions, that is, more than one active table with space. Or, an area with multiple casinos should be okay. What *won't work* is being shut out everywhere you go.

You will start at a $5 table, and your first bet will be $5 on the pass line. Hedging during the come-out is optional. Once the point is established, take single odds ($5 odds for the 4, 6, 8, & 10, and $6 odds for the 5 and 9). If you make that first point, bet the pass line and take odds, like before. When you do seven out (assuming that you previously made at least one point), continue to bet the pass line for at least two more tries before switching to the don't pass as your dominant choice.

If you start out *not* making the point, you're going to go with the (tentative) assumption that this is a *don't pass day* for you, and the *back line* will be your dominant choice.

What you're trying to do here is to estimate which of the two sides (the *Do* or the *Don't* side) will bring in more profit. As you accumulate information regarding your performance, you may find it necessary to make adjustments in your strategy. Just remember to consider the big picture (rather than react to the latest result). The primary question that should be on your mind as you play is, *"Is this a **pass**, or **don't pass** day?"*

For this exercise, carry a bank of $200 and buy in for $100 at each table. Your win goal is $75, and your loss limit is $75, but you must leave any table that serves up three consecutive losses, or a total of four losses (not including come-out losses to *craps, etc.*) For this one, there is no time limit.

The purpose of this exercise is to show you what legwork can (or might not) accomplish. Making money this way will be easier for some and harder for others, but I think you'll find this exercise to be a positive learning experience.

EXERCISE 5:
THE 5/9 PROGRESSION

This is a *closed progression*, which means that if you exhaust a series, you'll have to write off the loss.

You need a warm table for this, and that means spending some time checking out the tables. If you hear *"Seven out, line away"* every third or fourth roll, keep looking.

BETTING PARAMETERS

PROCEDURE: *THE 5/9 PROGRESSION*

TABLE GAME: *CRAPS*

BETTING LEVEL: *$5–$10–$15–$20 PROGRESSION ($50 TOTAL)*

WHAT TO BET: *If the point is 8, 9 or 10, bet the 5 for that come-out. If the point is 4, 5 or 6, bet the 9 for that come-out. At no time should you have more than one active bet.*

HOW TO BET: *Begin with a $5 place bet on either the 5 or 9, using the guidelines above to choose the betting target. If that bet wins, continue betting at that level. If it loses, proceed to the next level ($10). Continue through the progression until you win. When you do win, return to the $5 level, and repeat the process. If you exhaust the cycle before winning, the series is considered a loss, and you must leave the table.*

WHEN TO BET: *After the point is established, and keep the bet up continuously to win (except during come-outs). At each new come-out, follow the **what-to-bet** rules to determine whether that bet stays where it is or should be moved.*

BUY-IN: *$50 per table*

LOSS LIMIT: *$50 per table, $100 overall*

WIN GOAL: *$50*

DURATION OF PLAY: *30 TO 45 minutes per table*

We should have a clear sense of purpose before going further, so let's take a moment to reflect on what we've just done, what our goals are, and where we go from here.

If you have finished these first five exercises, you now have some experience at the tables. How did you do? Theoretically, the most you could lose from the five exercises is $400, because that is the sum total of the loss limits. But theory is not reality. It's a fairly safe bet that some readers did not heed the loss limits, or, pursued other betting options that weren't part of the program. But they all had good reasons for doing so. One guy blames the sparrow that somehow got inside and was being a nuisance. Another said his cocktail waitress brought him mixed drinks by mistake, and he was too busy to correct her. Then there's the lady who was distracted by the ringing of the slot machine that happened to be ten feet away from where she stood.

Yes, these are valid reasons to deviate from the procedure— as long as you're just a *recreational* gambler! But when you step across the threshhold to the *professional* way of doing things, you no longer have that luxury.

Either you get this or you don't: It's sink or swim.

Now, let's get back to the main question. *How did you do?* As stated, the maximum theoretical loss one could sustain is $400, but I don't believe it's possible for any of my readers to lose that much **IF** they followed the rules. In fact, I doubt that anyone lost even half that much. Chances are, your $400 bank hasn't fluctuated by more than $50 to $100, though it is certainly possible to exceed that amount, in either direction.

So, what do you think about your experience in the casino? Do you think you can stand this kind of life? It's still way early for you to know with any degree of certainty, but some readers may feel that they've seen enough. If that's the case, I say get out now and don't look back.

For those who remain, be advised that you may need as much as $800 to do all these exercises. But if there's a future for you in this field, it will be money well spent.

EXERCISE 6
CHINESE ROULETTE

At a $5 roulette table, buy in for $50 or $100. First chance you get, put a $5 bet on RED. Then follow up in accordance with the rules specified below:

BETTING PARAMETERS

PROCEDURE: *CHINESE ROULETTE*

TABLE GAME: *ROULETTE*

BETTING LEVEL: *$5*

HOW TO BET: *$5 on any of the six outside 1–1 bets, as shown:*

WHAT TO BET: *One of two betting cycles:*
1) Red–Even–Low, or 2) Black–Odd–High.
Start out with the first cycle, then switch to the second cycle if that bet loses. Keep switching to the other cycle after a loss.

NOTE: *If your first bet (on Red) wins, your next bet will be $5 on Even. If that first bet loses, you'll bet $5 on Odd.*

WHEN TO BET: *Continuously until you reach your loss limit, win goal, or a good stopping point.*

SESSION BUY-IN: *$50 OR $100*

SESSION LOSS LIMIT: *$50*

SESSION WIN GOAL: *$50*

There is no time limit for this. It may be helpful to consult the subchapter on *Chinese Roulette* (page 196) to refresh your memory of this procedure.

If you can, practice at home before going to live bets. Have a friend act as dealer, reciting the results–one by one–from a live game you charted in a casino. Then go through the motions as if you were in a live gaming situation.

EXERCISE 7
THE ANGEL AND SLEDGEHAMMER

Find an *active* $5 roulette table (with a scoresign) that hasn't produced a 0 or 00 in the last fifteen or more spins. Lay $100 on the table and ask the dealer for *"five stacks of one-dollar chips."* Then, await your wagering trigger: any number from 7 through 30. (You shouldn't have to wait too long.) When it appears, place two chips on each of the sixlines that comprise the *Sledgehammer A* (7–12, 13–18, 19–24, & 25–30). If that bet wins, repeat the bet, and continue to do so as long as you continue to win. When your bet loses, switch to the *Angel* (1–6 & 31–36), but you'll be putting *three* chips on each of those (two) sixlines.

For the record, your Sledge bet costs $8 (four $2 bets), and the Angel bet costs $6 (two $3 bets).

For this exercise, you'll be playing every spin, imitating the result that would have most recently produced a win. If you've hit a choppy table and lose three or four bets in a row, that's too bad. These things happen. Don't worry; your loss limits will protect you from serious damage to your bankroll.

BETTING PARAMETERS

PROCEDURE: *THE ANGEL AND THE SLEDGEHAMMER*

TABLE GAME: *ROULETTE*

BETTING LEVEL: *$6 (ANGEL), AND $8 (SLEDGEHAMMER)*

HOW TO BET: *As described above.*

WHAT TO BET: *As described above.*

WHEN TO BET: *As described above.*

SESSION BUY-IN: *$100*

SESSION LOSS LIMIT: *$75*

SESSION WIN GOAL: *$50*

EXERCISE 8
SLEDGEHAMMER, VERSIONS A AND B

This exercise is very similar to the last one (Exercise 7), except that you'll toggle between the *Sledgehammer A* and *B*. The former (Version *A*) is as described on the previous page, and the latter is the same except that you'll be covering these sixlines [1–6, 7–12, 25–30 & 31–36], instead.

Buy in as you did in Exercise 7, but this time you can start betting immediately. If the last number that won lies between 10 and 27, bet the *"A"* version (7–30). If the last number to win lies between 1–9 and 28–36, bet the *"B"* version. Use that formula to make your wagering choice as you play continuously, until you either win (roughly) $50, or lose $75.

Normally, when I play any sledgehammer version at roulette, I hedge the 0 and 00 with a bet that is large enough to return most of my bet if one of those wins. At this (low) level of play, however, hedging is not practical, or advisable.

Both *A* and *B* versions call for $2 bets on four sixlines, for a total bet of $8, which wins $4 if successful.

BETTING PARAMETERS

PROCEDURE: *SLEDGEHAMMER, Versions 'A' and 'B'*

TABLE GAME: *ROULETTE*

BETTING LEVEL: *$8 (four 2-chip bets, each spin)*

HOW & WHAT TO BET: *As described above.*

WHEN TO BET: *As described above.*

SESSION BUY-IN: *$100*

SESSION LOSS LIMIT: *$75*

SESSION WIN GOAL: *$50*

DURATION OF PLAY: *30 to 40 minutes, recommended maximum*

EXERCISE 9
THE FAVORED FIVE

This exercise may require some charting, even if the table has a scoresign. You are trying to find five numbers that have repeated (*recently* won more than once).

Before making a buy-in at a $5 table, use the crossout diagram on your scorecard to mark the numbers showing on the scoresign (as shown in Chapter 13). Then continue charting (if necessary) until you have spotted five numbers that have won more than once. When you have them, make your buy-in (*'Five stacks of $1 chips'*) and cover each number with a $1 chip. Continue to play until you either lose *seven* consecutive spins, or, after winning, you lose *three* consecutive spins. Please re-read that sentence, because it covers every possibility at any given table.

If you do nothing but lose at a table, eat the $35 loss and try it again at a second table, as before. If you win but don't show an immediate profit, continue on that basis at more tables until you either reach your $60 win goal or $105 (total) loss limit. Under no circumstances are you to play more than three sessions, if none of those three produced a win.

BETTING PARAMETERS

PROCEDURE: *THE FAVORED FIVE*

TABLE GAME: *ROULETTE*

BETTING LEVEL: *$1 per number, forming a $5 total bet*

WHAT TO BET: *Cover the five numbers that have repeated*

WHEN TO BET: *After you have identified five repeating numbers*

SESSION LOSS LIMIT: *$35 per table*

PROCEDURE LOSS LIMIT: *$105 total*

PROCEDURE WIN GOAL: *$60*

EXERCISE 10 (OPTIONAL): EXPLOITING THE ZEROES

This is an *optional* exercise, and there are two versions. One involves a progression—for those who can get to Las Vegas and play at some $1 or $2 tables. The other uses $5 flat bets, and it's for everyone else in the country, where the table minimums (for roulette) usually begin at $5.

Your wagering trigger is the appearance of a 0 or 00. When that is *the very last* table result, start your series (if you have value chips handy) or make your buy-in and then start.

Each series is comprised of (up to) six bets. You leave the table after: 1) a win, or 2) six losing bets. Then you move on, and seek another wagering opportunity elsewhere.

If you can get to a $1 table, start at the minimum and move upward in $1 increments after three bets. On that basis, your series would be $1–$1–$1–$2–$2–$2 at the first table, then $3–$3–$3–$4–$4–$4 at the next. It's an *up-as-you-lose* progression, which means that you go only as high as necessary to win. Naturally, we need a cutoff point so that you don't go upward forever. The loss limit is $84 for the Vegas version and $95 for the flat-bet version. One of those two figures is the most you will risk for this exercise, regardless the number of tables played.

With the Vegas version, you have 21 chances to win, which take you to the $7 level. If you are compelled to play at $5 tables, then you have 19 chances to get a win.

Your win goal, either way, is roughly $50. Or, you can quit whenever you'd like. That's the beauty of optional exercises. They are not mandatory or enforceable.

The purpose of this exercise is to help you achieve *big picture* awareness in the casino. Playing a progression that follows a very precise path as you move from table to table will help you do that. Even the flat bet version should help you see the continuity that exists between a multitude of isolated tables.

And, the effectiveness of this strategy may surprise you!

EXERCISE SUMMARY

Chance favors the prepared mind.

—from the movie *Under Siege II*

These exercises were designed to help you see the interplay of the various trends that occur at the tables, and, give you a taste of live gaming. Doing so should give you an idea what to expect when you go out on your own. Remember, the key to winning is to anticipate trend development.

If you adhered to your loss limits as instructed, the most you could technically lose is $800. But if you followed all the rules, it would not really be possible for you to lose that amount, because these strategies are too numerous and diverse to cause losses unanimously.

So, the key question is this: how did your discipline hold up? Chances are, if you suffered an overall loss of $200 or more, the problem can be traced to a lack of discipline. If so, you need to consider two more questions:

1) Can I handle the extraordinary amount of discipline that is necessary, day in and day out?
2) What changes can I make in how I handle myself, to stay in control, and true to my objectives?

Until you can answer those questions, you haven't completed your training. Even if you fulfilled the requirements of this chapter, you need to ask yourself, *Am I ready?* ✠

21

ODDS AND ENDS

Very soon now, I shall be able to release you to the custody of the casino. All that's left is odds and ends regarding casino etiquette and stuff like that.

CASINO COMPS

Back in the days when Las Vegas casinos booked their own horseplaying bets, I once witnessed something at the Barbary Coast casino that made an impression. A man had just won a $1000 bet on a 9–2 horse (which returned over $5500). I knew the guy was a regular, and wondered if casino management would ask him to leave after paying off the bet. How wrong could I be! Management broke out the champagne and hors d'oeuvres, and treated him like he was king of the world. This was the last thing I expected to see. But looking back, I have to say that it made perfect sense. If they could get him to stick around, they would have a chance to win some (or all) of their money back!

The freebies he received are known as *Complimentaries,* but everyone refers to them as *Comps.* They are part of a methodical reward system implemented by casino management to induce the players to keep gambling. The operative assumption is that the longer you play, the more you'll lose. But that's not how they sell the concept. To hear it from them, they're doing it because *you're special,* and deserve to be treated as such.

If you're in the habit of buying in at a table for $200 or more, it's only a matter of time before a floorperson will approach you and ask if you have a *player's card* (or whatever they call them), so that your play can be *rated.* If you act responsive, he or she will then try to sell you on the benefits of having this card.

What benefits? Well, you give the card to the floorperson as you make your buy-ins, and they keep track of your play. The more you play at their tables, the more points you accumulate. In time, you might rack up enough points to cover the cost of meals, hotel accomodations, or items from their gift shop.

If you're a high roller, you could really make out from all the enticements they're willing to offer, and you don't necessarily have to lose at the tables to qualify. We're talking luxury hotel suites, dining at its best, even free passage on cruise ships. All those things that epitomize the good life.

What's the catch? In this context, *Free* is just another word for *stuff that's paid for five times over at the tables.* Meaning, you're expected to lose at least five times the value of the comps. But that's just part of the problem. When you give in to all that deleterious crap, you forfeit your *low profile* and your *anonymity.* And that might be all it takes to kill your career. The *last* thing you need is for them to get a handle on how much money you take out of their casino each day.

And there's more. In trying to earn complimentary points, you're likely to spend more time at the tables. You lose your focus. That's a price you can hardly afford.

Nothing in this world is free. If you go after the comps, the greater chance is, you're gonna pay ✠

TIPPING

The free market works in accordance with the golden rule.
The more we help others, the more we advance ourselves.

—Percy L. Greaves, Jr.

Everybody seems to have a different view on tipping dealers, so I'll just tell you what I do, and why.

Knowing that—at this writing—the rate of pay for dealers is about $7.00 an hour, I like to help out. They have a pretty tough job, and it seems to me that most players seldom tip. So, part of my motivation to tip derives from empathy.

My main reason for tipping, though, is purely selfish. If the dealers know I am prone to tip generously, (I assume) they will be more courteous and accurate. They will be rooting for me to win, because when I do, there is a greatly enhanced likelihood that I'll send a meaningful tip their way.

But I don't always tip. There are times when a table treats me *so* bad, I'd feel like a hypocrite to do so. It's just not in my heart. At times like that, I don't think the dealers expect one.

How much to tip, and when? At a craps table, I often tip as I go, and depending on how I did, perhaps again as I leave the table. The *As I Go* tipping is always in the form of bets that I make for the dealers. For instance, during the come-out, I may toss some chips to the stickman and request, *"Two-way craps."* This is universally understood to mean a bet for the player and another for the dealers as a toke. (This bet must not be confused with *three-way craps*, which covers the craps numbers 2, 3 and 12.)

When I'm cleaning up because a shooter is making a lot of points, I frequently put down a *"Line bet for the dealers"*, and may even hedge it with the *two-way craps,* as just described. If it seems like it's too late in the game to do that, sometimes I place the point (or any other number that's hitting) for the dealers. And let me tell you: I sure wish my own bets had as high a win rate as the ones I make for the dealers. (But if I attempted to cash in on that, it would undoubtedly change my wagering impulses.)

At the end of a successful session, be it minibaccarat, roulette or craps, I usually give the dealers a little something. My standard tip ranges from $5 to $25, but I go outside that range when things go really well or really bad. That doesn't include the *As I Go* tips, which are made primarily at the craps table.

By the way, when you tip in the form of a wager, the dealers *never* leave it up beyond a single hit. If you toss a couple whites toward the stickman, saying *"Two-way craps"* and it wins on that roll, the stickman assumes that you want *your* bet repeated on the next roll, and he'll have the dealer give you $7. For the dealers' part of that bet, however, you'll hear the words, *"Eight dollars and down for the dealers."* Even if your tip takes the form of a place bet (which is a continuous wager), there are only two things that can happen to that bet: 1) it will lose; 2) it will win *once.* After the win, the bet and its profit go straight to the dealers' tip fund. There is *no chance* that a dealer's place bet will stay up to win as the bet was designed to be played. They wanna get their money while they can, and leave the gambling to the customers.

As for the cocktail waitresses, I usually tip them one, two or sometimes five bucks for each drink they bring, using whatever chips I've got handy. And this, again, is done for selfish reasons. When they're attuned to my drink preferences, some of them will bring me that drink without asking.

Whether to tip and how much is your call, of course, but I do recommend it. When you're up against such a powerful opponent, it sure is nice to feel that some of the enemy's warriors are actually rooting for your success ✠

CASINO ETIQUETTE

If you have no money, be polite.

—Danish proverb

What can I say about etiquette? I never give it a thought, except when I see some obnoxious boob making a scene. Only then do I think about it—just long enough to wonder why the concept of manners escapes him so exhaustively.

Escapes *him?* Did I say *him?* Come to think of it, I have to dig really deep into my memory banks to conjure an image of an obnoxious *her.* Seems like this sort of behavior is gender-biased, though I take no pleasure in admitting it.

Casinos do try to project an image as a fun and exciting place, but sometimes a player who had too much to drink takes the party atmosphere too much to heart.

For most of those who go to casinos, etiquette is a matter of common courtesy. For them, it's okay to get a little wild as long as they're sensitive to the reactions of the others around them. But for a professional gambler, the rules are different. The casino is his place of employment, and drinking on the job is forbidden in any line of work. (Serious) gambling is no exception.

At the seated table games such as minibaccarat, blackjack and roulette, the rules of etiquette are pretty simple. Treat the dealers and the players with respect and avoid behavior that is belligerent, pushy, or rude. If you get into an argument, be gracious. Be the peacemaker. Be the one to back down first. Whatever the problem, *nothing* is worth the risk or the indignity of being cast as the bad guy—by anyone who may be watching.

At the game of craps, the rules are a little more complicated. If you're not sure of something, take your cue from the players around you. But here are some rules you should know, because they are enforced by casino personnel:

1) When holding the dice, keep your hand over the layout and do not switch them to the other hand. This helps assure the table crew that you're not a *dice mechanic* (one who replaces the official casino dice with a crooked pair).

2) Do not spend a lot of time fixing the dice or engaging in an elaborate ritual before throwing. The casino crew (and the players) will be expecting you to roll the dice within about three seconds after receiving them.

The following is a continuation of the list, but these are not really enforceable:

3) Try to get the attention of the dealer before tossing out chips for wagers made through him.

4) Proposition bets should be made through the stickman, not the dealer, so try to make sure you have his attention before tossing your chips toward the center of the layout.

5) Unless you're shooting, do not hang your hands over the layout where they might end up in the path of the tumbling dice. And if *you* are the shooter and someone's hands are in the way, don't be afraid to call out *"Hands up"* before throwing.

6) Don't force your way into a crowded table. If there isn't room for you to put your chips in a separate section of the chip tray, you probably don't belong there.

7) To keep the game moving, know the correct amounts for bets, odds, and payoffs.

8) Do not try to take the dice away from the table.

9) Try to be discreet about your wins and losses.

10) One last admonition: while on duty, professional gamblers don't party, and they don't drink ✠

SECURITY

In Lyle Stuart's *Winning At Casino Gambling,* he talks about the dangers of exiting certain casinos at night in Atlantic City, as if there's a fair chance that someone's gonna shove a gun in your face. If I didn't know better, his words would make me paranoid as hell. Fortunately for me, I *do* know better.

This has never happened to me, in Atlantic City, Las Vegas or anywhere. I've spent hours just sitting on a boardwalk bench in Atlantic City after dark, and I've upped and downed the Las Vegas strip many times after midnight. Ain't nothing going on, nowhere. I'd know it if there was.

I haven't studied the statistics, but I think that casino towns, especially *near the casinos,* are some of the safest places in the US. They all have their own police force (in uniform *and* plainsclothes), and their cameras are everywhere. And although I *used* to feel a bit unsafe in the parking garage at Trump Plaza, I have never been threatened, or seen anything that resembled a dangerous situation. And I resent the implication that these places are unsafe. But then, I don't go around wearing tuxedos.

One must always be wary in today's world, especially when he carries a fair amount of cash. The hot tip is to dress down. There's a lot to be said for low profiles. If you project a modest image, you're much less likely to be a target. Just who're you trying to impress anyway?

The guy with the gun?

If you're discreet about your winnings and you dress down, the guns magically disappear.

To me, that's worth quite a bit ✠

RIGGED GAMES

I must complain that the cards are ill-shuffled, 'till I have a good hand.

—Swift

In the movie *Casablanca,* Rick, played by Humphrey Bogart, took pity on a young man, and told him to put all his roulette chips on one number. After that bet won, Rick advised him to let all his winnings ride, and behold—it won again!

That's the way casinos operate *in the movies.* But this is not to be confused with real life.

In the real world, a secret like that could never be kept from the media bloodhounds. After all, roulette dealers are real people like you and me, and all major casinos employ dozens of them. If the games were rigged, one of those dealers would squeal sooner or later. That would be the scoop of the century! And then the casino would lose its dearest possession: its gaming license.

There is simply no good reason for any casino to take that kind of risk in a world with regulations that are a lot more strict than those in Morocco during the Nazi occupation.

Don't buy in to the idea that rigged games exist in the casinos. They already have all the advantage they need.

Anything beyond that would be overkill ✠